THE GLORY GUYS

THE GLORY GUYS

THE STORY OF THE U.S. ARMY RANGERS

Mona D. Sizer

TAYLOR TRADE PUBLISHING

Lanham • New York • Boulder • Toronto • Plymouth, UK

Published by Taylor Trade Publishing
An imprint of The Rowman & Littlefield Publishing Group, Inc.
4501 Forbes Boulevard, Suite 200, Lanham, Maryland 20706
http://www.rlpgtrade.com

Estover Road, Plymouth PL6 7PY, United Kingdom

Distributed by National Book Network

British Library Cataloguing in Publication Information Available

Library of Congress Cataloging-in-Publication Data

Sizer, Mona D.
  The glory guys : the story of the U.S. Army Rangers / Mona D. Sizer.
    p.   cm.
  Includes bibliographical references and index.
  ISBN 978-1-58979-392-7 (cloth : alk. paper) — ISBN 978-1-58979-476-4
(electronic)
  1. United States. Army—Commando troops—History. 2. United States—History,
Military. 3. United States. Army—Commando troops—Biography.
I. Title.
  UA34.R36S59 2010
  356'.1670973—dc22

                                                              2009024609

♾ ™ The paper used in this publication meets the minimum requirements of
American National Standard for Information Sciences—Permanence of Paper
for Printed Library Materials, ANSI/NISO Z39.48-1992.

Printed in the United States of America

CONTENTS

CONTENTS

HOW THE BOOK
CAME TO BE

On a visit to Houston, Texas, to research another writing assignment, I visited Bayou Bend, the home of the late, much-beloved Miss Ima Hogg. The only daughter of a former Texas governor, this very wealthy lady had been an avid collector of early American antique furniture and accessories, patroness of the arts, and creator of one of the most beautiful homes in Texas and the United States. Located in the heart of downtown Houston, it is a mecca of beauty and grace in particular in the spring when the azaleas are in bloom in the exquisite formal gardens.

On a wall in a second-floor room, I caught sight of a lithograph of Captain Robert Rogers, the first Ranger. With me were my cousin Rexa Lee and her husband Lieutenant Colonel Robert L. Pickett USA (Ret.), who saw Ranger service as an LRRP in Viet Nam. When I pointed out Rogers' picture, Bob immediately began to recite the Rogers' Rules of Discipline.

Such knowledge was not part of the docent's talk. She listened, as we all did, in amazement.

Out of this moment on the tour grew the idea for *The Glory Guys*, to which Lieutenant Colonel Pickett has graciously added a chapter about the present Ranger school and training program.

From the eighteenth century to the twenty-first, Rangers are the special group of men who have led the way in America's most troubled times. They are men of dazzling courage and incredible toughness, determined to be the best in everything they do. Their missions are fraught with danger and awesome responsibility. If they fail, hundreds of ordinary soldiers may die. The challenges of their duty include scouting and spying on the enemy, leading the way onto the field of action, creating havoc behind the lines, thwarting the enemy's plans, in short, acting in every way possible to keep the enemy from waging war effectively. Those challenges require the most rigorous training and conditioning.

This book details nine of the Ranger officers whose names became associated forever with the men they commanded. From the French and Indian War to Iraq and Afghanistan, they have led the way in war after war united by comradeship, courage, patriotism, and pride.

Mona D. Sizer
Harlingen, Texas

A NEW KIND
OF WARRIOR

Captain Robert Rogers

THE SITUATION

In the Seven Years' War, 1.4 million people died. Every day, more than five hundred children died beside their mothers and their fathers, many of whom were actively engaged in killing and being killed. It was fought across Europe, in India, and over the seas in North America from 1754 to 1763. Nothing like it had ever been seen or imagined before. People who had only a distant knowledge of France and England died on foreign battlefields for reasons they never conceived or understood. Probably hundreds of thousands died for no reason at all.

In America the conflict began when the colonies of Virginia and Pennsylvania began a westward expansion. Since the beginning of the seventeenth century, Virginia had been extensively settled by farmers who needed more and more land to grow their most successful cash crop—tobacco. The exotic odor of these burning leaves filled the coffee houses of England with their fragrance. Moreover, the British Crown charged no tax for goods shipped from the mother country. Indeed, in most cases the "colonials" were living better in America than their counterparts could hope to do back in "Merrie Olde England."

These "colonists" were an entrepreneurial people who were beginning to think of themselves as Americans. Money was to be made on the land to the west. The manufacturing state to the north—Pennsylvania—produced Conestoga wagons that enabled the colonists to move with relative comfort and swiftness into that frontier. Not even the Appalachian Mountains could bar their way.

Long rifles made by German craftsmen living in the same state brought down game with deadly accuracy from as far away as four hundred yards. Fresh venison could more than sustain the pioneers along the weary miles along the banks of two rivers, the Allegheny and the Monongahela. Searching for their own piece of land among the fertile boundless acres, they came to the fork where the two rivers formed an even greater river— the Ohio. At the point where the three great rivers met stood a French outpost, Fort Duquesne.

Neither the American colonials nor the French fur trappers were the European discoverers of these waters. The first explorer was the Spaniard Hernando de Soto, who had stood at the mouth of a great "Father of Waters" and claimed all the land drained by the Mississippi and its numerous tributaries including the Ohio. He had no idea the extent of his claim and had no chance to explore it. When he died, his men buried him in the river and sailed back to Spain.

A newer and stronger claim was registered by France, whose stalwart explorer, Robert Cavelier, Sieur de la Salle, had traveled down the Ohio on his way to the Mississippi. Neither de Soto nor Cavelier had any thought that the Indians who had lived and hunted there for centuries might have a claim to the land. Those primitive people were of no importance to the Spanish, French, or British crowns. The conquering Europeans regarded the inhabitants of this new land as "savages." They even named it "America" for the Italian navigator and mapmaker Amerigo Vespucci.

The weaponry of this world war was in transition. The British army used the celebrated "Brown Bess" or long land pattern musket. It was a long-barreled muzzle loader that took considerable time to load. The soldier first set the cock in the safety position. He then opened the cover of the pan, poured in a small quantity of fine-grain priming powder from a priming flask or torn paper cartridge, and then closed the pan cover. Of course, a stiff breeze, a rain shower, or even a fine mist made that part of the operation tricky and sometimes impossible. He then poured the correct measure of powder from his powder flask (or powder horn) down the barrel. Finally, he used the ramrod, usually housed beneath the barrel, to ram the musket ball wrapped in a wad of cotton down the barrel onto the powder. The musket was *then* fully cocked and loaded and ready to fire. When the soldier pulled the trigger, the flint or match struck the pan and made the powder explode. The explosion drove the ball out of the barrel and, hopefully, to where the soldier had aimed. To fire a second time the process had to be repeated while the enemy was probably firing at the soldier.

The Americans, on the other hand, were beginning to use a gun made in Pennsylvania. Its octagonal barrel made it somewhat tricky to load because of the "rifling" in the barrel, but it was much more accurate than the smoothbore Brown Bess. As the Americans left Virginia and Pennsylvania and headed west across the mountains, they took with them the weapon that became known the world over as the Kentucky rifle.

The first skirmish between the French and the British in North America was fought outside Fort Duquesne (later to be called Pittsburgh after British Prime Minister William Pitt, the Elder). In the summer of 1755, British General Edward Braddock, his British troops, and colonial militiamen were caught in ambush just after crossing the Monongahela River. When Braddock died in the onslaught, twenty-three-year-old George Washington assumed command and defeated what proved to be a reconnaissance party rather than the main force.

The Seven Years' War had spread to the New World. The thunder of its gunfire—cannon, muskets, rifles, and small arms—shattered the peace of primeval forests. The first "world war" had begun.

In 1763, Great Britain, France, and Spain were the signatories of the Peace of Paris that ended the conflict. With remarkable lack of vision or sensitivity, their leaders left Paris and returned to their countries that were largely unaltered by what had happened. They would come to be amazed at how their colonies—in particular, the New World that had been divided among them—were profoundly and permanently altered.

In America thousands of acres of land changed hands after being wrested by force from the hands of the people who had lived there originally. Entire tribes disappeared due to European diseases; smallpox being the most virulent.

Not only native tribes, but European settlers were also displaced. When the British took Nova Scotia from the French, they deported the French inhabitants to plague-ridden, mosquito-infested New Orleans. A hundred years later American poet Henry Wadsworth Longfellow immortalized the event by his poem "Evangeline," a romantic narrative of two people's lives torn apart by thoughtless relocation.

All these events and many, many more created the New World in which a Massachusetts-born, New Hampshire frontiersman named Robert Rogers found himself compelled to invent a new way to fight its wars.

THE ACTION

In 1775 the Indians of North America assisted and, in some cases, were drafted by the French. Their unorthodox style of warfare resulted in great success in the wilderness with thick trees and heavy brush to shelter in.

The British were forced to learn the lesson of Machiavelli: "a good army . . . must attack the enemy sword in hand, and to seize hold of him boldly." Their thin red lines—marching straight at the enemy, halting, firing, then reloading while the enemy shot them down—were resulting in unacceptable numbers of casualties against the loose-knit Indian warriors. The savages—ignorant of the proper conduct of a battle—fell upon the red-coats without mercy with tomahawk and pistol, whooping and hollering to wake the dead, destroying the discipline of the well-ordered lines almost before they could pull their muskets off their shoulders much less load them. The Indians killed the hated "red-coats" and then melted away into the forest.

Clearly they were savages, but how could they be defeated if they wouldn't fight like soldiers?

Governor John Wentworth of New Hampshire was daring enough to offer a solution. He awarded a captaincy to Robert Rogers of the First Company of New Hampshire Regimental Rangers. Foremost among Rogers' skills was his ability to raise men. He immediately brought in twenty-four volunteers. They were men who could live in the north woods, trapping beaver, hunting game, defending themselves against the Indians. Eventually, the number of the company would grow to sixty, including Rogers' younger brother Richard and his friend John Stark, whose words "Live Free or Die" would become New Hampshire's state motto by order of the General Court in 1945.

Rogers' Rangers, armed with their own muskets, generally wore deerskin "frocks." These loose-fitting coats of earth tan and tree-trunk brown fell down around the knees and blended well in the deep forests in retreat. The first "ranging" mission that drew attention and met with approval was a reconnaissance north into French and hostile Indian territory.

Under cover of darkness, they approached the French at Crown Point and infiltrated the enemy picket line. Finally, they concealed themselves only 150 yards from the main fort. Throughout the evening, they remained perfectly concealed while Rogers made notes about the fortification. When he was satisfied that he had learned all he could from that vantage, he withdrew his team to a large hill a mile away, where he could observe the troop movements.

And move the British regulars did—all around Rogers' position. They never suspected that spies were again lying concealed while observing their movements within their own perimeter.

Finally, Rogers and his men withdrew under cover of darkness. By a different route, they passed within two miles of another fortress under construction on the narrow strip of land between the northern entrance to Lake George and the southern entrance to Lake Champlain. Though the French were calling it Fort Carillon, it would be renamed and come down in history when it became one of the great engagements of the French and Indian War—Fort Ticonderoga.

Rogers then led his small group of men overland cross-country to Fort William Henry. He had started out with only what he could carry on September 14. He returned with important information September 23. He and his men were tired and hungry, but otherwise, none the worse. They had moved over a hundred miles on foot and by *bateaux* with only the supplies they could carry. Most important since their primary mission at this time was spying and gathering information from which to plan an attack, they had returned without ever having been observed by the enemy.

Their action was not the prescribed way according to the European traditions, but its effectiveness could not be doubted. The patterned, gentlemanly way wars were to be fought was being changed forever.

Four days later, Rogers started out with only two men. They moved again to observe the new construction, which was now protected by a large advance guard. Again the three Rangers infiltrated the perimeter and actually spent the night within the partially completed fort. There they estimated they were surrounded by nearly one thousand men. Before dawn they crept out and started moving south on Lake George.

At first light they were observed. A birch bark canoe manned by nine Indians and a Frenchman gave chase. Rogers and his Rangers opened fire, killing four and wounding two. As the canoe swung around and began to move swiftly away, Rogers and his men gave chase. The remaining men escaped, for the gunfire had drawn attention from the fort. Rogers ordered his men immediately to turn and flee. They were pursued all the way back to the other end of Lake George. The enemy continued the chase until they were almost within sight of the British fortification at Crown Point.

Of course, the Rangers' exploits along with their narrow escape became the talk of General William Johnson's Crown Point Army. Immediately members of the British regulars wanted to join the Rangers. Rogers' daring leadership convinced twenty-eight more men to continue in service.

Even when Rogers told them they might not be paid, they insisted they had signed up to fight a war. They wanted to get on with it.

British officers all over New Hampshire were jealous and spread tales of Rogers' ordinary birth and his lack of status and breeding. As a result, so they declaimed, he could not be of good character. He was referred to disparagingly as the "colonial." This lack of respect angered many Americans, who regarded themselves as legitimate citizens of the British Crown. They were entitled to the same respect as any other citizen.

Fortunately, General Johnson maintained that Rogers was the "most active man in [his] army." With this recommendation Israel Putnam joined the troop. He would later become a major general in the Continental Army. In 1775 he was one of the leaders of the battle of Bunker (Breeds) Hill where he was famously credited with ordering his men, "Don't fire until you can see the whites of their eyes."

With General Johnson's approval, Rogers and some of his men went one more time to Fort Carillon because Rogers wanted to capture a prisoner for questioning. There he engaged in hand-to-hand combat with a huge Frenchman. Rogers was losing the struggle when Putnam smashed the butt of his musket into the back of the Frenchman's head, killing him instantly. Rogers struggled to his feet. The contingent beat a hasty retreat—

—but not before Rogers took the Frenchman's scalp.

His "uncivilized atrocity" shocked some and was scorned by many. Others admired and congratulated him when he took the fight to the enemy and gave him "a taste of his own medicine." The Indian enemies took the scalps of those they fought and killed. In particular they scalped those who had fought bravely. In taking one himself, Rogers signaled that he was fighting their kind of war. By his act he warned them that he was not going to abide by the rules of a British gentleman.

By December 14 Rogers had formed a unique company of forty-three officers and men eager to serve in the winter in northern New York. On the nineteenth they set out for Fort Ticonderoga in bateaux. Paddling fifteen miles, they hid their boats and traveled overland twenty miles the next day. Then as now, Rangers travel fast and light with only what they can carry.

By December 21 they were in sight of the fort and observed that the area was under active construction. They estimated at least five hundred Frenchmen were working at various tasks. By that time darkness had fallen. Rogers decided that they would not leave the area. He wanted to set up an ambush to capture at least one man and take scalps from others. Unfortunately, they were so close they "durst not" light a fire but had to gaze longingly at the blazing fires in the half-completed fort. During the night they could not sit still for fear that if they sat down, they would freeze.

The next day the weather had closed in so hard that no one came out of the half-constructed fort. Rogers was forced to leave for the lake at daybreak with snow still falling so hard they were almost blinded. They arrived back at Fort William Henry on Christmas Day 1755. They had been four days with very little food and almost no rest.

On January 14, 1756, Rogers started out again. This time he and a small group tied on skates at the lake's edge and skated briskly almost the whole distance, removing their skates only to portage around the waterfall. They noted construction had continued despite the weather. Fort Carillon would be finished in a matter of months.

At this point, Rogers decided he wasn't satisfied with merely observing the progress. He wanted to create havoc among the Frenchmen who believed themselves safe for the winter. He and his men intercepted two Frenchmen with a horse and sleigh loaded with fresh beef. Ruthlessly, he sank the horse and heavily loaded sleigh under the ice depriving the fort of provisions, took the two men captive, and escaped in the forest. On his way he went through a village and set fire to the houses and the barns that stored "abundant amounts of grain." His men killed fifty head of cattle. In the dead of winter, such supplies and animals were irreplaceable.

In another expedition he torched two houses and nine barns with eight hundred bushels of wheat, oats, and peas. From there he and his men marched eighteen miles and spent the night "in wetland" without a fire to warm them.

The next morning, Rogers sent his troop back to Crown Point while he and Putnam and seven other men remained behind. He refused to leave the area until he had found a "good wagon road." In the course of his fruitless search, he encountered tracks of a large force of upward of 150 French troops.

By this time the French were angry and confused. They were unable to decide how to combat this enemy who seemed to be everywhere destroying supplies absolutely essential for the garrison to survive through the winter. Desperate to rid themselves of the man they were coming to regard as their nemesis, they posted written warnings on trees stating if Rogers or any of his Rangers were caught "they would burn them directly."

The warnings were never a deterrent. Rogers' Rangers became famous for conducting their military campaigning when all other maneuvers had ceased for the winter. On March 17, 1756, Massachusetts Governor

William Shirley, acting as commander in chief of British forces in America, named Rogers commander of His Majesty's Independent Company of American Rangers.

His was the first commission of its kind and the one Rogers had come to recognize as necessary. If his Rangers were to continue to operate effectively, he needed to be independent of the regular army. Though British officers could give him orders, he was "free of the line." His men could not be ordered to the fore to take the first shots from the attackers.

He was authorized to raise a company of men who were accomplished in hunting and tracking, making long, swift marches, and—above all—conducting themselves with courage and loyalty beyond capacity of the ordinary soldier. Each was provided with ten Spanish dollars for clothing, blankets, and arms. For each Indian or French scalp they brought in, they would receive a reward of five pounds sterling silver. The handsome payment pleased and surprised them all especially those who were already in the company. They had volunteered despite Rogers' warning that they might receive no compensation.

Rogers' two lieutenants were his brother Richard and Stark. With the company they started out on a two-month reconnaissance mission. In the end the group had to scatter before the advancing French, and each man had to make his way back to Fort William Henry on his own.

As the war grew more heated, Governor Shirley had also managed to enlist the aid of fifty Stockbridge Indians to reconnoiter and bring back information. They were soon attached to Rogers' Rangers and remained with the force till the end of the war.

From the first group of Rangers to the present day, foreign troops with exceptional training and of exceptional quality have been attached or have attached themselves to the Ranger battalions. The Indians were exceedingly valuable as an advance guard because they could infiltrate among the French and Indians and learn much because they could understand the languages.

In June, Rogers' Rangers were given a surprisingly valuable gift. Six light whaleboats arrived overland from Albany. They were some of the finest small craft made at that time. Their keels made them swift and maneuverable, particularly in an engagement against the flat-bottomed French bateaux.

The whaleboats provided an unlooked for advantage as well. The French who saw them recognized them for ocean-going vessels. They were cause for great alarms. How could the British be operating whaleboats in Lake George? The garrison at Crown Point became convinced that Rogers had discovered a direct water route from Lake Champlain into the Atlantic Ocean. Until then they had believed that the lake emptied into the St. Lawrence River and thence into the Atlantic Ocean. Thrown into consternation and fearful of an all-out attack by British ships of the line, the commanding officer sent countless expeditions from the fort. Much of the summer was spent searching for the water route, wasting valuable time and energy in a futile quest.

When Rogers reported the success of those five boats, more began arriving. As commander of a "small inland fleet," he was promoted to brevet major. A brevetted position meant he actually was a captain and would receive a captain's pay, but he would be recognized as having the authority of a major. It was a common way to temporarily replace officers killed in the line and at the same time raise deserving officers although there was no promise that eventually the rank would become permanent. With his new rank Rogers was allowed to add four more lieutenants to his unit. Working in separate groups, they harried the French throughout the summer.

The ruthlessness with which Rogers operated confounded the French. At one point coming upon a cavalry unit's mounts, Rogers ordered forty horses killed. Not stolen. Not confiscated for his men. Not simply run off with the possibility that they might be rounded up later. He ordered them killed. His actions were not those that civilized men were accustomed to facing. They still had no strategies for repelling him.

In September, he and his men were transferred to an island in the Hudson River. It quickly became known as Rogers' Island. A blockhouse already erected there was supposed to be their headquarters and their barracks, but Rogers' men preferred to build themselves bark huts and sleep four to a hut. The seldom-used blockhouse later became a smallpox hospital.

The Rangers "ebbed and flowed" from their island. It suited the unit perfectly. It was impossible to approach without detection, ample to their needs, safe harbor for their whaleboats, and a perfect point of departure. Although officially they were attached to Fort William Henry, they were really running their own operation.

Not until 1757 did Rogers' men actually get uniforms of a sort. Their buckskin battledress was darkly greenish so as to blend into the woods through which they moved. At the same time they were issued individual muskets (either flintlocks or firelocks), scalping knives, and hatchets or tomahawks. Food rations—dried beef, sugar, rice, cornmeal, and peas—sufficient for two weeks were to be carried in a knapsack strapped over one shoulder. They carried their rum ration in wooden canteens. The lieutenants received compasses fixed in the large end of their powder horns. Eventually, all the other officers wanted them when they saw their efficiency.

In addition, Rogers' veteran group showed the new men how to make their own snowshoes. The major himself gave fighting lessons in how to wear, walk, and move in them to those inexperienced in winter fighting.

When the patrol of eighty-five men assembled on Fort William Henry's parade ground, Rogers himself inspected every man's equipment to be absolutely sure that all were properly equipped and provisioned. Then on January 17, 1757, in the dead of winter, they started marching into the first narrows of Lake George.

After the first night spent in the open wrapped in their blankets, which they regarded as their "campaign coat," every man was rousted out pre-dawn. Rogers explained that dawn was the favorite time for the French and Indians to attack; therefore, each man must be up earlier and ready for trouble.

While the men ate their breakfast of warm cornmeal mush cooked over the banked fires of the night before, Rogers inspected every man again. Eleven men were identified as lame. They were ordered to return to Fort William Henry. Even though every one of them protested, Rogers refused to take those who were not fit into battle.

At this time he began to devise mentally his legendary "Standing Orders" and "Rules of Discipline." These two documents have served as the basis for Ranger training throughout America, the British Isles, and quite a few other countries in the world.

When the remaining seventy-four Rangers marched within sight of the shoreline, they traveled single file or spread out across a fairly wide area. Rogers had ordered this lack of formation. It maintained a large enough interval between each man so that any two would not be hit by the same musket ball. Sent out to the front was an advance guard. Flanking parties moved on both sides approximately twenty yards distant.

The following morning they donned their snowshoes to move northwest eight miles cross-country through the hills to their next camp. Modern soldiers can only marvel at the strength these early frontier fighters called upon to make such "good time" through fresh, deep snow over hilly terrain above the frozen lake. The next morning they moved five more miles toward Lake Champlain. The spot today is called Five Mile Point because it lies equidistant between Crown Point and Fort Ticonderoga.

Bad weather prevailed. Rain and mist reduced visibility to a matter of yards. Though some of his men might have doubted that the spot was a good choice, Rogers had experience on this very spot. Within minutes of their arrival, scouts reported two sleighs bearing ten men from Ticonderoga coming toward them.

Quickly, Rogers organized an ambush from the very spot he had captured two sleighs the previous winter. Sending Lieutenant Stark with twenty men to circle past the enemy and get between him and Crown Point, he ordered Captain Thomas Speakman to remain in position where Putnam's Creek and La Barbue Creek emptied into the lake. Rogers himself with thirty men hurried north toward Ticonderoga to cut off any escape route.

What Rogers did not know was that a large supply unit—eight sleighs, eighty horses, and forty men—were headed toward Crown Point from Ticonderoga. Under cover of mist and rain, their presence was an unpleasant surprise. Rogers sent his two fastest men to Speakman and Stark with instructions to delay the ambush until all ten sleighs were in the trap.

Too late.

Speakman and Stark sprang the trap as the first two sleighs passed by. Three French soldiers saw themselves outnumbered and rather than stay and fight or surrender, jumped on the horses, cut the traces, and galloped away in the direction of Fort Ticonderoga.

All things considered the ambush was a bust. Still, Rogers had managed to capture seven prisoners, which he kept separated from each other. One of his legendary standing orders was to keep prisoners separate, so they couldn't "cook up a false story among themselves."

After he had questioned the prisoners, Rogers knew he was in a situation that would probably get himself and most of his men captured or killed or both. A prisoner revealed that two hundred Canadians and forty-five Indians had just arrived at Fort Ticonderoga. Another fifty were due to join them the next day. The combined forces at the two forts amounted to nearly a thousand French regulars that would be aligned against him in a matter of hours. He was badly outnumbered and in danger of being attacked from both sides with his own force split.

Quickly he sent messages to his lieutenants to hurry back to the first night's encampment. Once there, the men rekindled their fires and dried their powder and weapons. At this point he gave orders to the commander of his security detachment to kill the prisoners immediately if the enemy should attack. He reasoned that he could not cross the frozen lake without being observed. He believed that the only way to get out of his predicament was to march past Fort Ticonderoga in the dark with icy rain falling steadily. He ordered the men to load their weapons, cover them with their blankets, and then move out in four detachments.

Rogers led the way. Captain Speakman took the center. Lieutenant Stark brought up the rear of the main formation. Last came Sergeant Isaac Walker with his security detail guarding the prisoners.

Even as they moved off, a horseman was riding through the snow to Fort Ticonderoga to tell the commandant of the impending attack. By dawn two detachments of Indians, Canadians, and regulars under Captains De Basserode and La Granville were on their way to intercept the Rangers.

Around two o'clock in the afternoon, the Rangers were discovered as they tried to negotiate a seventy-five-foot-wide ravine that Rogers decided could offer them some concealment. His men struggled in their snowshoes over the uneven ground. Deep snow concealed rocks, undergrowth, even small trees. Still, Rogers thought for several minutes that his decision to go for concealment had been the correct one.

Just as the first lines climbed to a few feet below the summit, the French rose and opened fire. One of the first shots struck Rogers a glancing blow across his forehead, the only hit he sustained. Probably most of the muskets were aimed at him, but many weapons misfired because of the rain. Swiftly, he realized he had made a tactical error of monumental proportions. Two Rangers were killed before they could move more than a few steps, and several were wounded. Swiping the blood from his eyes, Rogers shouted orders to withdraw.

His force found they had no time to retreat. They were trapped on uneven ground. They had to aim upward at men who could stand on the edge of the cliff and fire down. They were targets in a stumbling, falling, turning, fleeing mêlée. The French and Indians could aim downward at targets that could not easily duck or get away. It was like shooting fish in a barrel.

When they had fired their muskets, the first line of French troops charged screaming and whooping into the ravine, letting gravity propel them down the slope and add to the strength of their attack. Slashing, stabbing, and shouting, De Basserode and La Granville's men closed with the Rangers. Veteran French regulars in uniforms, French Canadians in buckskin, and Indians in war paint created a mêlée from which there seemed to be no escape. Rogers shouted at his men to fire upon whatever enemy they could get a clear shot at.

At the rear of the cavalcade, Sergeant Walker's security detachment obeyed Rogers' order. Mercilessly, they shot and killed the prisoners. Leaving the dead without a backward look, they charged forward to aid their fellows.

In the meantime with their muskets fired, Rogers' Rangers began to withdraw, but where could they go? They were surrounded and in imminent danger of being overrun. The bottom of the ravine was four feet deep in snow. Those who had only got that far found they were hopelessly trapped. Trying to climb up either side of the ravine with their snowshoes still attached was nearly impossible. They floundered helplessly and screamed as they were shot from above.

They could not give "as good as they got" because they were fighting uphill against screaming, charging foes. The only hope seemed to be to spread out in the ravine and depend upon Lieutenant Stark, whose rearguard was still at the top of the ravine on the opposite side.

Spreading out proved to be the correct move. Stark's men could then aim down and across at the French and Indians who were charging into the same untenable position as the Rangers. Only obsolete technology and revolutionary tactics averted a slaughter. The muskets of the French and Indians had fallen silent after the first volley. The men struggled with their powder horns, balls, wadding, and ramrods to reload.

With time to organize the Rangers shocked their enemies. From the ravine came a round of shot. And then another. And then another.

Rogers had devised a system for his men. He had ordered them to fire in order. Half would fire first and then reload while the other half fired. True to their discipline every other man, although out of formation spread along the ravine, fired and then reloaded while the one who would have been next to him fired. In this manner they kept up a steady hail of fire. The enemy soldiers could answer it, but only after they had all managed to reload. The maneuver was so simple, and yet no one had thought of directing a small free-fighting force to do it until Rogers taught it to his Rangers.

Rogers himself was shot in the left wrist. He could no longer load his own musket, but he kept his wound concealed from his men so they wouldn't become discouraged. Moving constantly among them, he directed their fire to targets above them.

The situation was grave. Of the seventy-four Rangers at the start of the battle, ten had been killed and seven captured. Of the fifty-seven trapped along the length of the ravine, two were too seriously wounded to fight. One was Captain Speakman, Rogers' second in command.

In the French lines, however, all was not going well. De Basserode and La Granville tried three successive attacks on the trapped Rangers, but the ravine had provided some concealment although not as Rogers had initially planned. As the Rangers spread out and mist, fog, and powder smoke hung in the air, the targets were no longer sure.

Rather than attempting a fourth attack, De Basserode called for a parley. Shouting from the top of the ravine, he tried to talk Rogers into surrendering, promising the Rangers would be humanely treated. The Frenchman warned the Ranger captain that if he didn't surrender, all his men would die when the reinforcements from Fort Ticonderoga arrived.

Rogers' reply was that he had plenty of food and ammunition, and if the French tried another charge, he "would do some scalping." His men whooped and hollered at his defiant stand. Each man promised himself that he "would do some scalping too."

De Basserode was intimidated by the Rangers' bravery and defiance in the face of superior numbers and fire power. He was encouraged when he learned his reinforcements from the fort had arrived. Then his excitement gave way. Only an additional twenty-six soldiers—not enough to make a difference—had been sent. What good were twenty-six more soldiers when his two hundred had been largely ineffective against the Rangers?

He had little time to consider the matter. In the middle of the afternoon, a sniper mortally wounded him. Though his men held their positions, no one seemed eager to do more, and La Granville proved unequal to the position of leadership.

At sundown Rogers and his men took up their wounded and melted away into the darkness. Unfortunately, they could not locate Captain Speakman. He had been wounded in the first volley and had crawled away to hide. Later Rogers learned that when the captain had called for help, the French had found him and killed him with tomahawks.

Rogers was later disillusioned by the British estimate that the Battle of La Barbue Creek was of no strategic significance. For him, however, it proved to be a personal triumph. The word of it spread through the colonies. He and his men had been trapped. Without hope they would surely be killed or captured and then tortured to death. Then miraculously they had fought their way out, defeating a force many times larger than their own.

Poor Captain Speakman's story was told as an example of what the French and their savage Indian allies were capable of. More men picked up their muskets and came to enlist in their militias.

When Rogers' wrist wound did not heal properly, he was ordered to recuperate in Albany. Unfortunately, while he was there, he contracted a case of smallpox that kept him ill and severely weakened for forty days. Still, based on his success at La Barbue Creek, he managed to send out letters of recruitment to expand his forces. The battle had also increased his status with the British. He had received authorization for an additional one hundred Rangers. He was now a brevet major commanding a battalion. He needed good men in captains' positions. He recommended Lieutenant Stark to take Captain Speakman's company. Lieutenant Charles Bulkeley took command of the other company whose captain had died of smallpox. He too was promoted to captain.

In early spring of 1757, the French were determined to take Fort William Henry and rout the British. The first attack came on the day after St. Patrick's Day when almost everyone in the fort was either passed out unconscious or suffering a blinding hangover from too much to drink in the course of too much celebrating on the patron saint's day.

Only Rogers' Rangers were not drunk. In the end, newly promoted Captain Stark proved himself to be a canny commander. He had simply pleaded that he could not sign the Ranger company's requests for "spirituous liquors" because his wrist was lame. Therefore, they had no permission to get drunk, and few dared to do it. They sat around cold sober fuming and cursing the injustice of their lives while the British regulars got falling-down, passing-out drunk.

Unknown to anyone, but half-suspected by Stark and Bulkeley, the French force of 1,600 men lead by French Canada's Governor-General Pierre François de Rigaud was actually outside the fort under cover of darkness, listening to the sounds of revelry growing louder and louder. Finally, when all was quiet, they began to move.

An alert Ranger sentry detected movement. Stationed on the east side of the fort, he had seen a light moving across the frozen lake. Quickly, the Rangers had retreated from their encampment outside the walls of the fort and alerted the 346 regulars. With the sixty-three Rangers, the strength of the company was 409 although many were still drunk.

Not bothering to be particularly quiet, the French approached. The troops inside the fort opened fire. Believing themselves to have the element of surprise, the French were not prepared for resistance. They were routed within minutes.

A second attack began with the French beginning to burn the Rangers' encampment beneath the walls. The Rangers retaliated by storming out of the fort and attacking. Though they pulled back quickly before the superior numbers, the ferocity of the sortie impressed the French. They no longer dared to bother the Rangers' belongings.

Next the French tried to burn the British warehouses and their flotilla in dry-dock on the lakeshore. The Rangers again stormed out. They were unable to save the boats but did manage to drive off the French before they could burn the warehouses containing provisions not the least of which were all-important kegs of rum.

Issued to every man, the rum ration was erroneously believed to cure scurvy. No man objected to taking that particular medicine even though he could feel no difference in his deteriorating condition. Scurvy is a dietary disease caused by lack of vitamin C. It is unknown today anywhere in the civilized world. In Rogers' time, unless the disease was reversed, an entire company so afflicted would die.

Fortunately, relief came the first of April with supplies including oranges and limes. The scurvy almost miraculously disappeared. Rogers' Rangers recovered, and Rogers' new recruits joined them and worked themselves into a united force. One of the new lieutenants was James, Robert's youngest brother.

Richard, the brother just younger than Robert, was also sent with part of the troop to be stationed at Fort William Henry, where the company would serve as spies and reconnoiterers on Lake George and Lake Champlain. On April 22, 1757, the rest were redeployed for "Foreign Service."

They marched to Albany where their old commander Rogers again took command. History does not record whether he was badly scarred or much changed from his ordeal with smallpox. Certainly the length of time he suffered from the disease would indicate a particularly dangerous case.

Nevertheless, nothing seemed to stop him or discourage him. The Rangers boarded a ship and sailed down the Hudson where they linked up with a new company of "New Hampshire Rangers" to take the battle into Canada. The companies were extremely contemptuous of each other. Rogers was the nominal commander with his brevet major title, but Joseph Gorham, the captain of the New Hampshire Rangers, was angry and uncooperative. "Nothing but hollering" went on between the two companies. Finally, Rogers and Gorham took their problems to the commander who settled the matter by sending the two companies in different directions. The expedition was then abandoned since they no longer had the superiority of numbers.

Meanwhile, Richard Rogers in command of the Rangers at Fort William Henry was having his own problems with a troop of New Jersey Dutch

Bateaumen, who proved to be incapable of raising their skills to those required of Rangers. Richard himself was proving to be as able a commander as his brother. Tragically, in June he contracted a virulent case of smallpox and died of it on the twenty-second.

French General Louis-Joseph Montcalm decided that Fort William Henry at the southern tip of Lake George had been a thorn in the French side long enough. He surrounded it with 2,200 French regulars. The men within the fort had no hope of holding out or even mounting an effective defense. When Montcalm called for surrender, they agreed. They paid dearly. When the gates were opened, Montcalm allowed the Indians to swarm in and kill everyone inside including wounded and non-combatants.

In the end, the revenge backfired because the Indians came to believe that great treasure had been buried in the cemetery outside the fort. They dug up the bodies and robbed them of clothing and any other personal items that had been buried with them. Most of the victims had been buried with everything they possessed, since most of them had died of smallpox. The disease infected the grave robbers within days. One entire Indian nation, the Pouteotame, perished almost to one man in the resulting epidemic.

Though the spring and summer had wreaked serious setbacks to British efforts, Rogers had had time to establish his famous Ranging School. The British Prime Minister Pitt and John Campbell, Lord Loudoun, the commander in chief of British Forces in America, had decided that Rogers' Rangers were not only unique but also possessed the skills essential to fight and win in the British colonies in America.

On September 14, certificates were issued to British cadet volunteers who desired to become Rogers' Rangers. They were to be commanded by Rogers and "be ready to march at a minute's notice." They would become the first class to graduate from the first light-infantry school in history. Rogers along with some of his seasoned soldiers gave their cadets training in ranging, discipline, and methods of fighting.

At this time he codified his Ranging Rules based on his past experience. They were the foundation upon which Rangers were trained and disciplined. Twenty-eight Rules of Discipline presented detailed instructions that form the basis of the curriculum of Ranger school to this day.

Though these orders were the foundation for Rangers' operations, they were not to be adhered to blindly. Rogers himself repeated that stipulation over and over. He always maintained that a man might encounter a "thousand and one" conflicts that did not fit the rules. When those times came, he was ordered to deviate from them. His own common sense and judgment were to lead him to employ tactics correct for the situation in which he found himself. As such, a Ranger had to be a thinker. Above all, Rogers insisted that a Ranger must "preserve a firmness and presence of mind on every occasion."

Rogers was galled at the sight of Fort William Henry fallen into ruins after Montcalm's successful attack. He began to develop plans to take the French forts of Crown Point and, above all, Fort Ticonderoga. The idea he devised was to take Crown Point, garrisoned by only 150 men, cut the supply line from Lake Champlain south to Fort Ticonderoga, garrisoned by 450 men, and starve them out. Two birds with one stone so to speak. Of course, the entire mission was to be carried out in the dead of winter, something his Rangers were prepared to engage in with some success.

To his chagrin, his superior officers, Lord Loudoun and General James Abercrombie both recognized the feasibility of the plan, and Abercrombie decided he could and should be the one to carry it out. Rather than offend either man, Lord Loudoun would not authorize either of them to go forward with the idea. He himself played with the idea, made grandiose plans, but failed to lay the groundwork to proceed. Then spring came and the winter campaign was a thing of the past. Consequently, Rogers' audacious plan that might have made a successful end to the French in New York was never carried out.

On March 10, Rogers received orders to take "180 men, officers included" and capture Crown Point. Rogers knew he didn't have enough men to take the fort, and he knew that his superior officers knew it. He was sure he was being "set up" to walk into a trap and be slaughtered.

Unfortunately, he was now "in the line." He could not refuse the order. The best he could do was take steps to save as many of his men as possible. Even he could not work miracles. Of 180 men, 150 were killed in three subsequent attacks. Several of his officers, including Captain Bulkeley, were among the casualties. Though they fought hard and killed as many French regulars, the odds were too great. At last Rogers tried to withdraw, but the French followed with every intention of wiping the Rangers out permanently.

On March 24, Rogers made his famous escape—the action on which much of his legend is built. With his men either dead or captured and facing death by torture, he could do no more. He discarded his green jacket that contained his commission as a brevet major. When the French found it, they were sure he was dead, for he would not have left the valuable document behind.

He climbed the western slope of Bald Mountain, which is now called Rogers' Rock in his honor. At the summit he looked down at the sheer smooth wall of rock that descended a thousand feet to the frozen shores of Lake George. He could hear his pursuers stumbling up through the icy moonlight behind him. One found his trail and began shouting. Others joined him. They had him trapped. They were going to capture and kill the famous Rogers. What a blow to the English enemies!

The legend tells that he went over the side and slid down the slope, a dangerous act that would probably have broken his neck. Instead, he reversed his snowshoes and walked back in his tracks until he could swing himself off the trail and into a hollow. Through the defile leading out of the hollow, he descended to the lake and started for home.

The Indians didn't pursue him. They didn't want to tangle with him. In fact, most of them believed he had actually leaped off the rock and slid down the side of it and out onto the frozen lake. By "great magic" he had landed safely. Rogers became *Wobi Madaondo*—the legendary "White Devil."

Rogers returned to New York to meet the new commander who replaced Lord Loudoun. General George Howe was impressed that the Ranger officer had gotten out at all and succeeded in bringing back fifty-two survivors. The French claimed they had lost only eight Indians, but no one believed that. They had engaged the Rangers in running battles through the snow-filled forests. Crack shots that the Rangers were, the French were simply lying about their casualties to save their own face. They had had Rogers and his Rangers in an "inescapable trap" and had lost him.

After meeting with Howe and receiving compliments for his valiant stand, Rogers went back to General Abercrombie, who was now his immediate superior. Rogers was furiously angry and in no mood to play games. He wanted complete and unquestioned command of his independent companies. If he did not get it, he announced he would resign.

Abercrombie was thrown back on his heels. He had expected Rogers to be whipped after such a crushing defeat. Instead the Ranger was angry and ready to disappear from the state and probably take his brother and several important officers with him. No one could guess how many of his men would follow him or simply pick up their rifles and bedrolls and disappear. Abercrombie knew his own career could not survive that debacle. The Rangers' services were invaluable. Prime Minister Pitt had been explicit that the force should be maintained. Chagrinned, Abercrombie admitted to himself that the men would be "good for nothing" without Rogers.

Rogers had what Abercrombie could never have—the trust of his men.

On April 6, 1758, Rogers was commissioned "Major of the Rangers in His Majesty's Service." He was now the commander of a battalion with two ranks—captain and major. His almost equally famous second in command, Lieutenant Stark, was promoted to captain as well. With Rogers' new strength of command, his goal remained the same. He was determined to take the French forts.

He set about rebuilding his battalion and sent out five scouting parties to secure prisoners who could reveal the strengths and movements of Crown Point and Fort Ticonderoga. When he again took the field, he himself scouted around the ruins of old Fort William Henry, which had been taken and burned the previous year.

Divided into his three columns, moving approximately twenty yards apart, he and his men in the center column were attacked. One of his own lieutenants commanding the third column pulled back rather than come to the aid of his commander. Rogers and most of his men dispersed according to the Rangers' Rules of Discipline. Scattering like quail they melted into the forests. Since the territory was familiar to most of them either by experience or briefings from others in the battalion, they managed to escape and head back south.

The officer who had commanded the third column at the rear of the retreat had not come to Rogers' aid as he should have but had led his men away at the first sign of trouble. He, as well as the rest of his men, was exceedingly surprised and embarrassed when Rogers caught up to them unscathed a few days later. What Rogers said to the officer is not recorded for posterity, but the reader can imagine that the reprimand was very strongly worded.

On July 7, 1758, Rogers' Rangers participated in the attack of Fort Carillon, which the British, one and all, now called Fort Ticonderoga. From the beginning of the war, Rogers had watched it being built and had harried its forces, destroying their supplies, attacking parties that left the fort, even spending most of the night in the partially constructed stockade to spy on its progress.

Now at the head of ten companies of Rogers' Rangers, along with two revived Stockbridge Indian companies under the command of two leaders—father and son, named Naunauphtaunk—Rogers planned his attack so as to wreak the most havoc and do the most damage, both physical and psychological.

Rowing into the first narrows of Lake Champlain, Rogers' lead boat was fired upon. Returning fire, the Rangers drove the enemy down the lake.

Though the timing was off for the cannon to cause much destruction, the advance force of French and Indians retreated into the fort and left the narrows clear for the large-scale expedition to follow.

On July 17, Rogers was allocated forty-three whaleboats and bateaux for the Ticonderoga expedition. All was in readiness to storm the fort. Then the final Ranger scouting party reported that the French advance guard had withdrawn down the valley.

The next day Rogers' Rangers led the way for the larger British force led by Baron Jeffrey Amherst.

They landed on the shores of the lake in the Ticonderoga Valley. There the Rangers' exchanged shots with four hundred French and Indians attempting to secure the bridge across the Ticonderoga River. The Rangers' reputation must have preceded them, for the fight was half-hearted. The Rangers took the bridge and drove the French back.

With the way clear, Amherst and his army seized the heights and began to set up cannon to shell the fort. When the French saw him, they immediately withdrew from the entrenchments around the fort. As swiftly as the French withdrew from the entrenchments, the Rangers moved in and secured them for themselves. Though the French were essentially secured within the fort, how long could they expect to be safe with British cannon aimed down onto their movements?

The Rangers were given the first of several special missions. First, Rogers set up sixty Ranger sharpshooters to fire at the watchtowers and gun turrets to discourage the French defenders from showing themselves. Their cowering would allow more and more Rangers to filter in closer and closer to the fort's walls.

Rogers himself led a mission the next day to saw through the boom extending across the lake. Occupied with the task, he and his men heard a terrific explosion. From one of his three boats, he and his men watched the French abandon the fort they had built as a strategic bastion against the British invasion of Canada. They had blown up the ammunition magazine to keep it from falling into British hands. They were abandoning Fort Ticonderoga.

Rogers and his men in three whaleboats immediately took out after the French and harassed them in their retreat. Rogers actually captured ten boats and the men in them as the Frenchmen simply threw down their arms and surrendered. In addition to fifty barrels of powder and sixteen prisoners, he captured Commandant Hebecourt's portmanteau, a large leather suitcase that unfolded into a field desk. It contained many important letters regarding French intentions and plans for eventualities. Why it was not in the commandant's possession was a strategic oversight that Hebecourt undoubtedly came to regret.

The end of the story of Fort Ticonderoga was almost anti-climactic. The French had seemed to lose heart. By August 1, 1758, Crown Point had been abandoned and destroyed as well. From three forts in western New York, they now had none. The French had in effect abandoned their holdings in the American colonies.

THE AFTERMATH

The Abenakis at Saint-Francis in the province of Quebec were accepted as equals by the French. They lived in and around the town and were far removed from the lives they had once known as aboriginals. Moreover, they were exceptionally fierce and armed with French weapons with which they made many raids into New England.

In 1759, Major General Amherst, newly appointed commander in chief of British forces in North America, sent Rogers and his Rangers to attack the Indians, who had aided the French at the same time they had waged a war of terror on American civilians. The concept had been Rogers' all along. He had insisted that doing so would strike a psychological blow to the French as well as to the Indians.

Under Amherst's orders "to chasten those savages with some severity," Rogers and two hundred Rangers traveled deep into French territory. They reached the St. Francis River fifteen miles north of the town. Rogers was on the opposite side of the river with no time to build rafts and ferry his men across without being discovered. Since surprise was the main strength of this exercise, he had to get across the river without detection. Selecting his tallest Rangers, Rogers led the group across the river, ordering them to form a human chain. When the chain stood in the shallows on both sides, the rest of the Rangers forded the river passing hand to hand with the support of their fellows.

As luck would have it, a reconnaissance action discovered that the Indians were drunk in celebration of a wedding. Though one of the Stockbridge Indians turned traitor and warned the Abenakis of the upcoming attack and an Abenaki hunting party actually captured a Ranger, the tribe was not alarmed. They were deep in French territory. No raid was possible.

Misjudging Rogers' Rangers and his determination to attack proved a tragic mistake for more than a quarter of the St. Francis population. On October 3, 1759, Rogers burned the town, leaving the surviving inhabitants in desperate straits with winter hard upon them. Before the remaining Abenakis fled, they released the captured Ranger and killed the Stockbridge Indian who had tried to warn them.

Though Rogers had his men take enough food from the storehouses for eight days, it proved to be not enough—or perhaps the men underestimated the privations of the trip home. When they reached the Connecticut River, they divided into nine groups, each led by knowledgeable men who could scavenge and hunt and get themselves home.

Though some didn't make it, and others resorted to cannibalism, Rogers and his men eventually made connections with most of the group. Only seventeen men died in combat. Another thirty-two did not survive the journey home. Still Rogers' Rangers had acquitted themselves gallantly and, above all, successfully. He was at the height of his career having conducted a major raid without the assistance or support of any British regulars.

An unlooked for result of the successful raid was the effect it had on the colonists in New England. Until that time they had felt helpless, unable to resist the screaming, howling, and tomahawking attacks of the Abenakis as well as other Indian tribes in New England. Rogers' destruction of the town and many of its inhabitants gave them hope that if the Indians came again, they could be fought off.

Meanwhile, British General James Wolfe had undertaken an attack on the city of Quebec itself. He arrived with nine thousand soldiers and 140 ships sailing down the St. Lawrence and arriving on the Plains of Abraham before the city. Four companies of Rangers were attached to this group; one of them was led by James, Robert's youngest brother.

In the style of a European army commander, Wolfe laid siege and conducted raids that did little to soften the city. While he was conducting raids, Montcalm was conducting his own raids, attacking the British units and killing and capturing valuable men.

On September 12, Wolfe landed his troops in the darkness and arranged them on the Plains of Abraham in front of the city.

Montcalm's forces moved out rather in the way of a gentleman who had no care for his men. Within a few hours the French defenses were breached, and both Montcalm and Wolfe lay dying.

Only thirty-two years old, Wolfe was shot in the chest and was reported to have heard the cries from his men, "They run! They run!" He is said to have died happy having achieved his greatest victory.

Montcalm was also mortally wounded. When told he could not live, he is quoted as saying, "Thank God! I shall not live to see the surrender of Quebec." He died the following day.

Montreal fell to the British the following year. In charge of a Ranger unit, Rogers again was sent west to the newly named Fort Pitt (formerly Fort Duquesne). From there the fort commander Brigadier General Robert Monckton sent the Rangers under the command of Rogers to take the fort. Before the Rangers appeared, the commander had heard that Quebec had fallen. Deeming the situation useless, he elected to open the gates rather than resist.

The last French military commander at Fort Detroit surrendered the fort as well as the other forts on the Great Lakes on November 29, 1760. The British thereby gained control of the area.

With the war winding down, Rogers' Rangers had little to do. Rogers himself received several large grants of land in southern New Hampshire, married Elizabeth Browne in June of 1761, and established a home in Concord. Though he accepted commands from several colonial militias to quell various Indian tribes, he always returned home.

On February 10, 1763, the Treaty of Paris was signed leaving the French with nothing east of the Mississippi River except New Orleans and two small islands in the Caribbean.

In May of that year, Chief Pontiac and three hundred Ottawa warriors attempted a surprise attack to capture Fort Detroit by storming it. He failed, but the siege grew as more and more warriors from disaffected tribes joined him. Rogers offered his services and accompanied Captain James Dalyell to lift the siege. The Battle of Bloody Run ensued in July. The British were unable to win a decisive victory, but the name of the battle came from the story that the creek ran red with the blood of twenty dead and thirty-four wounded British soldiers.

The Pontiac Rebellion collapsed soon after and the infamous chief disappeared.

In 1765, Rogers sailed to England to capitalize on his fame. There he published his journals, his rules of discipline, and *A Concise Account of North America*. He also wrote a play called *Ponteach* (Pontiac). It was important as a drama that sympathetically portrayed the American Indians, in particular the "noble" war chief. King George III was quite impressed with Rogers and granted him the governorship of Michilimackinac (Mackinaw City, Michigan). Additionally he was to look for the Northwest Passage, a route around the continent of North America and on to the riches of China and India. Several men including Henry Hudson had died looking for it.

Rogers never even had a chance to look, although he did dispatch a couple of unsuccessful expeditions. He fell afoul of General Sir Thomas

Gage, who despised colonials and in particular Rogers, who had been a friend of Gage's successor Amherst.

Gage defamed Rogers at every opportunity.

Rogers' friendship with American Indians was one of the sources of trouble. Like most of the British officers, Gage regarded natives as treacherous vermin to be exterminated at the best opportunity.

Gage hired spies to bring evidence against Rogers. Though their evidence was unsubstantiated and viewed by many as nonsense, Gage had Rogers arrested for treason and taken back to Montreal in chains. Rogers' wife Elizabeth, pregnant with their child, went home to Portsmouth, New Hampshire, where a son was born to her. He became a lawyer and the Rogers' family line exists today.

Though Rogers was acquitted in Canada, he could not return to America. He began to drink heavily on his return to Britain. In 1776, he offered his services to the British Army. They accepted him hoping that he would live up to his reputation. They sent him back to America to form another Ranger company.

In September, he recognized Nathan Hale, the Connecticut schoolmaster. Rogers is said to have suborned Hale into admitting that he was collecting intelligence for the American army. Barely twenty-one years old, Hale was brutally hanged for treason after uttering the words that remain a tribute to courage and loyalty to this day: "I only regret that I have but one life to lose for my country."

Rogers' part in the arrest and trial became known and was sufficient to doom any hopes he might have had of remaining in America to live. For seven years he moved back and forth between Canada and Britain, trying to regain his position as a leader of Rangers, but losing everything including his self-respect and the respect of his peers as he descended deeper and deeper into alcoholism. When he died in London, he had not enough money to pay his rent or for his own burial—a tragic end to one of America's most gallant and innovative military men.

HISTORY'S ASSESSMENT

John Paul Jones named his American Revolutionary War frigate *The Ranger* in honor of Rogers to commemorate his fighting spirit defending America during the French and Indian War.

In 2005, a statue of Rogers was erected on Rogers Island in the Hudson, where Rogers set down his Rules of Discipline. Though his loyalties were with the British during the American Revolution, no one can fault him for being a daring and brilliant soldier—one of America's best.

ROGERS' RANGERS STANDING ORDERS

Rogers served as the protagonist for Kenneth Roberts' epic novel *Northwest Passage*. The book was later made into a movie of the same title directed by King Vidor starring Spencer Tracy as Rogers. Included in its text was an abbreviated list of the Rangers' Standing Orders as written by Rogers in 1757 under the title "Rogers' Rules of Discipline." They are now carved in a large stone plaque that stands in front of the Seventy-fifth Regiment Ranger Headquarters at Fort Benning, Georgia.

1. Don't forget nothing.
2. Have your musket clean as a whistle, hatchet scoured, sixty rounds powder and ball, and be ready to march at a minute's warning.
3. When you're on the march, act the way you would if you was sneaking up on a deer. See the enemy first.
4. Tell the truth about what you see and what you do. There is an army depending on us for correct information. You can lie all you please when you tell other folks about the Rangers, but don't never lie to a Ranger or officer.
5. Don't ever take a chance you don't have to.
6. When we're on the march we march single file, far enough apart so one shot can't go through two men.
7. If we strike swamps, or soft ground, we spread out abreast, so it's hard to track us.
8. When we camp, half the party stays awake while the other half sleeps.
9. If we take prisoners, we keep 'em separate till we have had time to examine them, so they can't cook up a story between 'em.
10. Don't ever march home the same way. Take a different route so you won't be ambushed.
11. No matter whether we travel in big parties or little ones, each party has to keep a scout 20 yards ahead, 20 yards on each flank, and 20 yards in the rear so the main body can't be surprised and wiped out.
12. Every night you'll be told where to meet if surrounded by a superior force.

13. Don't sit down and eat without posting sentries.
14. Don't sleep beyond dawn. Dawn's when the French and Indians attack.
15. Don't cross a river by a regular ford.
16. If somebody's trailing you, make a circle, come back onto your own tracks, and ambush the folks that aim to ambush you.
17. Don't stand up when the enemy's coming against you. Kneel down, lie down, hide behind a tree.
18. Let the enemy come till he's almost close enough to touch, then let him have it and jump out and finish him up with your hatchet.

—Major Robert Rogers

ROGERS' RULES OF DISCIPLINE

Given here are only a few of the twenty-eight rules set down by Rogers as part of his *French and Indian War Journals* printed in 1765. His rules were detailed, comprehensive, and exceptionally insightful—so insightful that they are still applicable to today's modern battlefield where unconventional scouting and skirmishing are still a significant part of every operation. These rules constituted the first military field manual written on the North American continent. The reader should be aware that these are in an abbreviated form.

1. All Rangers are to be subject to the rules and articles of war. . . . (Following were further specific duty details.)
2. Some time before you come to the place you would reconnoiter, make a stand and send one or two men . . . to seek out the best ground for making your observations.
3. If you have the good fortune to take any prisoners, keep them separate until they are examined. . . .
4. If you march in a large body of 300 or 400 with a plan to attack the enemy, divide your party into three columns, each headed by an officer. These columns march in single file, the columns to the right and left keeping 20 yards or more from the center column. . . .
5. If you force the enemy to retreat, be careful in pursuing them . . . and keep them from gaining the high ground, in which case they may be able to rally and repulse you in their turn.
6. At first light, awake your whole detachment. This is the time when the savages choose to fall upon their enemies. . . .

7. If your enemy is discovered by your detachments in the morning, you should not attack them until the evening. Then they will not know your numbers and if you are repulsed your retreat will be aided by the darkness of the night.

8. If you have to cross rivers, avoid the usual fords . . . in case the enemy has discovered them and is there expecting you.

9. If the enemy forces pursue your rear, circle around until you come to your own tracks and form an ambush there to receive them and give them the first fire.

10. When you encamp at night, fix your sentries so they will not be relieved from the main body until morning, profound secrecy and silence being often of the most importance in these cases. Each sentry should consist of six men, two of whom must be constantly alert. . . .

2

AMERICA'S MOST FAMOUS SOLDIER AFTER GEORGE WASHINGTON

"Swamp Fox" Marion

THE SITUATION

After almost two centuries, the thirteen colonies that had spread inward from the Atlantic Ocean, south from the forty-fifth parallel, and north from the Spanish colony of Florida, had decided enough was "more than enough."

Massachusetts, Rhode Island, Connecticut, New Hampshire, New York and Pennsylvania (where Robert Rogers and his Rangers fought the French), Delaware, New Jersey, Virginia, Maryland, North and South Carolina, and Georgia met together to discuss their mutual problems stemming from Mother England and "mad" King George III.

Their problems were many and of long standing. Wars and skirmishes with the Indians had remained constant for many years after the French had withdrawn. Colonial requests for the protection of professional soldiers of the British Army came with more frequency. Unfortunately, the British soldiers were simply too few in number and their lines stretched too thin to protect all the British interests all over the world. Moreover, their presence in the towns, villages, and homes of the Americans was more a burden than a blessing.

Their requests drew further unlooked for problems. In 1763, by royal proclamation, King George prohibited the establishment of any British settlements west of the Appalachians. The colonials were incensed. The land there belonged to nobody of consequence. It could be had for nothing. To add insult to injury, those who were planning to venture into those areas, including the redoubtable Daniel Boone, were ordered to remain in Virginia. Of course, Boone paid no attention as he traveled west to become a legend in Kentucky.

He was not alone in his lawbreaking. Many Americans were incensed enough to ignore this unenforceable act, since who would follow after them and bring them back? Sadly, besides leaving them on their own in conflict with hostile Indians, it set a precedent for their illegal behavior against the Crown. Unhappy about their lack of protection, they believed themselves oppressed by a series of intolerable acts in 1765.

First came the infamous Quartering Act, which required colonials to house and feed British troops in their homes. Besides the considerable expense of feeding healthy young men from the family larder, came the unavoidable problems for pretty daughters and wives within reach of those same men when the master was away. Following swiftly came a series of Parliament-generated taxes that created problems for the growing economy. These led to the famous rallying cry of "no taxation without representation." Bent on retaliation, the angry Americans increased their lawbreaking activities.

In May 1765, in the Virginia House of Burgesses, Patrick Henry presented seven resolutions proclaiming that only Virginia could tax Virginians. "If this be treason," he declaimed in one of several famous fiery speeches, "make the most of it!" Throughout the country in July, citizens calling themselves the Sons of Liberty formed illegal organizations. Dedicated to violence and intimidation, they forced tax collectors to resign and stopped merchants from ordering British goods.

In 1766 the first incident of tar and feathering occurred. In Norfolk, Virginia, a tax collector named Captain William Smith so angered the Virginians that he was "made an example of." Stripped and daubed with tar hot enough to raise blisters on his skin, he was then rolled in the stuffing of an old feather mattress. Humiliated and in pain, he was paraded through town before a jeering crowd and thrown into the harbor. Fortunately, a British ship rescued him from drowning.

All through that year, the peace was disturbed by the Sons of Liberty as well as by ordinary people who resented and refused to pay the taxes imposed upon them by the mad king so far, far away. In New York City in August, violence again broke out as the colonists refused to comply with the Quartering Act. In December, the New York legislature, the lawmaking body of that colony, was suspended. Antipathy toward Great Britain was in the very air the "colonials" breathed.

Incident after incident occurred through the following year. From the British Parliament new taxes were levied against paper, paints, glass, lead, and tea. The Americans retaliated by boycotting British luxury items. The boycotts were so effective that they began to damage the British economy.

Pocketbooks are forever man's Achilles' heel.

In February 1768, Samuel Adams of Massachusetts wrote a Circular Letter meant to be copied and circulated throughout the assemblies of the colonies. It called for united opposition against "taxation without representation." The Secretary of State for the Colonies, Lord Hillsborough, ordered colonial governors to confiscate the letters to stop their circulation. When his orders were found impossible to obey, he ordered the assemblies dissolved and the doors to their meeting rooms locked. His action drove them on to the village greens under the big oaks and elms that came to be called the Liberty Trees. The letters circulated everywhere, and the assemblies continued to meet. Civil disobedience increased as people became more disgruntled.

In May 1768, a British warship armed with fifty cannons sailed into Boston harbor to aid customs officials. These unfortunate gentlemen were being severely persecuted everywhere and were largely ineffective in their missions. Unrest prevailed all summer long. Then in September, more warships appeared, and two regiments of British infantry landed in Boston to be quartered there "permanently."

Massachusetts, the most British of American colonies, was under martial law.

In 1769, more colonies boycotted British goods as the taxes became more intolerable.

The end was already in sight when on March 5, 1770, British soldiers fired into the crowd of protesters on Boston Common. Five unarmed men were killed and six others injured. The soldiers withdrew immediately to the harbor islands; but not before British Captain Thomas Preston, who gave the order to fire, was stopped and arrested along with eight of his men. Lawyers John Adams and Josiah Quincy successfully defended them in the courts, and all were eventually released.

To this day, the tragedy has never been forgotten. The event is taught to American schoolchildren as the Boston Massacre.

Appalled at the idea of British troops firing on what were, after all, British citizens, Parliament retreated immediately thereafter from its adversarial positions. It repealed the many taxes, except the one on tea. It did not renew the Quartering Act. Many Americans came to believe that all could and would be well. Even though in June 1772, a British customs schooner was wrecked off the coast of Rhode Island and subsequently looted, people wanted to believe that this act was perpetrated by criminals rather than by good and loyal American citizens.

Then on May 10, 1773, the English levied a three-penny-per-pound import tax on teas *arriving in the colonies*. This strictly political tax was for the purpose of aiding and maintaining the British East India Company, which was near bankruptcy. In effect, politicians gave the company a monopoly on tea. The drink of choice throughout the English-speaking world was to be sold thereafter only to agents. Middlemen were bypassed; American merchants suffered because they were undersold. In September, the company shipped half a million pounds of tea to a special group of tea agents. The import tax alone was intolerable. The price the company chose to set on it was beyond anything imaginable a few years before.

In November, three ships docked in Boston harbor to be unloaded. The colonists led by the Sons of Liberty angrily proposed to load the tea on the *Dartmouth* and send it back to England without paying import duties. The British were doubtful of their resolve.

The Royal Governor of Massachusetts believed they were bluffing. The idea was ridiculous! Inconceivable! What would the wild colonials do without their tea?

On December 16, 1773, Bostonians dressed as Mohawk Indians boarded the *Dartmouth* and dumped the tea in Boston Harbor. As well as any hope for a peaceful settlement, 342 bales were destroyed. England, as well as the other American colonies, all heard the story of the Boston Tea Party.

Intolerable Acts or Coercive Acts were enacted immediately by Parliament all throughout 1774. The port of Boston was effectively shut down until Massachusetts paid the tax on the destroyed tea. At the head of four regiments of troops, General Thomas Gage, who despised colonials, arrived to put all of Massachusetts under military rule.

In May, Parliament passed the Quebec Act, which placed all rebellious America under rule by a centralized government located in Canada. It further extended the boundaries of that province to include territories claimed by Massachusetts, Connecticut, and Virginia. The Quartering Act was reinstated in full force and was more intrusive than before. To ensure that no resistance would be possible, General Gage seized Massachusetts' arsenal of weapons at Charlestown on the peninsula north of Boston.

On September 5, 1774, the First Continental Congress met in Philadelphia. The fifty-six delegates represented every colony except Georgia. In attendance were Henry, George Washington, Samuel Adams, and John Hancock. The congress declared that the Quebec Act and all acts stemming from it were not to be obeyed. It further asserted the colonists' rights to "life, liberty, and property." Finally in October, the delegates all agreed to boycott British imports entirely, to effect an embargo on exports to England, and to discontinue the slave trade. In one fell swoop, they had struck at the very heart of Mother England—her economy.

In February 1775, in Cambridge, Massachusetts, led by Hancock and Joseph Warren, a provincial congress ordered preparations for a state of war. On February 9, Britain declared the colonies to be in a state of rebellion. In the Virginia House of Burgesses on March 23, Henry uttered his deathless words, "Give me liberty or give me death!"

A week later, King George III banned fishing in the North Atlantic and ordered General Gage to suppress open rebellion by "all necessary force."

Quick to fire back, the representatives declared themselves the First Continental Congress and passed a resolution calling for "six companies of expert riflemen to be immediately raised in Pennsylvania, two in Maryland, and two in Virginia." They also authorized Provincial Congresses to be convened in all the colonies.

A company of Virginia riflemen joined Colonel Benedict Arnold on a secret expedition to Quebec. Fueled by the hot blood generated by all the oratory and the sense of abuse, they marched through the frozen November wilderness and attacked the heavily armed city. Ill planned and worse executed, the venture was a disaster!

In the end, the colonials had neither the numbers nor the necessary training to do the job. Only a relatively few survived. Among them was Arnold, who would live to fight another day and in the end betray the country he had proved himself willing to fight for and to love.

THE ACTION

Francis Marion had enlisted in the provincial militia in 1756 during the closing stages of the French and Indian War. He and his brother Gabriel planned to fight the Cherokees in South Carolina, but his brother married and never engaged in any sort of combat. Francis stayed on in the militia. He was twenty-nine years old in 1761 when he first saw action.

His commander, Colonel James Grant, led a long march up the Santee and Congaree Rivers to a Cherokee town named Echoe.

Grant took no pains to slip quietly along the riverbanks. In the time-honored style of British bright red-coated "lobsterbacks," he marched noisily along, boots tramping, metal equipment glinting and jingling. The Indians actually heard them before they saw them. They prepared an ambush above the defile through which the colonials had to pass. The headland above the small, deep ravine was a natural position to fortify, plus it offered high ground from which to attack. Grant realized he had to send a group of men to destroy the ambush or the remainder of the troop could not advance.

To lead the detail, he chose Lieutenant Marion, who by that time had five years' experience with weapons and had proved himself well disciplined. The operation was hazardous. The enemy was in place and had the advantage of the high ground. No doubt many of the force of thirty would be wounded and killed.

The detail was the first instance in American history of a "ranging" group sent to "lead the way." Marion had never been under fire before, but he took care to expose himself and his men as little as possible. The closer he could get to the ambush, the more efficiently he could scatter the enemy. Following his lead, and instead of marching along jingling and clanking, his men ducked from tree to tree, moved swiftly, darted, and zigzagged. All went well, until they were spotted at last.

With blood-curdling war whoops, the Cherokees fired on the advancing men. A less determined officer might have pulled back reporting to his commander that the enemy position was impregnable. Marion never entertained such thoughts. He allowed them neither to falter nor retreat. Though man after man fell, the rest kept following him, moving forward while they fired and reloaded, fired and reloaded. Marion himself led them past the defile, but twenty-one of his men lay wounded or dead.

Overawed by the Americans' determination, the Cherokees retreated from their position. Grant closed in behind Marion with his full force. All morning the fighting raged, until finally, the defenders ran for their lives. Grant then ordered his troop to destroy the Cherokees' home and crops.

Marion should have been exultant. In his first battle he had acquitted himself with distinction. Instead, he was deeply troubled. He wrote to his cousin and friend Peter Horry: "To me, [burning the Indian's cabins] appeared a shocking sight. Poor creatures! But when we came, according to orders, to cut down the fields of corn, I could scarcely refrain from tears.

. . . these sacred plants sinking under our swords with all their precious load, to wither and rot untasted in their mourning fields."

When Grant returned to Charleston, his commander William Moultrie accounted the job well done and immediately disbanded the regiment. Of Marion, he wrote the following commendation. "He was an active, brave, and hardy soldier, and an excellent Partisan officer."

Marion returned to farming.

But his quiet agrarian life was interrupted again. The people of St. Job's Parish in South Carolina didn't forget Marion and his brother, who was coincidentally named Job. On January 11, 1775, the brothers were sent to Charleston to represent the Whigs, the party favoring a constitutional monarchy (also referred to as the "Country Party"). The Tories were the King's men who favored, in principle, an absolute monarchy. They were known as the "Court Party." Since the King was mad, their real head was the famous parliamentarian William Pitt, the Younger.

Unfortunately, Marion's hopeful mood and perhaps the mood of all the Provincial Congresses everywhere was to be shattered when on "the eighteenth of April, in Seventy-five" Paul Revere and Williams Dawes rode through the night out of Boston to reach Lexington to wake and warn Samuel Adams and Hancock as well as the village militias.

"The British are coming! The British are coming!"

On the nineteenth, the Massachusetts militia fired on the King's soldiers. The guns of revolution were also the fireworks of liberty—

—and America was born.

On May 10, 1775, the Second Continental Congress convened in Philadelphia; Hancock was elected its president. On May 15, the delegates declared the colonies in a "state of defense."

Present front and center was the inheritor of the prosperous Virginia plantation Mount Vernon, George Washington. Unhappy as most colonials were with what they considered grossly unfair tactics and taxes imposed upon them by England, he appeared before the Continental Congress to volunteer for service and request a commission.

As befit an officer and a gentleman who had served with honor and distinction in the French and Indian War, he had assembled his own uniform and dressed most splendidly. On June 15, appropriately dazzled, the Congress unanimously named him General and Commander in Chief of the Continental Army.

Two days later the first major fight occurred at Breed's Hill (the famous but erroneously named Bunker Hill) where Captain William Prescott is supposed to have ordered the Americans not to fire until "you can see the whites of their eyes."*

The war would go on for five more years with more and worse defeats and fewer and more costly victories. When the news reached Charleston, the delegates to the Provincial Congress pledged to stand united in defense of South Carolina. They adopted the American Bill of Rights urged by the First Continental Congress the preceding year. By the Acts of Association, they bound themselves to the other colonies not to import goods, wares, and merchandise from England.

Following the lead of the First Continental Congress, the Provincial Congress of South Carolina immediately elected captains for an infantry and a cavalry regiment. Moultrie was elected colonel and ten captains were appointed. Among them was Marion.

Immediately, he set off northward, crossing rivers and riding through swamps to enlist men from among his own folk, the Huguenots, as well as the Scotch-Irish and English along the Santee, Black, and Pee Dee Rivers that drained the extensive Congaree Swamp. Easily enough because of his reputation, he recruited sixty men, including his nephew Gabriel Marion. He returned with them to Charleston and began drilling them. They were part of the Second South Carolina Regiment recruited for the defense of Fort Sullivan in the harbor.

In September, he and his men took part in the first overt act of rebellion in South Carolina. At eleven o'clock under cover of darkness, they boarded the packet at Gadsden Wharf. Their mission was to land a force on James Island on the south side of the Ashley River mouth and capture Fort Johnson. With it in American hands, Charleston Harbor could be closed to English traffic, although trade with Europe and other ports of the United States could go on as usual. The export of rice, that fabulous "Carolina Gold," would continue to bring in a steady flow of money and goods including weapons and ammunition to wage a successful war.

The action had been planned and conducted in utmost secrecy from its inception. But problems began immediately. Fearing the fort's cannons, the ship's captain refused to sail up to the island. He anchored almost a mile offshore. The men then had to be off-loaded in small boats. The operation took the rest of the night. Once the men of Captains Pinckney and Elliot were finally ashore, the attack was ordered without waiting for Captain Marion and his men.

---

*The command is also reported to have been given by then Major Israel Putnam in 1758 during the French and Indian War. Later it was attributed to now General Putnam again as he simplified Captain Prescott's command to conserve ammunition in 1775.

To everyone's astonishment, the gates of the fort were open, the cannons flung down from their platforms. Only a skeleton guard awaited them and offered no resistance.

During the night, the fort had been dismantled and abandoned by order of the Royal Governor Lord William Campbell. The garrison had retreated aboard the *Tamar* and the *Cherokee*, two sloops that now blockaded the river mouth.

Lord Campbell himself sent a courier to demand by what authority His Majesty's fort had been taken. Pinckney replied, "By the authority of the Council of Safety." All 150 members of the militia were now behind the walls, and the cannons had been replaced on their platforms, repaired, and primed. Only the order to fire was needed.

The captains of the sloops saw the Americans standing ready beside British guns aimed at British ships and men. Though the garrison commander on board might argue with the captains' decisions, the sloops turned away and anchored out of range. The standoff was likely to last quite some time.

Charleston prepared for siege. The Provincial Congress augmented its forces and strengthened the ramparts. Captain Marion, himself a member, was ordered to move his men from the fort to garrison a depot for military supplies and public records at Dorchester thirty miles up the Ashley River.

Marion narrowly escaped capture when Charleston fell on May 12, 1780. According to some sources, he broke his ankle leaping from a window to escape from British coming to arrest him. The ankle never healed properly and pained him for the rest of his life.

On May 29, the Battle of Waxhaws took place. Called the Waxhaw Massacre, it was one of the most controversial battles of the revolution. A group of 350 to 380 Virginia continentals came marching down to reinforce and lift the Siege of Charleston. Some miles outside the city, they learned that it had already fallen. The commander Lieutenant Colonel Abraham Buford ordered his men to turn back to Virginia since, in his opinion, they could do no good.

At that point in history, an adversary worthy of Marion entered the American Revolution. British Colonel Banastre Tarleton—twenty-three years old, hotheaded, and ambitious, a deadly combination—heard that Governor John Rutledge of Virginia was commanding the force. What a coup! He could capture the governor—and possibly seriously handicap the entire state. With his force of 250 Green Dragoons as well as mounted infantry, he pursued the retreating army. When he caught them, he ordered them to surrender, claiming that his force was three times the number he actually commanded.

Buford refused to surrender, but instead of preparing for battle, he kept on marching. What he thought would happen next will never be known.

A cavalry charge was undoubtedly the most powerful and devastating force in all of eighteenth-century warfare. With sabers drawn, Tarleton ordered his dragoons to attack. The Virginians broke and ran instead of turning their guns on the thundering assault. Their rout was total with over a hundred killed and all their guns, ammunition, and supplies lost.

Immediately, the story circulated that Buford had raised a white flag. Tarleton denied it. Instead, he claimed that the fight had been fair. His horse had been shot from under him, and his loyal men had turned murderous to exact revenge. A man's sympathies in the war dictated whom he believed, but "Bloody Ban's" reputation was established in the colonies.

In the spring of 1780, the Carolinas were again the objective of the British who were winning, winning, winning in the north despite Washington's best efforts. In South Carolina, the British warships sailed past the cannons of newly named Fort Moultrie and entered Charleston harbor. Within a month they had captured the fort and the garrison. The entire southern American Army—5,400 men—were either killed, captured, or surrendered by their officers. Four southern ships were also captured and the entire military arsenal was at the disposal of the enemy.

The Continental Congress responded by commissioning General Horatio Gates to command the Southern Army, although one no longer existed. The general was an odd choice. Wise heads called it a stupid one. Rumors had circulated among the upper echelons of the colonial army since October 1777.

Uncharitable souls told that though Gates was nominally in command on the scene of America's first major victory—the Battle of Saratoga—he had never actually taken the field. The credit, some maintained, belonged to General Arnold, who had defeated British General John Burgoyne and inflicted six hundred British casualties. Arnold would have put the entire army to rout had he not been wounded in the leg and forced to leave the field. Arnold was said to be a very disgruntled man "muttering about ungrateful colonials." He believed immutably that Gates had stolen honors that should have been his.

Now here was Gates surfacing again, placed in charge of hundreds of mostly green militiamen, with no sense of discipline or any idea of how to fight. With the Waxhaws Massacre in their minds, on August 16, 1780, as

Cornwallis' well-disciplined British lines came marching toward them, his green troops too broke and ran.

Some men charitably reported that Gates tried valiantly to rally them, but to no avail. What is known for certain is that by the evening of August 16, he had galloped over the colonial boundary and ridden into Charlotte, North Carolina, sixty miles away. By August 19, he was in Hillsborough, North Carolina, 180 miles away. He did not hold another command, though he was allowed to salvage his shattered reputation to return to Washington's staff just before the end of the war.

His defection left Marion as the leader of the only effective force in the state. Though his men were few, they were gathered around a core of twenty loyal, clever warriors who knew how to fight in the swamps of South Carolina. Sixty or so would join when called and then return to their farms and crops as needed. Marion and his men were holding the South.

Meanwhile, all was bleak in the North. Only two weeks later the winter camp of the northern Continental army in Morristown, New Jersey, erupted in mutiny. Two regiments marched through the camp, demanding full rations and their pay, now five months overdue. Though the revolt was put down by other troops and two of its leaders were hanged, the officers were increasingly reluctant to give any sort of orders that might be disobeyed or ignored.

Back in South Carolina, Lieutenant Colonel Tarleton took as his personal mission to kill or capture the elusive colonial partisan, Captain Marion, who led a troop that had come to be called Marion's men.

More than once, Bloody Ban was sure that he had Marion in his sights. At a gallop they chased him north from Black Mingo Creek into the South Carolina jungle to the fork of the Pee Dee River and Lynches Creek.

The small figure on the tired horse was there in front of them. Tarleton could almost taste his victory as he leaned tight over his own mount, a splendid animal brought with him from England. To intersect with Marion's path, he spurred the animal. It gave a leap—and sank to its belly in black swamp water that stank of rotting vegetation. While Tarleton fought the animal and tried to pull its head up, Marion and his horse simply vanished into the shifting, swirling mists. The sounds of the horse's hoofs echoed eerily and then ceased.

Punished by the heat, the mist, the swarms of stinging "no-see-ums," and the low-hanging branches festooned with Spanish moss filled with nearly invisible tiny red spiders called "chiggers," the heavily armed dragoons pulled their horses to a halt in the soggy, shifting swampland. They dared not risk straining or dislocating a mount's shoulder. In the event of such a catastrophe, the animal would have to be shot because the army had no provisions for resting and recuperating their mounts. Horses were extremely valuable because every one trained for battle had to be brought in by ship.

Tarleton probably cursed. Not knowing the nature of the swamps, he could not guess that Marion lingered resting his horse on dry land a hundred yards away. As the horses struggled, the men finally had to dismount in the morass, soiling their fancy uniforms, and help each other free their animals.

Then the cursing turned to cries of alarm. Their struggles in the water brought poisonous "cottonmouths" swimming toward them. Then what appeared to be a log moved. The whole troop bolted in screaming panic. No one among them had seen an alligator before.

At this point, Tarleton is said to have called for a retreat in good order, or as good as his men could make trying to pull their mounts out of the morass and to avoid the critters that frightened them as badly as anything in this colony of South Carolina.

"Come on, boys! Let's get out of here!" As he turned his horse, Bloody Ban is said to have shouted what he considered an insult. "The devil himself could not catch this swamp fox!"

Marion's men heard him, and so their captain's name was born.

Tarleton's consciously hurled invective did not have the effect he intended. To the Scotsman, foxes were simply vermin to be exterminated in a gentleman's hunt where the object was to run the creature to ground or to his burrow, dig him out, and throw him to the hounds to be torn to pieces as a reward for their staying power.

Instead, he bestowed the gift of fame in a sobriquet that would live in American history for a man of crafty wit and sly intelligence.

Swamp Fox Marion had earned a name that portrayed his ability to fight in the swamps and outwit much larger numbers of pursuers. He needed to play the fox, as did all Rangers, doubling back, covering trails, moving ahead and behind his enemy, ducking, dodging, shadowing, and clever and sly as the premier survivor among predators from the Atlantic to the Mississippi and beyond.

Once Governor Rutledge of Virginia heard of the episode, he commissioned Marion a brigadier general. Even with his new rank, Marion never commanded a regiment at full strength, simply because there were not enough patriots to go around. Contented with his smaller group of loyal men, his power was the cunning of a fox.

Still an officer in the American army, though a supernumerary, he re-tired to his home rather than become actively engaged in the skirmishing that was all that remained in South Carolina.

Sadly, the American Revolution went on and on. For that reason General Gates, escaping the humiliating rumors of his "personal retreat," was appointed to reunite and reinvigorate the southern Army. Marion rode into his camp with his troop of Scotch-Irish and Huguenot settlers, white and black, men and boys, who were ready to fight under his command.

What must the men of Gates' army have thought? In particular what did Gates, a career officer who had served in different armies in several European countries, think when this odd figure appeared?

More than twenty years had passed since Marion's original enlist-ment. The man who had ridden Bloody Ban and his Green Dragoons to a standstill looked every bit of his forty-eight years, a slight man, very thin, with a deeply tanned, lined face. His legs were bowed, and he still limped when he walked on the ankle broken during the Siege of Charleston. His personal troop of some twenty followers had no uniforms except the same sort of dark cap made of stiffened leather. The only way to distinguish Marion from his men was by a silver crescent. Above the bill of his cap, the points of the crescent turned upward like a horned moon. Those close to him could read the inscription in Patrick Henry's own words: "Liberty or death."

Their clothing, otherwise, was motley; their weapons a mixture of new and old, some dating back to the French and Indian War and even before. Marion carried a light sword in a scabbard belted to his waist. Gates doubted he could use it. He was completely fooled by the other man's unprepos-sessing size. He did not note his expression, his sharp, black eyes, and his square jaw all of which proclaimed him a man not to be trifled with.

All Marion's men rode their own horses, a decided advantage because horses were in short supply even though they were raised in the Americas. Almost all the horses did double duty for spring plowing and heavy draft work as well as riding mounts. They were in every color from light sorrels with pale blond manes, to dappled grays, to black.

Among the men in the company were Marion's cousin Lieutenant Colo-nel Peter Horry, Major James Vanderhorst, and three captains.

The troops of the regular army laughed and made rude remarks about the "swamp gators" until some of their officers, perhaps wise enough to see dedicated and determined fighters, ordered them to keep quiet.

Gates welcomed the Swamp Fox coldly, took his measure in the light of his own experiences, and within minutes decided how to use this old man and his rabble. Certainly Marion would not be present after the glorious victories. Gates himself would sit alone at the peace tables where he would order the British to accept his own terms of surrender.

For Marion's part after he and his captains had met with General Gates, he privately questioned the orders he was given. Gates seemed airily confident that he was going to win the oncoming battle at Camden. Before he even knew what odds he faced, he "fancied" himself already accepting Cornwallis' sword in surrender.

To ensure that this battle would be the only one, Gates was determined that no one should escape to fight again. They would all be prisoners of war—and Lord Cornwallis himself would be secured and held for the duration, which, Gates was sure, would be only a matter of days thereafter. His primary consideration seemed to be whether he could make suitable arrangements to hold Cornwallis as befit his rank. How he might actually defeat him was not a topic for discussion. Defeat seemed a foregone conclusion.

On August 17, 1780, Lieutenant Colonel Horry wrote that "Col. Francis Marion & Myself was ordered to go Down the Country to Destroy all boats and Craft of any kind . . . to prevent Cornwallis & his Troops Escaping him."

Marion led them off immediately. Indeed, he was pleased to do so. A messenger had arrived from the colonial militia of Williamsburg. They had decided to arm and fight if they could join and follow him. He was pleased to leave Gage and his fancies behind and join with people who knew that fighting came before winning. When night fell, his small troop quartered in the hall and garden of a Tory, who had to be locked up to keep him from escaping and warning the British farther upriver. The militiamen wrapped themselves in their blankets and coats, and posted a sentinel to prevent their being surprised.

At two o'clock in the morning, distant firing awakened them. Marion immediately got his men up and riding, sure that General Gates had attacked Williamsburg. When they arrived at Witherspoon's Ferry, the Williamsburg militia was already there. The men of the militia raised a cheer at the sight of Swamp Fox Marion. He and his men had galloped in to do battle. Washington himself wouldn't have created such a stir.

Major John James dashed up to welcome them and introduced his fifteen-year-old son. The boy later wrote in dazzled terms of his impressions on meeting the man who was already becoming a legend. Marion hesitated. He had no authority nor rank over James' troops, but James was more than willing to accede his authority. The Swamp Fox began to carry out General Gates' orders.

Ironically, he was again put in the position of destroying valuable property that had taken years for South Carolinians to build and acquire. Today's historians, who deprecate and censure Marion's acts, nevertheless cite the efficiency with which he carried out his orders. They call it zeal. According to documents written by the men and boys who served with him, no man ever knew the cost of war better nor deplored his task more than Marion.

He sent his cousin Lieutenant Colonel Horry farther south on the Lower Santee to begin the destruction of the boats. Horry was also instructed to collect as much gunpowder and as many weapons as his troop could carry for their own use. The rest he was to send upriver to Marion. If unable to send it, he was to destroy it. He was further instructed to post guards at every crossing to prevent people from reconstructing rafts. In particular Marion was concerned about American Tories, who might take up arms or engage in spying or rescue operations.

Forty-eight hours down the Santee, another band of Whig refugees came to him with a story he almost could not bring himself to believe. On the morning of August 16, General Gates and Lord Cornwallis had fought one of the bloodiest battles of the Revolutionary War. The gunfire he had heard in the night was from Gates' men. At dawn, the troops of Cornwallis and Gates had formed their lines. As the British moved forward in disciplined, determined lines, the Americans panicked. Untrained and unseasoned in professional warfare, they had thrown down the guns and tried to run away.

Sweeping from the left came Tarleton's Green Dragoons. They had attacked the Marylanders led by Baron Johann de Kalb, a friend of the Marquis de Lafayette. The German had come to America to aid the battle and stayed to fight. He was shot seven times in the body by the battle-maddened cavalry. Though Cornwallis himself had sent his own surgeon, De Kalb died the next day of wounds incurred at Camden.

Ironically, the baron too had been skeptical of Gates' appointment as Commander of the southern Army. He had judged the man no strategist with little experience and generally unprepared for battle. His estimation was proved correct, fatally so in his case.

De Kalb's Marylanders too fled. Tarleton pursued relentlessly and never halted his dragoons until they had reached Hanging Rock. Hacking and slashing his way through the fleeing farmers and townspeople armed, in many cases, with old and inadequate fowling pieces, he harried them all the way to the North Carolina border. Gates himself fled into North Carolina, leaving the way open for Cornwallis to follow him, take the state, and with it control of the entire southern United States. On that day, nine hundred Americans were killed and one thousand were captured.

Marion faced a dilemma. Should he tell his men of the disaster and send them home, or should he continue down the Santee and burn any boats he found that Horry had missed? To do so might prevent or at least slow Cornwallis' advance while he waited for supplies. He had just decided to keep the information to himself and proceed down the Santee as fast as possible when he was confronted by his own men. Bad news had traveled faster than he could have imagined.

Ahead of him, Horry had learned of Gage's rout from an old Huguenot planter. Outraged at the idea that his boats were going to be burned, the man snarled that Cornwallis was no longer interested in retreating down the Santee. The "English lobsterback" had already gone to North Carolina.

Ironically, despite his great victory, Cornwallis' army was in deep trouble. Some of the Americans taken prisoner had full-blown cases of smallpox. The British general had been unable to prevent it from spreading among his men. They had been decimated by the highly contagious disease. In addition to smallpox, the swamps of the Carolinas were rife with mosquitoes. Many of Cornwallis' men, including the general himself, were suffering malarial attacks.

By the middle of October, Cornwallis was desperately ill with malaria. When he ordered Lieutenant Colonel Tarleton to lead an attack to throw the Americans back from Charlotte, North Carolina, Bloody Ban could not even sit his saddle. He had almost died from an attack of yellow fever, another mosquito-borne disease of the swamps. The British were learning to their horror that when one fought in America, he fought a land as strange and alien as any on the planet.

Meanwhile, Marion and his men had reached General Thomas Sumter's house on an elevation above the Santee Swamp. It was in the possession of Tories. A sentinel spotted them and fired a warning shot. Too late. Marion and his men were able to close on the house both from the front and the rear. The Swamp Fox is supposed to have smiled when they found the enemy muskets stacked carelessly outside the front door.

Twenty-two guards and two Tory guides were killed or captured. Marion released 150 Marylanders. To his disgust, eighty-five of them refused even to consider joining with him. They had no stomach for fighting especially after having been defeated and captured. Claiming they were prisoners of war, they demanded to be allowed to go to Charleston to sit out the rest of the war as was the custom in those days when men gave their parole.

Still, the Rangers numbers were increased by sixty-five. Marion and his men turned back and retreated through the swamps, crossed Lynches River, and camped. From there he wrote to Horry, requesting that his cousin join him.

Before many days in the fever-laden swamps, the other sixty-five Marylanders began to desert. They were but a few of the men of whom Thomas Paine wrote in *Common Sense:* "These are the times that try men's souls. The summer soldier and the sunshine patriot will, in this crisis, shrink from the service of his country. . . . Tyranny, like Hell, is not easily conquered."

Disgusted but not discouraged or deterred, Marion led his small troop into the Drowning Creek area of the Little Pee Dee River. There he met Second Regiment veterans, who had served with him in 1776 as well as in the Savannah campaign. From there he wrote the official report of his expedition down the Santee. The Second Continental Congress, reeling from the news of the disaster in South Carolina, hailed his success. His was the only bright spot in a deluge of desperate news.

To keep up American spirits, Charles Thompson, the Secretary to Congress, forwarded parts of Marion's report as well as his victory to the *Boston Gazette, The Country Journal, The Connecticut Journal,* and *The Pennsylvania Journal.* For the first time, Marion and his exploits were read and cheered from New England to Georgia. Americans had a new revolutionary hero and a new kind of "ranging" warrior: The Swamp Fox.

Meanwhile, at Cornwallis' orders Major James Wemyss had been left in Williamsburg to gather intelligence. Patrolling and searching for Whigs, he fell under the influence of Captain Amos Gaskins, a conniving Tory, who bore a grudge against several of his neighbors. He guided Wemyss to cut off Marion's men as they rode south. When that short expedition failed, Gaskins guided Wemyss into Kingstree.

"This is a sedition shop," Gaskins informed the major, who promptly ordered the burning of the Presbyterian Church.

He then led Wemyss to the home of Major James, who was presently riding with Marion. The owner had been captured in the fall of Charleston and had been let out on parole. If he were found to have taken up weapons again, he would be hanged on the spot if he were caught. With his men behind him, trampling the front yard, Wemyss hallooed the house. Jean James, the major's wife, knew that to hide in the house with her children would not get her anything except perhaps a broken door. Fearing neither man nor the devil, she opened the front door.

Dressed in his bright red coat, tall black leather boots, and side arms, Wemyss dismounted and addressed her in a conciliatory tone, "If Major James will come in and lay down his arms, he shall have free pardon."

"I have no influence over my husband," came her answer. "In times like these his conscience compels him to take a part, and he has taken the part of his country."

Her answer angered him. He locked her and her children in one of the rooms without food and water. For two days, Wemyss waited for her husband to come to rescue his family. Unknown to the major, Captain David Campbell of Edisto pushed food and water through the window to the prisoners. Campbell, though a Tory, could not stomach the thought of a woman and her children tortured because of her husband's politics.

On the third day, Wemyss realized that he had wasted enough time. Moreover, he was in a dangerous position. Marion's men might pass this way and execute reprisals. Worse still, he had heard that a band of armed Whigs were known to be roaming the country, fighting Tories where they found them.

To save face, he convened a drumhead court at which he questioned and intimidated her slaves and questioned both Jean and her young children. No one in the house would say that her husband had broken his parole. The "court" acquitted James, but in a rage Wemyss burned her home before her eyes.

Her fifteen-year-old son who had gone with his father to join Marion had come to idolize the Swamp Fox and later wrote about his experiences in the company of Marion's men. He recorded later that Wemyss "burnt my stock of paper, and my little classical library, in my father's house . . . and for two years and a half afterwards, I had not the common implements of writing or of reading."

Frustrated and furious, Wemyss went on a rampage and burned a swath of homes and fields fifteen miles wide along the route from Kingstree to Cheraw. He hanged men that he "thought" might be leaders of rebellion and destroyed their property—breaking up their looms, firing the grist mills, and destroying the blacksmith shops. Even worse, he ordered his troops to shoot the milk cows and bayonet the sheep.

In the process of hanging a man named Adam Cusac, who had been paroled from Charleston, Wemyss became infuriated by the man's wife and children screaming and prostrating themselves at his feet. He was in the act of spurring his horse across their bodies, when a junior officer seized the major's bridle rein. At the same time Dr. James Wilson interceded for Cusac's life.

Wemyss allowed the condemned man to go free, but he destroyed the doctor's property. When Wemyss rode off leaving the ruins of the town, Wilson promptly went to join Marion's men.

Wemyss reported all he had done to "capture Marion" by letter to Cornwallis. The women, he wrote, were sullen, the slaves hiding out, the men run off to join Marion. Then he added in a postscript, "I have burnt and laid waste about 50 Houses and Plantations, mostly belonging to People who have either broke their Paroles or Oaths of Allegiance, and are now in Arms against us."

Lord Cornwallis replied by messenger that it gave him great pleasure to hear that Wemyss' detachment was healthy. Privately he remarked that, "I am much disappointed in that business."

While the Tories were elated by the business, the Whigs were now joining the Americans in record numbers. Former neighbors, friends, and family members committed atrocities they would never be able to reconcile with each other.

Unfortunately, some of the Whigs sought reprisals among their Tory neighbors. One of the most notorious in the Drowning Creek area was Major Maurice Murphy. He was powerful, raw-boned, and reckless. He was also the scourge of the Tories in that area. He had once used a bullwhip on an old Tory named Blackman, who refused to tell where his three sons were. (All were in North Carolina prepared to join Cornwallis' British troops.)

When Murphy stopped for breakfast with his uncle shortly after the incident at Blackman's, the uncle scolded him for his cruelty. Murphy stormed out of the house, shouting and cursing, then turned back, drew his pistol, and shot his uncle dead. The man's sons, Murphy's cousins, witnessed the murder but were too terrified to say anything. None of them made a later attempt to avenge the murder

Readers today think of the Civil War as the ultimate example of brother against brother in American history. They should remember that the American Revolution also turned brother against brother, father against son, and neighbor against neighbor.

On hearing of the atrocity, Marion wrote immediately to General Gates condemning Murphy and praising his own loyal men. He had established a camp in the Great White Marsh between the Pee Dee River on the north and the Santee River on the south where he was as safe as any man might be in the America of 1780. Smaller rivers and creeks ran through the marsh and the surrounding swamps were dark. A man or a troop who came to find them would lose their way very quickly among the cypress and the oaks. They had learned to be deathly afraid of the fangs of the water moccasins that swam silently through the still water. Equally, they dreaded the alligators that looked like half-submerged logs until they moved. Of particular danger, although not immediate, were the mosquitoes that drove both men and animals mad with their bites while they spread blood-borne diseases from one man to another.

On the other hand, on higher ground in the swamps, men found they could bed down under quilts or blankets if they had them or rake together beds of pine needles, leaves, and Spanish moss and sleep in relative comfort.

Colonial rations were probably as good as any army's anywhere in the world and much better than most. They cooked their own meats—beef and pork—to which they added hominy grits, corn meal, cow peas, and sweet potatoes.

Unfortunately, they had no salt, which was hard to come by in the best of circumstances. In the swamps it was impossible. Moreover, they too began to suffer from malaria from the mosquitoes that bred by the millions in the stagnant water.

Cornwallis had little faith in any of his officers now except Tarleton, who won no hearts and minds, but at least won battles wherever he chose or was able to fight them. The general sent orders to draw the different groups together believing they were too small and exposed throughout central South Carolina. He also believed that the real fight lay to the north. The south would be strictly a "mop-up" operation. His plan now was to slash through North Carolina into Virginia, where he was sure to find George Washington.

While Cornwallis was making preparations to leave, Marion was still carrying on small Ranger raids on the small exposed groups in South Carolina. One such raid was conducted at Red Horse Tavern west of Black Mingo Creek. A British Colonel named John Ball with a force of Tory militia had camped at Witherspoon's Ferry.

Marion's raid did not go as he had planned. When he and his men rode across the poorly maintained causeway, the loose, half-rotted boards rattled and thudded. The element of surprise was lost immediately, and the British got off one volley. Marion had foreseen their fire. He had divided his force into two troops. One drew the British fire. While the soldiers paused to load, the other troop came in on the right flank. As the British broke formation in alarm, Marion's first troop reloaded and charged as well.

Ball's men had no time to reload and fell back. Their discipline broke as well when shots found their marks, and their wounded comrades fell screaming. Throwing down their empty weapons, the survivors fled into Black Mingo Swamp.

The battle lasted only fifteen minutes. Two of Marion's men were killed and three of Ball's. But the Whig gains were substantial. Guns, ammunition, baggage, and—most important—horses were abandoned. In this instance Marion himself took Colonel Ball's horse, a powerful, spirited animal, as well as the colonel's excellent saddle and bridle. In a wry gesture Marion named the horse Ball and rode him throughout the rest of the South Carolina campaign.

Pleased with his successes and recognizing that his men were tired and many were ill, he dismissed them. Praising their fortitude and bravery, he told them, "Go home to your families."

He had done all he felt he could for the depredations wreaked by Cornwallis' men on South Carolina. With five of his officers and a dozen men who remained with him, he made his way back into the countryside.

On October 11, he received a letter from General Gates congratulating him on his successes and encouraging him to continue to harry the enemy wherever he found them. But when Marion called for his men to muster, he found they were reluctant to come. The war had passed South Carolina by. They were tired. They saw no reason to risk their lives needlessly.

Discouraged, he discussed resigning his commission and leaving the area entirely, fading away into the west. How much more could a forty-eight-year-old man with a crippled ankle continue to do?

He might have done so despite the protests and arguments of his cousins Peter and Hugh Horry, had not another Tory militia under the command of Colonel Ball (whose horse Marion had appropriated) and Colonel Wigfall moved their troops into the Low Country. They had misunderstood Cornwallis' orders. He had not wanted them to venture there because of Wemyss' treatment of the people, particularly women and children, in those areas.

When they moved, Marion took a mission for himself. He would protect the citizenry from any depredations that Wemyss might decide to repeat. Word went out of his intentions. From a small group of loyal followers who had decided to remain with him, the numbers grew. Marion's reputation was enough to bring out every man who could command a musket.

Cornwallis was all too aware of what Wemyss' house-burning raids had caused. The entire Low Country was filled with frightened, angry men who had nothing to lose by defending their homes, wives, and children.

In retaliation, Marion's men had replied with strength, although not such violence. The Tories were nevertheless frightened of what might happen to them. The general ordered Wemyss to return to Camden. Too late. Retaliation began.

The situation in South Carolina convinced Cornwallis that he should leave Charlotte, North Carolina, and return to conduct the mop-up operations himself.

To bolster the British morale and numbers, a Loyalist militia under the command of Colonel Samuel Tynes was formed of volunteers from the High Hills, from the headwaters of the Pocotaligo River, and from the swamps of Lynches River. Some didn't know whether they lived in North or South Carolina. Unfortunately, they were generally unseasoned younger sons (possibly those who had grown beards since 1763).

From the depot at Camden they were issued brand-new English musket, powder and shot, new blankets, bridles, and saddles. Delighted as schoolboys with all their new gear, they camped in rip-roaring, non-military fashion on a meadow of crabgrass backing up on Tearcoat Swamp.

Marion could not have been more pleased. Here was an opportunity for his men to have good reason to muster, take care of a problem if these wild men were turned loose among the colonials of South Carolina, and win a significant victory with light casualties. The boost to morale would be significant. The British might abandon the idea of holding the South for the foreseeable future.

His call was heeded; 150 of his men responded. The Tories' position in a meadow with their backs to the Tearcoat Swamp was easy to attack. Retreating even a few yards would have them in the swamp, which would handicap their fighting and probably take the wind out of them.

Marion kept his plans to himself, spreading rumors that he and his newly mustered men were going in another direction entirely, even sending messengers to McCallum's Ferry to be ready to take them across the river in the opposite direction.

At Kingstree he turned north, traveling at brisk canter, scouts out ahead of him, galloping in and out with information about any Tories or British who might be on the highway ahead. That night, October 25, 1780, he turned abruptly northwest and forded the Black River.

Just out of hearing distance, he halted his men and sent runners ahead to check out the Tory camp. The report could not have been more favorable. Overconfident in the extreme, the officers seemed to have assigned no pickets. Campfires were blazing. Like "farm boys on a fishing trip," the men were laughing, singing, telling stories, and playing cards.

As Marion's men closed in around them drawing the net tighter to push the whole lot of them into the swamp, they heard Captain Amos Gaskins cry, "Hurrah! At him again, damme! Aye, that's a dandy! My trick, by God!"

Marion waited until midnight to attack. He had divided his troop into three parties in the fashion recommended by Rogers' Rules of Discipline. Two small groups would go in at the flanks. He would lead the main force straight in. At the flash of his pistol all three divisions charged simultaneously, shouting, screaming, and firing as they thundered forward.

Completely surprised, Tynes' men stumbled up and fell, turned and ran, yelled in dismay and then in pain as some were shot. No one seemed to have the presence of mind to reach for his weapon, even had it been loaded and at his side. Like stampeding cattle they blundered into the swamp. Colonel Tynes made no attempt to pull his men together or offer a defense. He simply vanished into the night.

Among the many dead and wounded was Captain Gaskins, who had been so excited about his cards. He died with them in his hand. He held high, low, and jack.

"But Death played the joker," was the end of the tale when it was told across South Carolina.

As gory as the rout was, the important result was the capture of eighty excellent horses with all their tack and eighty muskets.

The British were even more discouraged to hear that many of the boys who had been driven into the swamp came wading back out in the morning and volunteered to join Marion's men.

Marion's only regret was that he had missed Ball at Black Mingo. Now he had missed Tynes at Tearcoat Swamp but was able to send a party after him into the High Hills. His aim was to capture officers and destroy the leadership. Without leaders, many a Tory would simply change sides, thereby leaving fewer men willing to fight for Cornwallis and mad King George.

For the British general, the news from Tearcoat Swamp was devastating. Still convalescent from malaria and with pessimism obvious in every word, he wrote to Sir Henry Clinton, who had organized a British expeditionary force with the idea of acquiring land for himself in the Americas when the colonials had been subdued. "Bad as the state of our affairs was on the Northern Frontier, the Eastern was much worse."

Marion, who had been only a name and a vague reference to "some backwoods colonel" in Cornwallis' dispatches, was now the scourge of the British. He seemed everywhere, preparing ambushes, moving stealthily through the darkness on his fine British horse, and leading successful midnight attacks. The British wagoners were afraid to cross the Congaree River except at the most northern ferry. As a consequence the supplies took much longer to arrive, and the hungry troops were restive.

Colonel George Turnbull wrote to Tarleton on November 1. He begged the leader of the Green Dragoons to come with all haste and chase the rebels from the supply line. Tarleton forwarded the request to Cornwallis. "I can make nothing of this [except] that he describes Parties of ten or twelve Rebels, which it is not intended to employ the Legion to hunt."

Cornwallis had no choice. While giving Bloody Ban the order to go a-hunting, he stipulated, "You will of course not be long absent."

Tarleton and his dragoons rode south and crossed the Wateree at Camden the very next day. From there he sent a spy into Marion's camp. The spy came back with the intelligence that Marion would be at Singleton's Mills. Tarleton followed the Santee Road to the Mills but found no rebels.

In the meantime, Marion was moving fearlessly up the Santee Road in the opposite direction from the way Tarleton had gone down it the day before. His plan was to disrupt and delay traffic and halt the flow of supplies as much as possible. From there he went into bivouac at Jack Creek.

Tarleton had received intelligence that Marion was at Jack Creek. Spreading rumors that he and his men were returning to Camden, he moved to the plantation of the late Brigadier General Richard Richardson. On the evening of November 7, he emplaced two cannon to cover the road and lay with his men in full armor, ready to ride.

Unfortunately for the plan, which might have worked all too well, the widow Richardson sent her own son, a paroled former Continental officer, to warn Marion.

Marion was not afraid of Tarleton. He had every confidence in his men, particularly if he used several different strategies besides a head-on attack against the Green Dragoons, but his mission was not about fighting. It was about disrupting supplies, destroying morale, and distressing and discouraging the enemy.

Immediately, he turned his troop and led them across the Richbourg's Mill Dam across Jack Creek.

A Tory prisoner managed to escape and carry the news to Tarleton, who rose before dawn, issued a call to arms, and galloped at full charge toward the mill dam.

The chase went on for seven hours. Tarleton trailed. Marion turned right and left, doubled back, and played the fox until his enemy was exhausted. At last he urged his mount into the cold waters of the Pocotaligo River and from there trotted into his familiar haunts—the Swamps of Black River.

At Ox Swamp, Tarleton gave up. His horse was winded and heaving, standing straddle-legged with head drooping. Behind him all the horses were in the same or worse condition. He had gone as far as he was prepared to go, indeed as far as he could go. Finally, he had to admit that he could not catch the "damned old fox."

"The devil himself could not catch him!" he shouted, brandishing his fist at the still, green water with the mist drifting across it and the Spanish moss hanging in thick gray masses from the dripping trees.

In retaliation, he returned to the widow Richardson's house, insulted and terrified her, forced her servants to fix him a dinner, and then drove all her livestock—cattle, hogs, and poultry—into her barn and set it afire. He wrote to Cornwallis that he had "laid waste to the Houses and Plantations of violent rebels about Richardson's and Jack Creek."

What Cornwallis thought of his use of Tarleton must remain unknown. What he did say for publication was that "the total Destruction of Mr. Marion has been accomplished."

The destruction of "Mr. Marion" had not been accomplished, but at this time Cornwallis found it politic to recall Tarleton from the area. "I do not see any advantage we can derive from a partial destruction of the country."

On November 14, Lieutenant Colonel Tarleton and his Green Dragoons cantered out of Camden and passed from the region of the Santee forever.

In a very real sense, Marion had defeated him by driving him as well as other commanders to such excesses and such atrocities that they destroyed any hope the British might have had of returning America to a peaceful and amenable relationship as a part of the British Empire. The Tories who could not stomach Whig rule returned to England or emigrated to Canada. The Revolutionary War might end to be followed in short order by the War of 1812, but the ties that bound the former colonists to the mother country were forever severed.

Tarleton and Marion were obvious enemies in most people's minds. Men who took their time to judge such things calculated they were essentially equal in guile, cunning, and their ability to command loyalty from their men. Tarleton was hated because he burned and destroyed homes and supplies. Marion's men, when they requisitioned supplies or destroyed them to keep them out of British hands, gave the owners receipts for them. After the war, most of the receipts were redeemed by the new state government.

So successful was Marion in his warfare and his honest treatment of the people in the Low Country that South Carolina Governor Rutledge from exile in North Carolina commissioned Marion a brigadier general of the state troops.

In January 1781, General Nathaniel Greene took command of the southern Continental army (such as it was after Gates fiasco). Swamp Fox Marion and Lieutenant Colonel "Light Horse Harry" Lee were ordered to attack Georgetown. They were unsuccessful in taking it, but the attack was deemed a success because they broke communication between the British armies in the Carolinas by taking both Forts Watson and Motte.

By June 1781, Greene's forces had gained virtual control of South Carolina. The British forces were sick both physically and emotionally of the summer heat, but their commanders were determined to make one more attempt on Charleston. In September, they camped in the cool shade of Eutaw Springs.

Barely five hundred miles away Washington was preparing to launch his American-French campaign to encircle Cornwallis at Yorktown. He had already sent Marquis de Lafayette, Baron von Steuben, and "Mad" Anthony Wayne into Virginia. Privy to the plan, Greene called for resumption of offensive operations by Marion and his men. These had to be undertaken with all speed, for British Lieutenant Colonel Alexander Stewart had broken out of his camp north on the Congaree River. He had to be stopped. If he got to the coast, he and his men would commandeer ships to take them up to the Chesapeake Bay.

Greene was determined that they should not get the chance. He sent messengers immediately to Marion, who was bivouacked in the swamps at Peyre's Plantation. When Greene's order came, the Swamp Fox and his men set out immediately.

Stewart fled as fast as he could, desperately trying to avoid a confrontation that would reduce his numbers and keep him from coming to Cornwallis' aid. He managed to travel thirty miles down the Santee. There he secured a strong position and camped for the night at Eutaw Springs. Only a few more hours and he could easily slip down the Ashley River and on to Charleston.

In one day, Marion's men moved up the Santee, bypassed Stewart, and waited for Greene seventeen miles north of Eutaw Springs. Greene was provoked that Marion had not attacked immediately, but the Swamp Fox would let no more of his men die unnecessarily in engagements when they would be outnumbered. Stewart's men were the last in South Carolina. If Cornwallis was defeated, the chance for peace was immediate.

Taking one of the dreaded Swamp Fox's tactics as part of his battle plan, Greene divided his men into three groups. Marion's men were stationed on the right; General Jethro Sumner's men were on the left; and Greene would hold the middle of the attack. At the rear waited a small legion of mounted men under the command of Lieutenant Colonel Lee.

While Greene was still four miles north and not even in position, two American deserters warned Stewart of the impending attack. Amazingly, the colonel did not take the warning seriously. Instead, he prepared a detachment to meet what he assumed was to be a small American force that would break and run before the psychological intimidation of a deliberate forward march. Few rabble troops could face a line of disciplined British regulars firing on command and pausing to reload while the line behind them stepped forward to fire.

The British were not only better armed, they were much better dressed. The sight of bright uniforms with polished buttons and tri-corn hats had worked their spell before. Most of the men including Marion's men and Greene's regulars were ragged and filthy. Many were barefooted. Above all, they were hungry.

Responding to Marion's suggestion, Greene moved his men into position at four in the morning on September 8, 1781. Marion's men then advanced from the left and spearheaded the attack in darkness, aiming for figures in the firelight and silhouettes in the streaks of dawn. Purposefully and methodically, they drove the British skirmishers back into the lines.

The British opened fire, but true to the courage Swamp Fox had shown since his first encounter in the ambush outside the Cherokee village twenty years before, he led his men to hold their ground when they fired and to dodge like denizens of the swamps while they reloaded. As the British fell back, Marion and his men continued their advance through the woods in the teeth of the very hottest fire the lines could throw at him. Later he would write General von Steuben, "Such conduct would have graced the veterans of the Great King of Prussia."

They fired seventeen volleys. Then, mission accomplished, they withdrew as Greene's regulars and militiamen surged forward. Shaken by the disciplined and well-organized attack, Stewart's flank retreated as the center line buckled and fell back in disarray. Seeing his opportunity, Light Horse Harry threw his cavalry into the struggle charging full tilt into the already shattered left flank.

The entire line gave way when, on command, Greene's Marylanders fired one terrific volley. The whole rout would have been complete, had not Stewart's retreat gone through the middle of their camp where a mess tent had been set up with drink and warm food that the cooks had been preparing before the battle commenced.

The starving Americans could not resist the temptation to stop and grab what they could. The offensive fell apart. With all control gone, Marion ordered his men back into the woods. The others soon fell back under heavy sniper fire.

Stewart claimed he had won a great victory. After all, his enemy had retreated. But claim what he would, statistically, his army had been shattered. The number of his dead is unknown because he did not stop to collect their bodies. Seventy wounded were left "under flag" for the Americans to care for.

The Swamp Fox took his men back into the swamp at Peyre's Plantation where he posted marksmen to protect his back door against reprisals. On the morning of August 29, he sent a reconnaissance detachment to Strawberry Ferry. A force of one hundred dragoons had been spotted in the vicinity. The detachment led the dragoons straight into ambush. Their first volley dropped twenty men.

Unfortunately, it also spooked the horses pulling the ammunition wagon. With nothing left to shoot, Marion ordered their retreat to the Santee. He had fired his last shot at another human being.

On September 14, Washington's army of seventeen thousand men began the siege of Yorktown. French cannons bombarded Cornwallis' nine thousand men. Though he held for several days, no help arrived. On October 17, Washington and Cornwallis worked out terms. As their band played, "The World Turned Upside Down," the British army marched out and surrendered.

On December 14, 1782, the Swamp Fox dismissed his men, bid them happiness, prosperity, and God's grace. With that he mounted Ball and road away from military life.

His home had been looted and damaged, but he rebuilt it and married his cousin Mary Esther Videau. After several terms in the state Senate he was made commander of Fort Johnson, a courtesy title with a salary of five hundred dollars per annum.

He died on his estate in 1795.

No man ever led a more exciting life. Free to command men and do what he deemed correct, he made his judgments and did his duty. Fortunately, for America, he made the right decisions in her behalf.

HISTORY'S ASSESSMENT

American literature is full of poems, stories, dramas, and novels as well as endless numbers of historical and biographical accounts of the participants. Every school child has heard and some have memorized "Paul Revere's Ride" by America's most beloved poet of the time Henry Wadsworth Longfellow. Walter D. Edmonds, one of America's premier historical novelists of the twentieth century, wrote the richly researched *Drums along the Mohawk*, set in upstate New York during the American Revolution. It was a *New York Times* bestseller for two years. In 1939, *Drums* was made into an exceedingly successful movie directed by John Ford and starring Henry Fonda.

However, thoughtful historical scholarship does not heartily endorse either Marion or his British nemesis Tarleton. The British historian Christopher Hibbert believes that the Americans who admire Marion are unaware of some of the really bad things he did. Hibbert regards efforts to honor him repugnant in the light of his personal life and the fact that he owned slaves.

Though a daring and effective leader, Tarleton receives censure for his ownership of slaves, as well as the known fact that he gave orders for several attacks that killed many civilians as well as American soldiers. (He did not, however, burn a Presbyterian church as depicted in *The Patriot*.)

Still and all, their uniquely individual personalities and personal styles are made for tales, fiction, and creative non-fiction. Likewise, their legendary adversarial relationship is linked forever in the minds of writers and moviemakers. Tarleton has appeared as a character in several movies invariably played as someone handsome, suave, and more than a little like Lord Byron as "dangerous to know." No less distinguished an actor than Michael Caine played him in *Sweet Liberty*. On the other hand, he has appeared as a despicable church-burning villain in *The Patriot* and a slave owner and trader in *Amazing Grace*.

In *The Patriot*, Mel Gibson's script and his heroic character is based on the life of Marion, although Marion never galloped in carrying his own tattered American flag. As part of the special Sunday evening series that also introduced Davy Crockett, the "King of the Wild Frontier," Walt Disney created eight episodes of a television series titled *The Swamp Fox*.

While towns, counties, lakes, and parks are named Marion all over the eastern half of the United States, still one signal honor awaits him. In March 2007, the Brigadier General Francis Marion Memorial Act passed the U.S. House of Representatives. It awaits a vote in the Senate but has been placed on the general calendar. The people of South Carolina believe it will pass, and the president will certainly sign it into law.

It has been a long time coming for a man who rode and fought so gallantly through some of America's most dangerous country in some of her darkest days.

3

OLD ROUGH AND READY'S "LAWLESS SET"

Captain Ben McCulloch and the Texas Rangers

THE SITUATION

During March and April of 1836, the Mexican state of Coahuila y Tejas split forever. All the land north and east of the Rio Grande became the Republic of Texas as she formally declared her independence from Mexico as well as the state of Coahuila. Almost before they could react, the Texans, many of whom came from all over the sixty-year-old America, found themselves engaged in a war against the largest standing army on the North American continent.

Most battles these new Texans lost—badly. At the Alamo, 180 men fought to the last man on the sixth of March. At Goliad, 342 Texans surrendered and were marched out onto the road and shot or clubbed to death on the twenty-seventh. The victorious Mexican army burned the bodies in both cases, while the Anglo families, many of whom had been in Texas for decades, made a mad dash for the Sabine River.

Finally, with no real hope of victory but with vengeance eating at their hearts, the men sent their wives and children across the Sabine and gathered behind General Sam Houston for one last act of defiance and revenge. Under his command, the angry ragtag group halted their helter-skelter retreat across Texas. They knew they would be facing the might of Mexico, the largest standing army on both American continents.

On April 21, 1836, on the plain of San Jacinto, they stopped and turned and attacked the Mexican army exhausted from weeks of marching over a thousand miles from Mexico City and disheartened by losses of personnel and arms. Overconfident and worn out, the army was taking a siesta. The battle lasted only seventeen minutes, only long enough for the Mexicans to drop their guns, throw up their hands, and cry, "No Alamo! No Alamo!"

Wounded in the initial charge and in pain, Houston sent a sortie into the heart of the Mexican camps and captured the man responsible for all their troubles, the ruler of Mexico—Generalissimo Antonio López de Santa Anna. He might have escaped in the uniform of a private, had not his own men recognized him and betrayed him.

When the king is captured, no matter how many pieces remain on the board, the game has gone to checkmate!

And the Republic of Texas, born just four days before at Washington-on-the-Brazos, won its first and most satisfying war, virtually bloodless after so much blood had been shed.

For eleven years Texas functioned as a nation, although a poor one. Surfacing immediately were all the financial and logistical problems of running a government and creating a state. The new republic fell deeply into debt. Some talked of petitioning America at once to become a state among the others. But many objected, calling such an option a last resort. While many of its citizens were American born, its population included European as well as Mexican groups scattered in small privately organized and governed areas around the state.

During these years, Santa Anna never really gave up the idea of returning and retaking the fledgling state. He was already beating the war drums in Mexico City. In this he was unsuccessful. His efforts to make himself president of Mexico failed when the Mexican congress elected a liberal José Joaquin Herrera. Santa Anna went into hiding in the hills above Veracruz.

America might have been content to leave Texas alone were it not deeply concerned with the diplomatic efforts of Great Britain to offer all sorts of aid to the infant republic. Though Britain had lost the battle of New Orleans in 1815, it had never given up its ambition to take back its "colonies"—to reconquer America. If the beleaguered republic agreed to overtures to become a British Protectorate, Britain would have what it most wanted—a back door—Galveston, one of the largest towns in Texas, to anchor a navy and to ford a river and march an army overland.

Galveston wasn't New Orleans, but any port will do in a storm.

In 1841, President William Henry Harrison had died of pneumonia just one month after his inaugural parade. When his successor, the "accidental" president, John Tyler, had annexed Texas by joint resolution of a "lame duck" Congress in 1845, he had known within reason he was leaving a war to the man who followed him. For Tyler, the act was at least partially malicious, a final defiance against the country and the political party that had denied him its respect and cooperation all four years of his term.

Tyler's successor, James K. Polk, had been handed a big, nasty can of worms. He assumed the presidency of a country in conflict, faced immediately with a huge indefensible western frontier alive with Comanches, Apaches, and Southern Cheyenne, Great Britain's looming presence in the Gulf, and south of the Rio Grande a war with Mexico presided over by another president—an angry, unstable alcoholic—Mariano Paredes y Arrillaga.

Though President Polk sent an ambassador to Mexico City, the representative was not received. Having made the effort to effect a peace, Polk then moved some of his armed forces into positions to wage a war. In July 1845, he sent "Old Rough and Ready," General Zachary Taylor, to Texas to defend the border at the Rio Grande. While Polk had not sought the war, he was fully aware of the threats that could be turned into disastrous action if the new state of Texas was not defended against Mexico. Above all, he wanted no diplomatic arrangements between Texas and England.

When Taylor arrived at Corpus Christi, at the mouth of the Nueces River, he sought to enlist the aid of Texans to fight for their own freedom and union. The first group he turned to was a paramilitary group that called themselves the Texas Rangers. Though they were an undisciplined lot, Taylor needed fighting men who could move swiftly.

Reluctantly, he mustered several companies of John Coffee Hays' Rangers into national service. Though they might be considered a part of the U.S. Army, he first left them at their locations west of San Antonio to guard the frontier against the Indians.

He was unfamiliar and therefore suspicious of their weapon of choice, a new-fangled revolver that shot six bullets before it had to be reloaded. It had been made by Samuel Colt of New York with improvements practically demanded by the Texas Rangers. He doubted the reputation and the weaponry of this hugger-mugger group.

Old Rough and Ready had never seen them fight.

They were all deadly shots and their weapon had been designed and handmade to their specifications back in 1838. Ranger Samuel H. Walker had been sent to New York with a list of faults and merits to present to

Colt. With the original Colt guns, the barrel had to be taken off to allow the empty cylinder to be replaced with a full one while the rider held all three parts in his hands. If any part fell to the ground during the process, the weapon was useless. Walker wanted Colt to construct a weapon that was not light and flimsy (as the original Colts were). More important, it had to be loaded on horseback while riding hell-for-leather through the brush with thorny mesquite and huisache limbs swatting its owner in the face.

The two Samuels labored long and hard over the new gun.

A month later, Walker returned to Austin with the new Colt, a completely altered weapon. The frame was heavier and stronger. The grip was a convenient shape. The trigger was protected by a trigger guard. The cylinder took .44 charges, big enough to stop almost any attacker dead in his tracks. Its lever rammer *attached to the barrel* seated all the bullets in the chamber without removing the cylinder.

The year 1845 would prove what it could do.

Unfortunately, though they craved them with desire akin to bloodlust, most Rangers did not have them. The Republic of Texas had had no money to purchase them.

When Texas Rangers Big Foot Wallace and John Salmon Ford reported for duty to Taylor, they demanded that he arm their Ranger companies with this weapon. Reluctantly, Taylor authorized them to send Walker again to New York to find Colt, whose factory had gone bankrupt and had closed. Imagine his unbelievable delight when he received an order for a thousand revolvers—two for each of the new Texas Rangers. He was back in business again.

The "Old Army Type" with new specifications became known as the Walker Colt. It was manufactured, of all places, in Eli Whitney's cotton gin factory. Though Colt lost money on the deal, his fortune was ultimately made. Every one of the weapons bore the hallmark: *Address Samuel Colt, New York.* His name and his weapons became legend.

Another technological revolution in warfare had begun in America. With 2 six-shooters each, five hundred Texans were able to ride into battle armed with six thousand bullets to use against their foes before they had to pause to reload.

Meanwhile, after drilling his disparate groups for nine months and determining the political situation was not improving, Taylor moved south. While Texas claimed the Rio Grande as its southern boundary, Mexico disputed that claim in favor of the Nueces 150 miles north. In the eyes of Mexico, Taylor had invaded their territory by crossing into the disputed area. Undeterred, Taylor fixed a base at Point Isabel, where the Brazos de

Santiago pass permitted entry into Bahía Grande, a deep water bay only a quick overland march from the mouth of the mighty Rio Grande.

As a matter of record when Brevet Second Lieutenant George B. Mc-Clellan of the Corps of Engineers, fresh out of West Point arrived, he was shocked that the troops should establish its first camp in Texas at that spot. In his opinion, Brazos de Santiago was "the very worst port" on the entire American coast. It was a barren sand bar occupied by clouds of sand flies. "The water is very bad . . . brackish . . . unhealthy. The island is often overflowed to the depth of one or two feet." The only good thing about it was that the men could run down the beach, bathe, and frolic in the surf every morning. The beach, he asserted, almost made the whole expedition worthwhile.

Taylor really had no choice. He was finding his feet in totally unfamiliar territory. First, he established a detachment under the command of Major Jacob Brown in a bend of the river directly across from the city of Matamoros. Their purpose was to keep close watch on the large Mexican forces gathering there. Utilizing every enlisted man as well as civilians, he ordered the construction of earthworks to protect the people from sniper fire from across the river. Christened Fort Texas, its purpose was a show of defiance. Behind the earthworks Brown made a camp, erected a flagpole, and ordered the Stars and Stripes raised and lowered each day accompanied by fife and drum. The Mexicans in Matamoros were constantly aware of what was happening.

In a towering and probably drunken rage, President Paredes promptly sent the Mexican Army of the North into the border state of Tamaulipas. In command was General Mariano Arista, a famous firebrand, who could be counted on to strike the invading enemy swiftly. Paredes prophesied that the result would be a massacre—a disaster to send the Texans fleeing back across the Nueces. Both the president and the general were determined that this victory would make Mexico forget the shameful debacle of San Jacinto.

THE ACTION

Daily, Old Rough and Ready sent the Texas Rangers under Walker out to scout the land. They rode through the chaparral and canebrakes, noting the Mexican army movements and bringing back valuable information. An observer from above would have been amused and confused. The thick brush country where every plant was covered with thorns was crisscrossed by narrow game trails. The paths of white-tailed deer were used by the scouting parties of Texans and Mexicans. Most of the parties were made up of hunters making very little sound and leaving small "footprints" that others might miss.

Meanwhile, mindful of the delicate political situation in Washington, Taylor notified and received instructions from Polk. Regular information was carried by packets, small steamers that carried mail and passengers along a regular route on the Texas coast.

Polk received the notice that a Mexican army had crossed the Rio Grande less than a week after the invasion. Still the president waited. He could not ask Congress for a declaration of war unless the shooting started.

On April 24, sixty of Taylor's dragoons out on patrol were attacked by a Mexican cavalry organized into an ambush. The dragoons could do nothing but surrender when shots were exchanged. While Arista thought his men had made a decisive move, the ambush was like a gift. Taylor informed Polk immediately. In the eyes of the Texans and, more important, the American public, the Mexican army had invaded America and interfered with American soldiers in the act of carrying out their orders. Taylor informed Polk, "hostilities may now be considered as commenced."

McCulloch's Texas Rangers received orders to come with dispatch. His mounted company was composed of the best and bravest young men living on the Guadalupe River. In addition to Anglos, it included fighters of both Indian and Mexican descent. Every man prided himself that he could live and function with very little support from a large military quartermaster with supplies and ordnance.

Their horses were the best the western frontier had to offer. Many were mounted on half-wild mustangs that could gallop all day. Just as many rode equally powerful blooded stock brought with them from Kentucky and Tennessee. Every man who had joined the Rangers had furnished his own tack and arms and his own bedrolls. He carried his own supplies in his saddlebags. Every man sworn in was ready to take the field. Unfortunately, they would not make the battle in time.

As further indication that hostilities had begun hot and heavy, Arista ordered the batteries in Matamoros to begin firing at the hastily erected earthworks on the north side of the river. At the orders of the commander Major Brown, the Americans returned fire. The cannonade served as an agreed-upon signal to General Taylor. Fort Texas was under attack. On May 6, during a particularly violent bombardment, Brown was wounded so severely that his leg later had to be amputated.

On May 8, under presidential orders, Old Rough and Ready considered that he could not wait for the Rangers to reinforce his troops. He decided to meet the invading army at Palo Alto prairie; 2,300 disciplined troops engaged the Mexicans on a broad, level grass-covered plain in what was the first real battle of the war. Taylor's troops were eager for the fight. He seized the opportunity.

Though he did not know of it, dissension was already rising in the upper echelons of the Mexican army. They were not ready to fight. Command had changed three times in the past month. Arista could not with certainty know that his troops would obey his commands since the men originally in command had been shuffled off and demoted in rank and pay. Furious with the treatment, the now-subordinate officers constantly countermanded and undermined his orders. As can be imagined, morale was low.

Many grizzled Mexican veterans had cause to remember the Alamo. Though Santa Anna had won the battle for the mission and presidio, he had lost hundreds of men in the effort. At San Jacinto, he had grossly underestimated the determination of the Texans. His exhausted and demoralized soldiers were caught flat-footed and unable to mount a defense.

At Palo Alto on May 8, the Mexican lancers' charge that should have shattered the Americans' will to fight ended in disaster. The strength of a cavalry charge is a wall of men on horses galloping abreast straight at their enemies. Grossly incompetent officers ordered the men to funnel down between a mesquite thicket and a bog.

American Major Samuel Ringgold's artillery aimed for the opening in the funnel where they wrought terrible destruction. Their shot slashed through the bodies of the leading riders killing them instantly. Directly behind them, the same shot smashed into the men ordered to charge directly behind them. Each shot killed two and three times as many men and horses as if they had been strung out in a line across a field.

Meanwhile, the Mexican artillery lobbed hot shot that started several fires in the tall grasses behind Taylor's infantry. While the wind was at the soldiers' backs and several were severely burned, most avoided the smoke and flames that rushed straight on. Drawing fuel from the dry grass and high wind, the smoke blinded the Mexican soldiers as the fire attacked them. It forced them to retreat screaming. The result was exactly the opposite of what Arista had planned. Both cavalry and infantry were put to rout while the Texans suffered negligible casualties. Unfortunately, one was Major Ringgold, a popular fellow with his men and other officers. His specialty was a "flying artillery" form of attack used to great advantage by the Americans.

The battle of Palo Alto can be called a draw because both sides retreated with no decisive victory and relatively few casualties. Still, first blood is always the most shocking to the men who survive to fight again. The sight of their dead in pools of blood on the scorched prairie earth took away whatever desire they might have had for glory. Since many Mexican soldiers were untried men who had little stomach for what they were about, their morale disappeared along with their lack of trust for their leaders.

Possibly more significant was the fact that the Texans had a personal reason to fight. They considered this their land, the land of their heroes David Crockett, William Barrett Travis, and Houston. They had a standard to live up to.

Four hours' march from Palo Alto, Arista's demoralized although not severely depleted force halted where the road back to the Rio Grande crossed the Resaca de la Palma. *Resacas* are the paths or trenches cut by rushing water blown in from the Gulf by hurricane winds and storms. At La Palma, the bottom of the ravine was now dry except for a few pools from the recent rain. To Arista it seemed the ideal spot for an ambush to teach the oncoming Americans a painful lesson. The banks were lined with mesquite thickets that would conceal his troops at the same time limiting the effectiveness of the American artillery. In order to cross the resaca, the Americans would have to move between emplacements of infantry and artillery.

On May 9, the first Texas Ranger performed heroic and valuable service. Walker and a small company had waited west of Point Isabel for McCulloch to arrive. Taylor ordered him to scout the Mexican forces and discover their plans if possible. Employing his frontier skills, Walker crept up on Arista's ambush, scouted the situation, and returned to inform Taylor.

While he was receiving the news of the Mexican troops ahead, Taylor heard Major Brown's guns at Fort Texas open up across the river from Matamoros. Immediately, he sent Walker and six Rangers accompanied by an escort of dragoons to tell Brown that help was on its way.

Walker led the way overland through the chaparral, avoiding Mexican sentries and outriders. He reached Brown with Taylor's assurances. Brown sent back the word that he would hold until they arrived. Walker's news marked by the successful return from his mission spread through the ranks. Taylor had known everything he needed to know to wage a successful battle. He gave the Rangers full credit in his dispatches, which were passed on to newspapers in Washington and New York. Their reputation began to build for the first time beyond the boundaries of Texas.

On May 9, Taylor's 2,300 men overwhelmed and shattered Arista's army for the second time. His carefully prepared ambush never took place because thanks to Ranger scouts, Taylor knew where it was set up.

With a charge so fast, they were through the chaparral before the Mexicans could fire and the Americans captured nine of the cannons. Screaming like banshees and shooting and bayoneting the Mexican gunners, they sprang from their horses and wheeled the loaded cannons around to face the Mexican cavalry waiting impatiently for orders.

No orders came.

Instead the Americans opened fire on the cavalry with deadly results. While the infantry watched stunned, the American troops tore the heart out of the Mexican army with its own ordnance. Though Arista himself took command and tried to lead a charge to reclaim the advantage, he had no success. His own cannons supplemented by American firepower moved into position by this time forced him to retreat. Panic-stricken, many Mexican soldiers ran the three miles to the Rio Grande, where at least three hundred men drowned trying to swim across.

Impressed in spite of himself was young Brevet Second Lieutenant Ulysses Simpson Grant. Much, much later in his famous memoirs, he damned Old Rough and Ready with faint praise. He wrote that he had no doubt that "the battle of Resaca de la Palma would have been won just as it was, if I had not been there."

Having driven the Mexican army out of Texas, Taylor marched his army in good form into Fort Texas to find its flag flying but Major Brown lying mortally wounded. He died the next day, and Taylor changed the name of the earthworks to Fort Brown. At this point Taylor decided to rest his troops.

Meanwhile, the news of the successful battles "fought in self-defense against an invading army" had reached Washington. The Congress could no longer dilly-dally. American blood had been shed. American honor had to be maintained. Retaliation was the only course. Mexico must be taught that her neighbor to the north would not tolerate a violation of her territory.

Despite the protests of congressmen from the Northern states fearing the admission of another slave state into the Union, the Southern states and states whose only concern was American sovereignty outnumbered the North. On April 26, 1846, at the disposition of President Polk, Congress declared war on Mexico.

On May 19, McCulloch's company of Texas Rangers arrived at Point Isabel. He was bitterly disappointed that he and his men had arrived ten days too late for what he presumed was the last battle of the war. According to a contemporary report by Samuel C. Reid, Jr., published in 1848, Taylor had been unimpressed with the idea of a regiment of Rangers. On the other hand, the excellent work of Walker and his scouts, overlooked by Reid, had convinced Taylor that the Texans were valuable soldiers.

Especially impressive among the new arrivals was Captain McCulloch, whom most Texans looked up to as an ideal "partisan" leader. He was naturally calm in any emergency. According to Reid, the Ranger captain was almost preternaturally aware of where his men would be in relation to the enemy. He planned the lightning strategies that would give them the upper hand in any eminent danger.

Whether Taylor actually admired McCulloch or his men or the men of other Texas regiments that came later under the command of Governor J. Pinckney Henderson is open to conjecture. He certainly made no effort to see whether they were outfitted or billeted as they should have been. They had to construct their own shelters. The American government did not furnish "so much as a patch of canvas" during the whole expedition. Furthermore, they were not furnished rations or cooking utensils such as the American expeditionary forces carried.

The result was a ragtag outfit spread out around the orderly billets of the Americans. Indian wigwam-like structures, rude lean-tos made out of scrounged poles, or cane with saddle blankets stretched across them to keep out the sun or the very occasional rain shower. They looked frankly more like an encampment of camp followers than one of the most fearsome legions of fighters on this or any other continent.

The Rangers make-do living conditions gave the American soldiers an excuse to look down on them and disparage their contributions. The jeers and catcalls irritated the Texans, but otherwise they showed no reaction. When they were forced to pilfer provisions from the countryside when none were supplied, their thievery also gave the group a bad name.

They cared nothing for the slurs. They were dedicated to revenge for the Alamo and Goliad massacres. They would see this campaign through to the end.

Taylor's troops be damned!

On the very first expedition, the Rangers proved their worth as they utilized many of "Rogers' Rules of Discipline." No accounts reveal whether McCulloch had ever read or even heard of Robert Rogers. Many of the rules are techniques that a clever backwoodsman would use to stalk game, avoid hostiles, live off the land, and generally behave in a careful, practical manner.

His cleverness was unsurprising to those who knew of him. From his father, a clever backwoodsman, McCulloch had learned all of those techniques and some of his own in his early life. Born in Rutherford County, Tennessee, in 1811, his formal education was limited to two months in a rural school. The traditional three r's—readin', 'ritin', and 'rithmetic—were taught without books, blackboards, paper, and pens. Most people cannot conceive how modern education with thousands of books, computers, and supplies of all kinds plus extensive teaching materials has evolved from these primitive recitations.

Like most men who lived their lives in the wilderness, McCulloch really had no need of any more education, although he claimed to have read the books from his father's library. Since he had time to read only at night, his father cautioned him against straining his eyes in flickering firelight. During the day he made his living on the land—hunting, trapping, and logging—and on the rivers poling his furs, lumber, and farm products by raft down to New Orleans.

In 1835, he and his brother followed the trail of Colonel Crockett, who had lost his bid for reelection to Congress and a return to Washington. Disgusted, Crockett and his Tennessee volunteers went to Washington-on-the Brazos, signed up as citizens of Texas, and traveled immediately to join the hopeless fight with Colonel Travis at the Alamo. Too late. The siege was already in progress.

When McCulloch reached Nacogdoches, he fell ill with a severe attack of measles. By the time he recovered, the Alamo had fallen. Like almost everyone else in Texas, he joined the Runaway Scrape heading for the Sabine River. At San Jacinto, when General Houston fought Santa Anna, McCulloch was in the ranks that charged. He had come to consider himself a citizen of the Republic of Texas. Now he looked to be back in America.

Taylor ordered the Texas army across the Rio Grande to occupy the city of Matamoros. In doing so, he had invaded Mexico. The invasion was more an effort to keep his men supplied and billeted than an actual act of war; 2,300 men with a long wagon train behind them required quarters that the meager settlement around the newly christened Fort Brown could not accommodate.

For his part, Mexican General Arista made no attempt to defend the city. With indecent haste he ordered his shattered, disorganized cavalry and infantry to make their way south. Their progress was slow, bogged down as they were by wounded and absent important supplies. He himself felt no obligation to lead his army in retreat. Accompanied by a squad mounted on fast horses, he galloped toward Monterrey.

Taylor was in no hurry to pursue him. Polk's declaration of war required that American garrison troops stationed along the coast of the Gulf of Mexico set sail for the mouth of the Rio Grande. The troops landed not at Matamoros, but on the sand at Brazos de Santiago where river steamers constantly loaded and moved goods northwest upriver past Matamoros to Reynosa and even Camargo.

The troops that came were moved upriver, too, in order to establish the river as a boundary between America and Mexico. Implicit was the idea that the Rio Grande would be the boundary for all of Texas. The northern part of the river drained half of present-day New Mexico and the city of Santa Fé, a Spanish settlement established by Don Francisco Coronado. It had become a town in 1607, the same year that Jamestown was founded in Virginia.

Once Polk had accepted the idea that war was inevitable, his sights were set on the ideals of newspaper columnists who wrote enthusiastically about America's "Manifest Destiny" to extend the nation from the Mississippi River to the Pacific Ocean. The Texans might have thought they were the objective of all this movement of armies. Instead they were the excuse, the opening that Polk, one of America's most undervalued presidents, needed.

Meanwhile, McCulloch led his men across the Rio Grande at Fort Brown and scouted the most practical route for the invading army to travel to Monterrey.

He knew Arista's army was retreating south toward Linares. He did not know that Arista himself had galloped on with a squad of fast riders to Monterrey. The man in charge of the remaining men was General Antonio Canales, the bloody "Chaparral Fox," who had been relentless in his attacks on Texans back and forth across the river. With an opportunity for an ambush, McCulloch led his men across the Rio Grande and upriver southwest from Matamoros to Reynosa. Several miles up the river, he made camp off the road where they could ambush anyone trying to travel by it. Their choice of campsite was in this case governed by the fruit and vegetables available to forage out of the fields.

The next morning, his scouting expeditions learned that they were "going in the wrong direction." He turned sharply to the south and rode through the brush to intercept the fleeing Arista.

In the early dawn of the second day, McCulloch's troop of forty Rangers discovered the armed camp of Blas Falcón, a Mexican *ranchero* who had raided and robbed the Americans across the border. Before Falcón could set up lines and fight in the approved matter, McCulloch yelled, "Charge!"

The Rangers went thundering at them, whooping and hollering and firing their pistols.

Falcón had no luck in screaming orders to his men. Among cries of "*los Tejanos diablos*," translated as the Texan devils, some of his men began screaming "*¡Los malditos Americanos!*" translated as the wicked Americans. By and large, the Mexicans were so badly frightened that they fled into the brush leaving their guns, pistols, spurs, even horses behind them. The tactics were classic Ranger from the days of Rogers. Get up early in the morning and attack before the enemy is awake and can think what to do.

McCulloch made no effort to keep secret his movements. In fact, he gloried in them as he moved back and forth across the countryside. Raiding and terrorizing, he moved his Rangers southward toward Monterrey. As they did, they noted that it was easy enough to follow because the desperate men were shedding clothing and equipment to lighten their loads as they quick-marched to stay ahead of the army they knew was coming.

McCulloch reasoned that Arista, traveling straight southwest, making for Monterrey, would plan ambushes to discourage any army attempting to follow him. As Rogers advised in his Rules of Discipline, the Rangers crossed and crisscrossed the Mexicans' trail rather than follow directly in their wake. He also learned from some farmers that the road to Linares was an impossible route. No water or food was to be found over the last fifty miles. Not trusting the Mexicans' word, he sent a Ranger south to be sure. The man rode for forty miles but found only one dry waterhole.

McCulloch turned his men back west and made for Reynosa, where Taylor was headed with a small force. It was the longest day of the year, June 21. That night as they slept, the skies opened up with a flood of rain. The men dismounted, filled their canteens, drank their fill, and watered their horses.

The next day the Rangers found the Monterrey road, then turned back northeast to inform Taylor at Reynosa. They had spent ten days on the scouting expedition and had ridden at least 250 miles. During that time they had never taken off their coats or boots. The information they brought Taylor was invaluable. He knew where his enemy was. He knew the way his men could go and, just as important, he knew the way they couldn't.

At Reynosa, the Rangers gained a reputation that followed them through the rest of their service to their state and their country. They became known as troublemakers and assassins. When the ill-fated Mier expedition of 1842 had been captured, they had been treated cruelly in Reynosa. Some of the former prisoners were among the Rangers. Though the order was to treat everyone in the town as non-combatants, some men were found shot and others hanged out in the chaparral.

When Taylor ordered an investigation, all his representatives could discover by questioning members of the Ranger troop was that probably the dead men had experienced fits of remorse and taken their own lives. Repeated efforts and questions were thereafter met with a shrug and the rhetorical question, "¿Quién sabe?" translated as who knows?

At this point Taylor confessed in a letter written in July 1846, "I have not the power to remedy it [the Rangers' behavior]. . . . I fear they are a lawless set."

Despite their shocking ruthlessness, he valued the information they brought him. Though he found them insubordinate, he was forced to turn a blind eye to their deeds. He even doubted their battle worthiness: "I fear that they are and will continue to be too licentious to do much good." His use of the word "licentious" is construed to mean they were too freewheeling in their actions to be of much use.

On July 4, he observed that they celebrated by shooting their guns in salutes to the day. "Accidentally" they killed Mexican pigs and chickens, which they roasted and washed down by drinking two horse-buckets full of whiskey sweetened with sugar loaf and only slightly diluted by water.

On July 9, Taylor moved northwest to Camargo, the head of navigation for steamboats on the Rio Grande. Purposefully, he had left units of American soldiers at every village and town all the way from Point Isabel. Not only were they a deterrent, but they were also a signal to the government in Mexico City that Texas belonged to America. Her border was defended and invaders would be met with strong resistance.

Taylor sent McCulloch out from Camargo to investigate routes to Monterrey. On McCulloch's return with no ambushes or movements of troops noticed, Taylor ordered the march south. On September 13, in two parallel divisions, the invading Americans started for Monterrey. The groups moved through the countryside, presenting no single target and causing no undue hardship on the villages and ranches they passed. The idea was to have no groups behind them angry enough to pursue and attack from the rear.

On September 14, leading the way in true Ranger fashion, McCulloch's men were far out ahead. As the "point of the spear," they scouted the town of Ramos just north of Monterrey. Without warning, thirty-five Rangers attacked the town, rousting out two hundred Mexican cavalry, sending them fleeing southward. Though several were wounded, they all managed to get away. No Rangers were hurt.

On September 17, Taylor and his staff surrounded by McCulloch's Rangers stared across the plain toward the "*silla del cielo*," translated as the saddle of the sky, rising above Monterrey. The city's walls faced them too, lined with Mexican soldiers while the Mexican cavalry made a sortie as a show of strength calculated to test the invaders. It was quickly aborted when the Rangers spread out in front of General Taylor and drew their weapons. The sortie quickly retreated. The Texans' reputation had preceded them.

For two days Taylor rested his troops at a spring in Walnut Grove, the picnic grounds of the fashionable set in Monterrey. Campfires blazed on the carefully manicured lawns, and soldiers took no care of the trees and shrubs they hacked down for firewood. Both columns were united now, and the general was planning his strategies.

To intimidate both the city's non-combatants and the garrisoned soldiers, all of whom were watching, Taylor allowed the Texans to "play games" to worry and torment the Mexicans watching from the city walls, the towers, and the belfries. Howling like banshees, the Texans galloped back and forth, charging the walls, then riding out again. Some rode like Comanches, with only one leg and one arm visible on the side of the horse as it galloped past the walls. Some rode two horses at once at a full gallop, transferring from one to the other without ever dismounting. They performed tricks like circus performers, hanging over the back of the horse and turning backward in the saddle and aiming their rifles at the walls. They made the Mexicans duck again and again.

Taylor observed that the northern ramparts were too well fortified to be easily taken. He encouraged the Texans to continue their play until General T. J. Worth began to lead two brigades off to the west around the city. The Texans abruptly formed up and rode off at a good clip. They galloped to the head of the American brigades and again took the point.

They must have been an intimidating sight. McCulloch's Rangers, heavily armed, led the way, "desperately courageous on steel-muscled ponies." Behind them came the uniformed and armed Americans in good order. Their destination was the road that ran approximately fifty miles through the mountains to Saltillo.

Arista and his officers must have despaired when they saw their strategy. Taylor was encircling what was left of the Army of the North. No reinforcements could aid them. No supplies could be brought in. Moreover, the presence of a large force at their backs also prevented the Mexicans from turning tail and retreating.

On the road from Reynosa, Taylor ordered his troops to prepare "the advance of the army tomorrow" and to be ready to move at sunrise.

On the Saltillo road, Worth gave the same instruction. The next morning at six he sent the Texas Rangers around a small hill. To their amazement they found themselves facing a body of mounted lancers supported by infantry. Both units halted, but McCulloch recovered first. Unimpressed by the Mexicans' brilliant uniforms and the fluttering pennons on their lances, the Ranger captain yelled the order and charged out ahead. Like a Comanche counting coup, he broke through the Mexican line, scattered the soldiers like geese, wheeled his horse, and rode back through without a scratch.

Then the armies met with terrific impact. Horses screamed and reared, curveted, and crashed to the ground. Men were thrown from the saddles and crushed under their mounts' hooves. Every man used every weapon he possessed—sword, knife, pistol, and lance.

The mêlée was all too much for the Mexicans. Less determined and less well trained, the first men broke. Then the rest soon fled back down the road. The Rangers sprang from their horses, shouldered their rifles, and picked off many of the terrified enemy with deadly accuracy. No quarter had been shown at Alamo. Cold-blooded murder had been done at Goliad. Vengeance was swift and sweet.

Worth was eight miles from Taylor's force with four days provisions. Why waste the opportunity? In swift order he took Federation Hill with its strategic gun emplacement overlooking the road. The Rangers immediately turned the cannon on Fort Soldado outside the city walls.

The Mexicans in the fort as well as those fleeing toward it were too confused and too frightened to mount any sort of effective defense. Moreover, the dissension in the Mexican army had left no one really in charge, no cadre of officers who could give orders and expect that they would be obeyed. Many were political appointees who had never been in combat before, certainly not against the shrieking, shooting wild men firing at them with deadly accuracy with guns that fired repeatedly without being loaded. They had no idea what to do.

Those inside the fort watched in horror as their comrades raced for safety. The Texas Rangers accompanied by a troop of Louisiana volunteers, yelling and shrieking like Comanches, chased the fleeing artillery and infantry toward the city walls. As the Mexicans fell back and turned and fled some without firing their weapons, the regimental flags of the various American units were hoisted on the walls of the fort. Without planning to do so, the Rangers had won the day.

When the attack finally subsided, the Rangers were sent back to care for their horses and prepare for the attack the following day. A thunderstorm blew up, but the men slept through it with their heads pillowed on their guns.

Opposite Federation Hill, now in American hands, was Independence Hill and beyond it was the Bishop's palace. At three the next morning, the attack on the next objective began. It would be led by two Texas Ranger companies of Colonel Hays and Lieutenant Walker. Just fewer than half the attacking force would be made up of Rangers, but they were to be in the middle and forward parties. Again they would be the point of the spear.

Two columns advanced as silently as possible. Every man was cautioned to make no noise until everyone was in place. The idea was to climb to the summit by daylight. Unfortunately, Independence Hill was a truncated mesa. The ascent was so steep that the Rangers were only halfway up its side at daylight when they believed they had been spotted. A single shot was fired, but they kept going. Within twenty yards of the top, their commanders erupted with wild yells that spread among the Texans, who began to climb fast and furiously. After a brief, violent struggle, the Mexicans fled.

Whether the shot fired had been an accident or a warning that went unheeded was never known. The Americans were triumphant, but too exhausted to give chase. Though one of the fleeing Mexicans got away with one of the cannons, the other cannon was captured and brought back. The Stars and Stripes was run up the flagpole. Cheer after cheer echoed over the walls of the city. On the opposite side, Taylor's men heard it and returned it.

During the next few hours the skirmishes that were fought were more like combat planned for a Hollywood movie. To read of them today strains credulity. The battle for Monterrey was a dramatic one with elaborate costumes, deeds of individual daring, and lightning movements of troops. For the Mexicans it was a long, horrendous retreat, during which they sustained unacceptable numbers of casualties.

General Worth organized a thousand men by noon. At his orders, a howitzer began throwing shells against the walls and through the windows of the Bishop's palace.

He suspected that the Mexicans would try to take the offensive and drive his forces from the hill. He therefore divided his force in two with the Texas Rangers concealed in forward positions. Hays' men were on one side; Walker's were on the other. Behind the Rangers were five companies of regular army. The Louisiana volunteers formed up in the center. They alone were visible to the enemy. It made no difference. By this time, every man was dressed in clothing that had seen many days of traveling and sleeping out in oppressive heat, dust, and rain. They all looked the same—scruffy, shabby, and unshorn.

The Mexicans had been rallied in the meantime and prepared to take the offensive. They had donned the uniforms that Santa Anna, in his role as the "Napoleon of the West," had spent inordinate amounts of money on. They looked like soldiers out of picture books prepared to fight wars in Flanders and Artois.

"Battalions of infantry formed in front of the Palace, their crowded ranks and glistening bayonets presenting a bold and fearless front, while squadrons of light-horsemen, with lances bright and fluttering flags, and heavy cavalry, with . . . broadswords gleaming in the sun, richly contrasting with the gaudy Mexican uniforms, made a most imposing sight."

The Mexicans were poorly armed in contrast to being better dressed. Lances and broadswords put to use against the rifles and pistols, in particular the six-shooter Walker Colts of army regulars and Texan and Louisiana volunteer soldiers, would be tragically ineffective. The white plastrons attached by gold ornamental buttons to the fronts of the dark green coats would make excellent targets for the Texans and Americans in the streets of Monterrey.

Still, they were spectacular. The Louisiana volunteers fell back as the Mexican trumpets sounded. The Mexican army came on. Saddle leather creaked. Iron-shod hooves thudded in the dusty street.

Then, twenty yards in front of them, men armed with bayonets filed out to block the way. At the same time, the Rangers and regulars rose from hiding and fired rifles in concert. Someone yelled "Charge!" and the fixed bayonets dashed forward. The Mexicans broke and ran back in through the gate of the Bishop's palace. The guards closed the gates. The howitzer pounded it open, and the Americans poured into the yard. Yelling in fear, the Mexicans dashed for the back of the palace.

The entire garrison except for some thirty prisoners ran down the hill.

This victory, however, was small. If intelligence was correct, Worth was in a desperate situation. A large Mexican force was approaching from the southwest along the Saltillo road. At about the same time, Taylor began his attack on the east. Cannon thundered. When Worth heard it, he interpreted it as an order to move into the city.

Two columns—Hays' on the right down the Calle de Monterrey and Walker on the left down the Calle de Iturbide—advanced into the city. McCulloch reported that the Mexicans had withdrawn as far as Cemetery Plaza. From there they scattered into every house and crouched at the windows. Finally, they drew their guns. Their barrels bristled from every window.

From there the real battle began. Every house, every block, had to be taken by force. The Texas Rangers and the Louisiana volunteers fought like the men of great courage that they were. Sharpshooters climbed onto the roofs of houses and aimed down in through the windows. Teams armed with axes and crowbars broke in the doors and tunneled through the adobe walls. Again and again the Mexicans were forced to fall back, leaving their dead and wounded behind them. Through the city they fought until nightfall.

By dawn the next morning, the Texans and regulars waited on the roofs and the firing began again into every window where a Mexican with a rifle might conceivably take cover. During the night several men had picked a hole in the masonry of a very large building. At dawn a team armed with sticks of dynamite with lighted fuses dashed across the street and threw the explosives into the building. Its occupants dashed out and were shot dead in the streets.

Before Taylor could set up a parley, the Mexicans were ready to surrender. A letter arrived under a flag of truce for General Taylor from General Pedro Ampudía. He offered to lead his men to evacuate the city with the honors of war and provision for eight weeks' truce. Taylor agreed only to suffer a firestorm of harsh criticism and angry protests on all fronts.

What was the point of fighting so hard, expending men and ammunition, if the enemy was allowed to crawl away and reform? Many Texas Rangers, who had already overstayed their enlistment to be part of the fight, quit and went home on October 2, a week after the surrender.

For his own part, Taylor could not have been happier. In fact, he was almost insulting in his desire to get rid of his lawless set. One thousand Texas Rangers with nothing to do was a group that Taylor was just as relieved not to have to deal with. He granted their discharge immediately, although others among them still had a week left of their enlistment. For that week, they displayed their hatred and resentment for all things Mexican, fighting, damaging property, and generally creating enemies for all "Americanos."

Even so, Taylor could not deny their essential services without which his battles might not have been won. He extolled them for the services they had done, the dangers they had faced, the hardships they had endured, and the sacrifices that they had made. He recognized that they were not, by and large, crude, ignorant hooligans. Among them were lawyers, doctors, poets, surveyors, and legislators. He was also aware that while they had been on campaign their families remained behind more or less undefended from attacks by Indians living in the western part of the great territory of Texas.

Taylor waited for five months in Monterrey. During that time he learned that the government of Mexico had been dissolved. Ironically, he could find no one with whom to negotiate a peace with honor.

In Mexico City, Paredes had been acknowledged as a drunken tyrant. He had been pushed out by the Mexican Congress who promptly announced a new liberal president Valentín Gómez Farias, who reinstated the Constitution of 1824. The Texans had revolted against Mexico in the first place because that constitution had been rejected. That date had been on the flag that flew over the Alamo. For a brief period of days, everything seemed wonderful. Peace with honor seemed a possibility.

Then Farias quixotically recalled for the commander in chief of the Mexican armies none other than Santa Anna!

¡Caramba!

As if the losses at the Alamo and the embarrassment of San Jacinto had never happened, Mexico embraced Santa Anna's return. His popularity and his charisma were such that he was able to raise an army of eighteen thousand men. More important was the fact that to pay and outfit them, he was able to cajole money from the federal and state governments—even from the Church. For a short time he was again The Napoleon of the West.

His presence as the returning hero enabled him to push Gómez Farias out of office. Then as the new president, he promised to drive the "*loco Tejanos*" and their American invaders into the Gulf of Mexico.

Subsequent investigation uncovered the interesting information that Santa Anna was back in power through the intervention of none other than President Polk. Exiled to Cuba, Santa Anna had written letters to Polk that somehow convinced the president that the man who ordered the massacre at the Alamo was a reformed man. Moreover, he declared that he was only man with the power and intelligence to bring peace and stability to Mexico.

(This author could find no copy of the letter, but its contents must have been one of the most persuasive documents of all time.)

Meanwhile, back in Monterrey, Taylor waited no longer. On November 13, he notified Santa Anna that offensive operations would be resumed. Three days later his army occupied Saltillo. In a month he was in Ciudad Victoria headed for Tampico and from there a few miles farther south to Veracruz.

At that moment in history, Winfield Scott arrived at the mouth of the Rio Grande. The politics of the situation in Washington were exceedingly hostile to Polk, a member of the Whig party. Scott's specific orders from the Democrat Congress were to deny Old Rough and Ready any more victories. Instead, Taylor was ordered by his commander in chief to halt at Monterrey rather than march on to the capital. There he was to remain in command, so to speak, while he sent nine thousand of his best troops on to Veracruz. They were to be thereafter under the command of Scott, who was already being trumpeted as the man who would replace Polk as the president's term of office expired in 1848.

Scott, a loyal Democrat, needed a victory to catapult him into the White House as Polk's term of office expired in 1848. Of course, he demanded a more substantial one than the "little skirmishes" Taylor had commanded in Texas and northern Mexico. Furthermore, he knew that with Taylor's well-disciplined troops he could take Mexico City itself.

So the Democrat Congress ordered Taylor back to Monterrey with further instructions not to advance farther. In January, the old man, who was sixty-three by this time, wrote the Congress humbly regretting that he no longer had their confidence and expressing his disappointment that he had not been allowed to return to his home and his retirement.

Congress had a very good reason not to recall him. Although they felt a certain sense of shame at letting Scott seize the victory from Taylor, politics was politics. They were determined that Taylor should appear to be ineffectual. Therefore, by implication he would be an ineffectual president.

Governance from more than two thousand miles away as the crow flies is all but impossible. The Congress could not know that Taylor had allowed the thousand disgruntled Rangers to return to Texas. Their bravery and unorthodox tactics that had done so much to win him the victory would loom large as Scott was soon to discover. Few among the nine thousand American troops that marched to Veracruz were qualified to act as scouts, guides, messengers, and translators. Couriers were killed, dispatches intercepted, and scouting parties who did not know the lay of the land were cut off, captured, and humiliated.

The mission of Lieutenant John A. Richey, McCulloch's friend and one of his most successful scouts, ended in disaster. Richey was roped off his horse by Mexican *vaqueros* and died a brutal death dragged through the cactus and trampled. His courier's pouch was stolen and its messages eventually delivered to Santa Anna. Of singular importance was a message from Scott reiterating the congressional order that Taylor was to go no farther south.

When Santa Anna learned that the general was to be left in Monterrey with a skeleton force, he decided to move his army overland to crush and capture Taylor.

Who knew Santa Anna's mind? Possibly he thought to further impress the people by parading the famous American general as a captive in Mexico City. Such a glorious occasion would secure his position for the rest of his life. He made plans to take his newly recruited army north.

On January 1, 1847, McCulloch returned to Mexico. To keep his promise to Taylor, he and twenty-seven Rangers met the old general at Saltillo on his enforced retreat from Victoria. Old Rough and Ready was desperate for the information the Rangers could provide him. So long as he was in the field, he would never give up the fight no matter what humiliation politicians might heap upon him. The Rangers at first refused to enlist, but he insisted that he would take them on their own terms if they would be his eyes and ears as they had been from his arrival in Texas.

By January 28, Santa Anna had left San Luis Potosí. Just thirty-five miles of desert separated him from Taylor's small force. But neither man knew where the other was.

Taylor sent McCulloch and his Rangers to bring back intelligence. On February 16, they found Santa Anna at Encarnación. Taylor then sent McCulloch again to learn the size of the force that he would have to oppose.

Leaving the other Rangers to wait, McCulloch rode alone in the dark and slipped through the picket lines without being seen or heard. Once inside, he rode around like a shadow, judging from the dimensions of the camp the size and numbers of the Mexican forces. He estimated Santa Anna had a force of at least twenty thousand men. Armed with this information, Taylor determined to protect his force for as long as possible.

When Santa Anna arrived at the site of Taylor's former camp, he immediately thought the general had abandoned it in retreat. Eager for the battle, Santa Anna followed. When the Mexican army struck, Taylor, the old strategist, was in a very favorable position. He had led them into an impregnable position at the *hacienda* of Buena Vista, a position from which they could not be flanked or turned.

Santa Anna sent a unit of soldiers under a flag of truce to give Taylor one hour to make up his mind to surrender. Taylor's less than polite reply was, "Tell Santa Anna to go to hell."

Taylor inspired his men who fought as he did—with the courage of an old and very clever lion. Though they saw themselves as outnumbered, they gained experience by his tactics. Men under his command went on to greater glory in battle. Foremost among his troops was Jefferson Davis's Mississippi volunteers who not only held their line but advanced. Supported by Captain Braxton Bragg's artillery, the Mexican forces were cut to pieces by grape shot and fled under cover of night in a thunderstorm.

Santa Anna's forces collapsed. He was as always a brilliant politician but a poor field commander. As the battle raged for over twenty-four hours, conditions changed constantly. Neither he nor any of his officers could adapt their strategies to meet those changes. In the end he returned to Mexico City, his credibility severely damaged.

Old Rough and Ready, a man with a name made for the political campaign trail, returned from the war triumphant.

HISTORY'S ASSESSMENT

Taylor's victory at Buena Vista was one of the most significant in world history. The future course of great nations was decided that day, although neither opponent had any idea what would follow.

Mexico suffered a disastrous defeat. Her monstrous army, armed with the best weaponry, spectacularly uniformed, and numbering twenty thousand strong was hurled back by a relatively small force. Psychologically, the defeat was devastating. Even with strength and superior numbers, the men of Mexico concluded that they were no match for the Tejanos and Americanos.

Though Santa Anna led his men back to Vera Cruz, he discovered to his humiliation that his defeat at Buena Vista had not been a fluke. His disheartened army was no match for Scott's fresh troops, many of whom were Taylor-trained. Taylor's men sang their general's praises and told stories of the Congress's unfair treatment of Taylor to make Scott seem more worthy to be a president.

Scott's own men, who were mostly volunteers, referred to him scornfully as "Old Fuss and Feathers" because of his insistence on uniforms and strict discipline. Reporters with the troops relayed that name to the American voters, who were instantly influenced by the demeaning nickname.

Captain Walker missed both Monterrey and Buena Vista. He had been commissioned and assigned to a regiment of mounted rifles. As a handsome Texas Ranger, he became an icon that newspapers used in story after story. The government used him too as a recruiter in Maryland. Once that tour was completed, he spent time with Colt to order another thousand Walker Colts to arm the Rangers disembarking at Veracruz.

Again Colt was desperately grateful. The creation of another six-shooter—this one a .44 caliber designed for saddle holster—was the impetus his business needed. The weapon's publicity along with the handsome captain's name attached to it reached all the way to Mexico. There it gave the Americans another psychological advantage. Weapons called *revolveres* able to shoot six times without reloading terrified the Mexican soldiers. What did revolvere mean? Were they developing a weapon that could shoot around objects, around corners, hunt down its target?

¡*Madre de Dios!* Better to surrender than die.

Unfortunately, the large weapons had some drawbacks, but their reputations made them fearsome, and the Texas Rangers made them work for them.

The Walker Colts were also supplied to many of the regular army. Though Walker was now technically an American captain, everyone continued to think of him as a Texas Ranger. In May 1847, he returned to Scott's invading force that occupied Mexico City. Santa Anna withdrew his forces to Puebla, and Scott determined to complete the mop-up operation and capture him, reasoning correctly that the war would be over when a more reasonable man was in power.

In October, Walker led his troops in a battle against a large body of Mexican lancers. Walker was shot through the head and chest by Mexican sharpshooters. His men burst into tears at the news of his death. His commanding officer's eulogy named him "one of the most chivalric, noble-hearted men that graced the profession of arms."

The order that ended Scott's presidential hopes was one he gave at the last battle of the Mexican War. As Fort Chapultepec was taken on the heights above Mexico City and the victors raised the American flag, the Irish immigrants of St. Patrick's Battalion who had deserted from the American ranks were hanged. Nearly fifty men of whom more than half were Catholics from Ireland had been enticed with promising of money, land, and officers commissions. Some had been simply captured and coerced into joining the Mexican army. Again the news made the American papers and Scott's presidential hopes were dashed. In 1998, Irish director Sam Hool made a movie about the tragedy *One Man's Hero* starring Tom Berenger.

In 1848, the Treaty of Guadalupe Hidalgo negotiated by Santa Anna, who was then president of Mexico, was not so much a peace treaty as an exchange of land for money. The war had bankrupted the Mexican government. America was willing to pay $15 million for what quickly became territories of New Mexico, Arizona, Utah, Nevada, Wyoming, Colorado, and the golden coast of the North Pacific—California. The territory was four times the size of France. Almost as an afterthought, the boundary of Texas was forever set at the Rio Grande.

The Mexican War had been such a small short war. Its importance was scarcely acknowledged until people came to recognize the Manifest Destiny that Polk and others had hoped for. America stretched "from sea to shining sea." Mexico made rumbling noises about retaking California, but in 1849 gold was discovered at Sutter's Mill. Its glitter drove Americans to take ships to round the Horn of South America and covered wagons to across the Great Plains to make their fortunes. The West was settled almost before anyone could imagine.

Today Santa Anna's $15 million seems like highway robbery. Sadly, it was one of the greatest prices Mexico has yet paid for perpetuating the form of government that allowed despotism to take root.

The effect of the war was far-reaching on America.

An unusual number and range of men remembered in our history gained their experience and chose their careers on the basis of their service in Mexico.

Brown, who died so heroically in the standoff behind the earthworks of Fort Texas, has a town Brownsville and the university on the site of the fort named for him. Ringgold's name remains on a fort farther upriver in Starr County.

Robert E. Lee, the son of "Light-Horse Harry" Lee, a signer of the Declaration of Independence, was stationed at Fort Brown before he was called to head the Army of Virginia and eventually to take command against the Union during the Civil War.

Taylor's heroic battles at Monterrey and Buena Vista won the hearts of the American public. Despite his languishing in northern Mexico, Old Rough and Ready became President of the United States succeeding President Polk. The Whig party had one more triumph before fading into history.

Old Fuss and Feathers Scott got the credit for capturing Vera Cruz and subsequently Mexico City. Unfortunately, for his political aspirations, he gained a reputation for indolence when he was reported to be arising at six p.m. and eating a plate of soup to tide him over till supper. His corpulence was also a distraction. Many people found him repulsive and his military credits never carried him into the White House. Though he won the nomination for president in 1852, he was defeated by one of his own officers, Franklin Pierce, a man few had even heard of, and fewer still remember.

Scott redeemed himself, however, during the Civil War. He is remembered as the "Grand Old Man of the Army" who envisioned and set in motion the blockade of the Southern ports that did much to starve the South into surrender.

Grant and McClellan, brevet second lieutenants under Taylor and Scott, went on to become generals by the time the Civil War began. Grant rose to the rank of general, covered himself with glory, and rode into the White House. McClellan organized Lincoln's Army of the Potomac, but then was too timorous to use it. He proved himself incapable of moving his army. He allowed much ground to be lost in northern Virginia. The Civil War probably went on far longer than it should have because of his failure to act.

Davis returned to Mississippi where he found himself President of the Confederate States of America.

Texas Ranger McCulloch was promoted to the rank of brigadier general in the Confederate Army. He participated in the Battle of Pea Ridge, fought March 7 and 8, 1862, in Arkansas. Though the South outnumbered the North, the lack of cohesion on the part of the southern officers lost the battle.

On March 7, McCulloch rode forward to scout enemy positions. He had always disliked army uniforms, so he had chosen to dress in a black velvet suit, silk tophat, and Wellington boots. He paid a high price for his vanity. He was shot out of the saddle, dead before he hit the ground.

In the effort to recover his body, one other officer was killed and another was captured. With no one remaining to lead the troops, they withdrew. The Confederate forces lost not only McCulloch, but also the battle and the undefended state of Arkansas.

His body was buried at Pea Ridge but much later was reinterred in Texas State Cemetery in Austin.

The Texas Rangers, aggrandized in song and story, have their own museum in Waco, Texas. They remain today a part of the state for which so many of them fought and died.

4

THE UN-CIVIL WAR

Vast differences existed between the representatives from the various states that came together in September of 1774 to unite to become a new nation. They were more or less operating in the dark, for if they succeeded they would become a nation unlike anything the world had ever seen.

How bold they were to declare themselves independent from one of the most powerful nations in the world!

How did they dare to leave Mother England?

First, they decided that the new confederation, the United States of America, would have to agree on everything at least at first. "United" meant what it said. The idea was theoretically correct, but implementing it meant compromises would have to be made. Immediately a thorny problem presented itself. Members of the First Continental Congress introduced legislation discontinuing the slave trade. Censure came from all sides, immediate and noisy. Many influential Englishmen made fabulous, albeit unconscionable, amounts of money on this business.

For years, thousands of blacks had been imported from East Africa to harvest southern America's boundless acres of rice, tobacco, and cotton. Anti-slavery legislation would destroy the economy of the three southern colonies. Virginia as well as South and North Carolina depended on a steady stream of slaves to replenish those who died from poor working and living conditions as well as various North American diseases for which they had no immunities.

England then imported the cheap American goods harvested by slave labor to sell for another large percentage of profit. Besides food and a luxury addiction that kept the whole country inhaling fragrant smoke, New England manufacturers enjoyed the products of their "cruel mills," which employed poor children to sit for hours a day in loathsome working conditions to produce fabrics that sold for high prices. The balance of trade between England and her colonies amounted to blatant exploitation.

Many Americans saw the evils of slavery and sought to abolish it. Massachusetts, whose citizenry had no need of slaves, had already done so. Unfortunately, in 1776, the southern delegates, now including Georgia, would not sign the Declaration of Independence unless the article prohibiting slavery was stricken from it.

To the signers, solidarity was all-important. England must know that they stood united at that time. Unfortunately, its deletion proved to be the document's fatal flaw. Over the succeeding years slavery became seen more and more to be a sin and a disgrace.

During the next ten years, other northern states enacted legislation to abolish slavery. They required an educated labor force to manufacture goods, and slaves proved too expensive to educate as well as too totally unsuited to the northern climate. Hypocritically, however, the North continued to trade extensively with the South whose agrarian exports were harvested by slaves.

For fifty years, America tiptoed around the problem while the slave populations grew. The Census of 1820 recorded their number at 1,538,000. Many laws were enacted to forbid or to limit the spread of slavery into new states forming east of the Appalachians, but they were almost never enforced. As Americans spread westward, they took their slaves with them. No one seriously tried to stop them.

In that same year, the Missouri Compromise tried to set rules for statehood requiring that one free state and one slave state must enter the United States at the same time. In demanding this stipulation, Southerners hoped to maintain a balance of votes at least in the Senate where any bill passed by the House could be stalled. The compromise also drew an imaginary line across the center of the country. No one could own slaves north of the 36" 30' parallel.

A symbolic "line in the sand" had been drawn. Many learned and concerned people were conscious that the country was headed for a dreadful reckoning.

Ten years later, tempers flared more hotly. Daniel Webster from Massachusetts, the consummate American statesman, denounced the idea that Americans must make a choice. On January 27, 1830, he spoke on the floor of Congress demanding that Americans embrace a righteous tenet. "Liberty and Union," he thundered, "now and forever, one and inseparable!"

The next year Nat Turner led a slave revolt in Southampton County, Virginia. Though his uprising was put down, it—as well as the rising tides of outraged Christian sensibilities—created a hostile atmosphere despite the importance of slavery to the general economy.

"Abolitionists" might publish their creeds, but Southerners stubbornly hung together. When their very way of life was threatened, they rose to defend it, no matter whether they owned slaves or not. Defenders appeared to claim slavery as a "positive good" rather than a "necessary evil." As the rhetoric raged, the idea of a United States of America began to seem less permanent.

In 1844, the debate galloped into the churches. The Methodist Episcopal Church South broke with the northern church. Nearly a hundred years would pass before they could heal themselves and reunite as the Methodist church. In 1845, the Southern Baptist Convention broke away to form a separate entity. To this day, it has not reunited with any other groups of the Baptist church.

As antipathy built between the two sections of the country, Southerners were warned against depending on the North economically. Thoughtful people could see the North's manufacturing, shipping, banking, and international trade was diversification that would allow it to grow and prosper in many different directions whereas the entire Southern economy was based almost totally on agriculture that could not exist without imported unpaid workers living in deplorable conditions.

Then, in 1848, the President of Mexico, General Antonio López de Santa Anna, sold America the northern half of his country. Since Mexico's first constitution had prohibited slavery, one of his stipulations for the sale was that no states made from the "Mexican Cession" could work slaves.

No one was overly concerned about this stipulation until the next year. In 1849, gold was discovered in California. The state immediately applied for statehood. The precarious balance that had been artificially maintained at such economic cost was about to be disrupted. Southern Senators were incensed. No free state could enter the United States unless a slave state was added to balance it.

A compromise of a sort was cobbled together. Within two years California—already extensively settled by a well-to-do, amiable, and cosmopolitan Mexican/Spanish society, rich with gold, ocean shipping, and agriculture—entered the United States as a free state. Simultaneously, the desert and mountain country around Santa Fe was named the New Mexico Territory. The plan was that it would enter as a slave state when its population would grow to warrant statehood. It was not a good plan, but it soothed Southern congressmen for a time.

The year 1850 also saw the pot begin to boil as Northerners, too, broke the laws of the land. They refused to obey the Fugitive Slave Law, which called for the return of the slave to his master if he was apprehended in a free state. Some states passed laws that declared that a slave was free once he passed over their borders. Religious groups, in particular the Quakers, operated safe houses for runaway slaves in the North. By following the North Star, the Big Dipper, the Drinking Gourd, or whatever name they called it, black men and women "boarded" the Underground Railroad to freedom.

Then the lid blew off this bubbling cauldron.

Harriet Beecher Stowe, a protestant minister's daughter, wrote *Uncle Tom's Cabin*. Though a novel, it detailed the evils of slavery in dramatic, memorable terms. One of the most important novels in the English language and in the course of human history, to this day it remains on many reading lists. Northerners who had no knowledge of the problem were converted upon reading her book. Southerners were inflamed by her denunciation of their way of life.

It sold half a million copies in America and England, stiffened the opposition to slavery in both countries, and partly caused the defeat of the venerable Whig party candidate in the election of 1852. General Winfield Scott, one of the heroes of the Mexican War, lost to an unknown Democrat, Franklin Pierce. The Whigs were never able to mount a credible campaign again.

The next attempt to bring a pair of states into the United States—in this case, Kansas and Nebraska—ended in a demand for "popular sovereignty," whereby the states were to be allowed to vote upon entrance whether they would be free or slave.

The entire South was incensed as it read the handwriting on the wall. In a very few years, an anti-slavery bill would be introduced. It would pass, and their economy would be destroyed.

As if on cue, the new Republican Party was formed in the North with anti-slavery as its base. The next year, the roots of the Civil War took hold in "Bleeding Kansas" as neighbor fought neighbor over the issue.

The explosion was averted in 1856 when the Republicans lost the presidential election to the Democrats. President James Buchanan based his campaign on holding the nation together and averting civil war. His election did nothing to calm tempers in the Senate. In a fit of rage, Preston Brooks of South Carolina took his cane to Charles Sumner of Massachusetts and thrashed him until he lay bleeding on the floor of that august body. A less than effective statesman, President Buchanan had no influence over his legislators. He served only a single term in office. His four years were also torn by judicial storms including the *Dred Scott* decision.

Dred Scott, a slave, sued to be free because he had been taken from a slave state into a free state and then back into a slave state again. The Supreme Court dodged the issue by ruling that Scott did not have the right to sue because he was an African and therefore not a U.S. citizen. It further ruled that buying a slave in one state and moving him into a free state did not free the slave because the slave was property, and the concept of freedom did not apply to property.

Thoughtful people asked, "How could a man be property in a country whose watchword was *freedom?*"

As the nation moved closer to war, rhetoric reached an all-time high in 1858 when Democrat Stephen A. Douglas and newly minted Republican Abraham Lincoln debated throughout Illinois for the state's Senate seat. The topic of each debate was slavery—the morality of it, the logic of it, and the relative values of it. Their discourse drew from philosophy, government, and societal values rather than statistics and refutation of points. Their speeches made national headlines.

Though Lincoln narrowly lost the election, he emerged as a national spokesman for the Republican Party. He had demanded answers to several cleverly pointed questions that forced Douglas to go on record supporting the righteousness of slavery. Though Douglas won the Senate seat, his own words came back to defeat him in his subsequent bid for the presidency.

The next year an explosion occurred that made the war inevitable no matter who won. A wild-eyed minister named John Brown attempted to start a slave rebellion in Virginia. To gain weapons to lead a revolt, he attacked the federal armory at Harper's Ferry. All his efforts went to waste. The slaves did not rise up either in rebellion or in defense of Brown. He was hanged by the Virginia courts for committing treason against the sovereign state. In hanging him, the South gave the North a martyr who had the support of the Boston Abolitionists.

The presidential election of November 6, 1860, was marked by bitter rhetoric, fear, and violence. The traditional Democrat political party was split three ways with no candidate accumulating a sufficient number of votes to defeat the small new Republican Party. Lincoln who said, "Government cannot endure permanently half slave, half free" was elected. He received 180 of 303 possible electoral votes, but only 40 percent of the popular vote.

On December 20, South Carolina started the process to declare "that the Union now subsisting between South Carolina and other states under the name of the 'United States of America' is hereby dissolved."

5

SCOTT'S ANACONDA, THE BLOCKADE, AND THE MAN WHO MADE IT WORK

Commander William Barker Cushing

THE SITUATION

In the spring of 1861, a political cartoonist for a New York newspaper showed a snake charmer, a bulbous figure in billowing pantaloons, and a turban "tootle-ling" on a flute. Out of the instrument's throat came a giant black snake encircling the southern United States and weaving its way up the Mississippi River to St. Louis.

General Winfield Scott, the erstwhile hero of the Mexican War, was the barely recognizable figure. The depiction was not complimentary. In his last years, Scott had become a pathetic embarrassment. From a tall, athletic figure as a young man, he had turned into a grossly fat inept soldier whom few paid attention to.

The Anaconda Plan, however, proved to be the high point of his advisory position to President Abraham Lincoln, who saw the wisdom of it immediately. The anaconda, a South American cousin of the boa constrictor, encircled its prey and strangled it into submission. In this case, the rebellious Confederate States, with access to the Atlantic Ocean and the Gulf of Mexico that far exceeded the United States, were the prey. The plan was simple enough to conceive but difficult to execute, yet Lincoln realized as Scott had envisioned it, it would and must succeed in shortening the tragic and costly war. Hopefully, fewer Americans would die as a result of it. It was to be executed in two parts.

The first part called for a rigorous naval blockade of all southern ports from Hampton Roads at the mouth of the Chesapeake Bay to Corpus Christi Bay in Texas. No Southern ships would be allowed out with trade goods to sell to European markets, and no foreign ships would be allowed to sail in with food, medicines, armaments, and ammunition. If the barriers could be rendered effective, the South must surrender in months or face starvation.

The second part called for an army of eighty thousand men to use the Mississippi River as a highway to thrust completely through the Confederacy, thereby dividing and cutting the rebellion in two. Scott thought the culminating battle would be at New Orleans, after which the entire river would be in federal hands south of St. Louis.

Because the North had not enough ships to carry out either part of the plan, the press ridiculed it as a pipe dream, and Scott was portrayed in cartoons of the day as blowing nothing but smoke out of his pipe. In no way would the Anaconda damage the South or bring about a quick surrender.

And yet, Lincoln ordered the blockade put into action April 19, 1861, despite the ridicule, and despite the fact that the North had only one efficient warship, the *Brooklyn*. Amazingly for a nation whose greatest centers of population lay within sight of salt water, the United States had only forty-two vessels of all types, including many obsolete ships scattered across the seven seas. In order for the blockade to succeed, she must acquire enough ships to traverse the coast of the southern United States, a distance of 3,549 statute miles with 189 inlets.

Though the task seemed hopeless, Lincoln was willing to try anything to keep from being the cause of what was sure to be a ruinous and tragic war. Already it was obvious to people in the North who knew about such things that the situation in the South had deteriorated much more rapidly than anyone could have imagined. Men stood on street corners in New York and Philadelphia discussing the suicidal attitude of the Southerners who seemed blind to the full impact the war would have on their society in a very few months—even days.

By the fall of 1861, luxuries were already scarce in the new Confederate States of America. "Butter was made of persimmon seeds, tea of berry leaves, coffee of a variety of parched seeds." Shoes were made of canvas with wooden soles. No one could buy any bacon. Since salt had to be "tried out" from the earth beneath old smokehouses, there was no means of preserving meats. No one had any matches. Housewives struck fire with flint and steel. Money was no longer available, for the Northern greenback dollar disappeared as viable currency.

Something as basic and important as the principal means of general communication also became scarce. Paper mills were mostly in the North. Therefore, newspapers had to be cut to half size as newsprint became ever scarcer.

The job of postmaster or mistress had been by political appointment since the time of Andrew Jackson. Northern appointees shut their windows and doors refusing to deliver or accept mail. Postage stamps, also issued by the U.S. Government, disappeared as well. Nobody could have mailed a letter even if there had been any stationery or ordinary paper to write on. People tore pages from tablets or used scraps cut from pieces of wallpaper if they had something they needed to write down.

Soon, the Confederacy began to print money, but with all the shortages it was poor stuff, badly printed using inferior inks and dyes that smeared. Also, the paper was of such poor quality that it fell apart in the hand. Ironically, counterfeit bills were actually somewhat more desirable because they were of better quality.

Cotton, the South's cash crop, could not be shipped until it could be harvested and ginned. But slaves were needed to pick it, gin it, and load it, and fuel was needed to operate the gins. With little going out, little could come in. In order to make a profit, merchant ships had to carry in imports and carry out exports.

Most crippling to a rebel nation preparing to fight a war was the shortage of iron ore and lack of foundries. Even scrap iron was scarce, so manufacturing rails to repair railroads to transport materials around the South was virtually impossible.

And how could a man make a gun or procure the parts to repair a gun? The gunmakers—Colt, Spencer, Remington, and Winchester—were all in the North.

While the South waited and writhed in frustration, the blockade began to take shape, although not without difficulties.

First, men had to be recruited to maintain the watches, which were arduous because of the extreme monotony of the job. Then came the problems of instructing the new crews and their officers recruited from the merchant navy. The work was unpopular because of the hours spent doing absolutely nothing except searching the rolling, never-changing sea. Likewise, the ships that had been converted from merchant to ships-of-war had no real instruction manual. Every day was "train-as-you-go."

Occasionally, a blockade runner would be chased down and captured, but at first, an estimated nine out of ten got in and out unscathed. And many ran the blockade in the early days. If a runner succeeded, the profits to be made were enormous. In addition to the food, guns, ammunition, and clothing of his usual cargo, he was a fool if he did not carry lace, perfume, and spices that he could sell for fabulous prices to the wealthy, who still had gold and silver stashes.

As the war progressed and Scott's Anaconda tightened its coils, the odds of the blockade runners went down, while the crews of the ships of war became more adept at their assignments. The odds dropped as one in eight was captured in 1862, one in four in 1863, one in three in 1864, and one in two in 1865. The number of blockaders' vessels captured or destroyed by the Union was at least 1,500. Their value was an estimated $31 million.

The initial successes were further decreased as control of peninsulas and estuaries along the Atlantic seaboard was lost to the invading Union armies. The factories in the North switched into wartime production mode, and more ports were closed. Cape Hatteras on the coast of North Carolina fell in November 1861. Next came Port Royal and Beaufort, South Carolina. Soon after, venerable Roanoke Island and the old town of New Bern in North Carolina fell. When Fort Pulaski surrendered, the mouth of the Savannah River as well as the heavy river traffic to and from one of the South's greatest cities ceased. In the spring, Pensacola and Apalachicola on the Gulf of Mexico were captured. Biloxi and Pass Christian, Mississippi, followed in quick order.

When Charleston passed under siege in the summer of 1862, even Rhett Butler, Margaret Mitchell's fictional blockade runner of *Gone with the Wind*, would have had no chance to make it through.

Still the South fought on, gallantly, stubbornly, foolishly, piling misery upon misery for its people and building a hundred years of resentment and downright hatred to last into the middle of the twentieth century.

THE ACTION

No less promising a naval cadet ever attended the U.S. Naval Academy than William Barker Cushing. He was a brawler, once getting into a fight with his aunt's neighbor because the man sneered at Cushing's uniform jacket. When the cadets left their living quarters without permission for a night on the town, creating all sorts of disturbances, Cushing was always in the van of those expeditions. And, of course, he was almost always involved in the all-night whiskey and cigar parties. At the center of everything, he joined in the loud songs and told the bawdiest of stories.

After four years at the academy, he was expelled in March 1861, for those pranks and the poor scholarship that resulted from them. His was the oft-told story of a university career ruined by self-indulgence. Had not the war broken out shortly thereafter and created a high demand for trained personnel, he might never have been heard of again.

Fortunately, he seized the chance to fight a war. He applied to Secretary of the Navy Gideon Welles himself. Cushing promised that he would prove worthy of the service. Whatever he said to Welles moved the secretary. Probably the need for young men to command ships to create Scott's Anaconda had much to do with Cushing's reinstatement. Since he had never graduated, he was never given a commission. Though his men would call him "Sir," he never had official rank in the U.S. Navy.

Thereafter, Welles took a personal interest in the young man whom he considered his protégé. Cushing was attached to the North Atlantic Blockading Squadron, where he served throughout the war.

After such a less-than-stellar educational experience, he was not really expected to perform with distinction. Even those who knew him best expected nothing of any importance from him. He soon realized that challenge was what he had always lived for. He was nineteen in November 1861 when he was put in command of the U.S.S. *Ellis*. The gunboat herself was a recently captured prize. The master's mate Edward Valentine was twice as old as the boy who commanded her.

Cushing described the boat with a teenager's pride. She was "of iron" with "an 80-pounder rifle forward and a 12-pounder rifle howitzer aft." With a sense of excitement, he sailed her into the New Topsail Inlet on the coast of North Carolina. His orders were to capture whatever vessels lay at anchor north of Wilmington. They might be potentially useful to the Union, but more important they would not be available for blockade runners.

Cushing soon spotted a Confederate schooner lying at anchor with no protecting vessels. He set his helm for the *Adelaide* and ran up to within a hundred yards of her. Her captain, in a panic, ordered the crew to set her afire and abandon her. They went over the side in two small boats and rowed for their lives. Cushing coolly ordered his own crew to board her. They extinguished the blaze with little or no trouble. She was an English ship out of Halifax carrying six hundred barrels of turpentine in the hold, thirty-six bales of cotton, and a smaller amount of tobacco.

Unfortunately, he couldn't get her out of the inlet. He was frustrated beyond belief at the thought of not being able to bring "home" his prize. He had operated with notable efficiency despite the fact that he—like many, many other boat and ship captains—had no pilot. (The pilots for the inlets, bays, and rivers of the South were all born and reared in sight of them.) Loaded as the *Adelaide* was, her draft was too deep. No wonder, her crew had abandoned ship. They had believed that the Confederates would give up and leave.

Cushing struggled with his conscience for a minute. Then rather than allow her to escape back to England, he ordered the turpentine set afire. Too late, he realized that the destruction of a valuable schooner as well as her cargo worth an estimated one hundred thousand dollars was going to be difficult to explain. He was young and inexperienced with a less than sterling record behind him.

To his relief, when he returned from his expedition, Commander Davenport approved the action ordering: "continue to act in accordance with the dictates of your best judgment."

Within a week, Cushing was back along the coast. His primary assignment this time was the destruction of the salt works, a particularly vital industry in provisioning the South. He steamed into New Topsail Inlet again and made straight for the salt works that supplied the entire city of Wilmington, North Carolina.

Here he exhibited his ability to operate above and beyond his orders. Seizing the opportunity, he and his men captured three schooners, perhaps to make up for burning the *Adelaide*. With the prizes safely attached to the *Ellis*, Cushing himself led an armed party ashore in small boats. As the workers in the salt works escaped, Cushing ordered his men to tear down the brickwork, destroy the copper and iron kettles and pans, cut holes in the flatboats, and burn the buildings.

"The 10 or 15 bushels of salt that had been made that morning, I turned into a ditch," he reported. He obeyed his orders though aware that civilians would go hungry because of his act of war.

Unfortunately, the destruction had taken too much time. The workers had come back with Confederate troops armed with two artillery pieces. Cushing and his men sprang into the boats and rowed for the *Ellis*. Shots fired at them succeeded only in splashing water over them. Climbing on board his ship, Cushing turned his gun on them. When one of his shells exploded in their midst, they ran. He had more than enough time to bring home his prizes in triumph.

Fired up by his easy and exciting victories, he next decided to take the gunboat down the coast of North Carolina to Onslow Bay. From there he turned the *Ellis* up the New River Inlet through a narrow, shallow area called "The Rocks." By this time, he had "found and persuaded" a pair of pilots to steer for him. He was going to "sweep the river, capture any vessels there, capture the town of Jacksonville, and destroy any salt works," he might find along the way.

On the way in, he came upon a vessel that suddenly burst into flames before he reached her. She had been loaded with turpentine and cotton. The combination was swiftly destroying her as her crew abandoned ship. He knew a moment of disappointment that he could not claim her as a prize and haul her off down the inlet.

Reluctantly, he sailed on up to Jacksonville, a sleepy little town with no one of importance available to stop him. Ever audacious, he ran the Stars and Stripes up on the flagpole, took all the mail in the post office, saying it belonged to the United States, confiscated the store of twenty-five guns in the courthouse, and seized two small schooners tied up at one dock. He also "freed" the postmaster's Negro slaves.

Still brimming with excitement and self-satisfaction, he cruised back down the inlet past the still-burning cargo ship now settling low at the waterline.

Even as he took fire from the bank as he passed over The Rocks, he must have thought it had all been too easy. The tide was fast going out, but the entire expedition looked to be an unqualified success—

—until one of the pilots took a wrong turn in a channel.

Cushing ran aground just after he had chased the enemy away from two artillery pieces with which they had opened fire at close range. He loaded everything except the pivot gun, coal, and ammunition into one of the schooners. Still, he couldn't get the *Ellis* to float out over the bar.

At last, he turned to the crew. Probably shaking with excitement, he called for volunteers to remain with him and fight to the last. In a heartwarming show of support every man stepped forward, and he picked six. Hurriedly, he sent the schooner on her way with orders to drop down the river and keep watch. If he and his volunteer gunners were overpowered, she was to proceed on her way.

Through the long night they waited. At dawn the federal troops opened up from four different points—a crossfire that began to cut the *Ellis* to pieces. With devil-may-care enthusiasm, the six men stood in that hail of fire and swung the pivot gun around and back to return fire. The battle might have continued until one or both parties ran out of ammunition had not Cushing realized they would either have to surrender or row in an open boat for the schooner.

He had already devised a plan. He trained the pivot gun on an enemy emplacement and loaded her to fire with a long fuse that trailed across the deck. As his men took their places in the rowboat, he set fire to his ship in five places. Leaving his battle flag still flying from her mast, he abandoned her. The crew rowed away into the mist-shrouded river while the federal troops poured more fire into the flaming gunboat.

When the *Ellis* exploded and the cheers went up from the shore, Cushing's men rowed for their lives in the covering darkness. Wonder of wonders, they reached the schooner. A strong wind had sprung up with the sun. They were blown out over The Rocks and in four hours made Beaufort, South Carolina.

He was commended by the department for "his courage, coolness, and gallantry." Welles swelled with pride. His protégé was doing him proud. Word of his successful actions spread through the navy inspiring more men to act with initiative.

Then next January, Cushing proposed to execute an enterprise that he himself had planned—to capture some pilots out of Wilmington, North Carolina. He tried three times and failed each time—to his chagrin. The last time he was determined not to return to port without accomplishing something.

He took his plan to Rear-Admiral Samuel Phillips Lee (no relation to General Robert E. Lee), who must have blinked, stared, and smiled. Cushing proposed that he and his crew take one of the captured schooners, the *Home*, disguise it as a blockade runner, and sail it up the Little River past Wilmington to Fort Caswell. The captain at the pilot station there would not perceive the trick until Cushing and his men had entered the station. His purpose was to take prisoner several pilots.

Admiral Lee wrote to Cushing's immediate superior, "Young Cushing's scheme ventures more than it promises, but liking the morale of the thing I would not stop the project."

Under cover of darkness, Cushing sailed upriver half a mile with two dozen men. When he was observed, the guards opened fire with muskets. Instead of retreating, he turned his boats into the bank two hundred yards upriver from the source and landed his crews. Once on shore, he scarcely knew what to say. Gamely, he shouted, "Forward, double-quick, charge!"

None of his men had ever charged before. Nor had they any idea what they were charging at. Yelling, they ran through a small wooded area and burst out upon a fort, with camp fires blazing brightly around the walls. Instead of being daunted, Cushing yelled again, "Forward! Charge!"

The enemy, however, was daunted. Thinking at least a regiment was attacking them, they fled over the opposite side of the walls while Cushing and his men broke in the gates. Neither he nor his men fired a shot. He found he had taken an earthwork fort with a blockhouse in the center, holding the company's stores, clothing, ammunition, and part of their arms.

Probably congratulating himself on his brilliance, he ordered his men to load up what they could carry and destroy the rest.

He returned to a certain amount of gratifying adulation.

Again word spread of Cushing's bravery and initiative on land as well as sea. His successful venture garnished his already growing reputation. Men were eager to serve under him.

These actions and his potential for inspiring others to follow drew him a flattering offer. He was twenty now and almost a man. Major General John G. Foster, army commander of the department of North Carolina, offered Cushing the command of a squadron of five steam-powered army gunboats. These were essentially landing craft. The army needed men who could handle boats as well as lead a charge. Men with both talents were few and far between.

Though extremely pleased with the confidence placed in him, Cushing refused. The navy had become his life. It offered him all the excitement he could wish for. "I did not wish to relinquish actual naval service," he told his brother Alonzo.

At the same time, he asked permission to go to New York to purchase a new uniform since he had lost all his clothes when the *Ellis* went down.

Rear-Admiral Lee granted permission and probably chuckled as he told the indefatigable Gustavus Fox, Assistant Secretary of the Navy, his young protégé's ill-kept secret. "Rashness in a young officer is rather commendable. Young Cushing went off to New York not to get clothes, but to see his sweetheart."

On that particular trip, Cushing did indeed visit his sweetheart who, by the way, was not the girl he eventually married. More important he had a good visit with his brother Milton. Then he took the train down to Washington to see his brother Alonzo, whom Lincoln had brevetted a captain for "gallant and meritorious services at the battle of Fredericksburg." Unfortunately, he arrived too late. His brother was on a train bound for his next assignment. All his life, Cushing regretted that he did not arrive in time to make the connection.

On Cushing's return, Welles called him in to offer him his choice of two ships. Of the two he chose the heavier *Commodore Barney*. The ship was to be patrolling Hampton Roads, where her superior firepower would be most effective.

Hampton Roads is not a series of roads. It is one of the world's biggest natural harbors. The Elizabeth and the James Rivers empty into it and through the "roads" into Chesapeake Bay past Norfolk, Virginia, and the Atlantic Ocean. It was vitally important if Scott's Anaconda was to succeed. Cushing's obvious successes undoubtedly prompted Welles to send his protégé into that area.

A second reason Cushing chose the *Commodore Barney* was that he had heard, although he was not supposed to know, that the Union expected heavy fighting south of Norfolk before very long. The young lieutenant didn't hesitate to ask Welles if the rumor was true.

Though the information was strictly classified, Welles did not contradict Cushing. Instead, he was pleased that his protégé displayed curiosity and good sense about many things military. To the secretary's way of thinking, the young man had his ears and eyes open wherever he went. At the same time, Welles mentally vowed to make life unpleasant for whoever was responsible for the leaks.

Cushing knew what he had been given in the *Barney*. She was a powerful steamer of 512 tons with five 100-pounder smoothbore guns, a 100-pounder Parrott rifle, and a 12-pound howitzer. She carried a crew of thirteen officers and 125 men. Somewhere a naval captain awaiting a boat was gnashing his teeth in frustration. Meanwhile, Cushing was the *only* lieutenant in the navy with a separate command.

Hardly, had he gotten the steamer into position when he was ordered to take her into the Suffolk area to assist the land force. For this task he was sent four more vessels—a river steamer, a converted ferry, and two tugboats. They were all civilian boats, commandeered for service, but Cushing had no complaints. Not yet twenty-one, he was in charge of a flotilla.

Of course, he would not be satisfied with lying downriver if fighting broke out. When he suggested that he might move closer, Rear-Admiral Lee refused and warned him against doing so. Lee had no way of knowing that Union General John J. Peck had immediately moved his troops in defiance of orders to occupy and control the riverbank. With Cushing's boats in the river, the Confederate sharpshooters popped off shots at them causing several casualties. Cushing returned fire and moved his flotilla upriver as he engaged in battle.

Shortly thereafter, the South had moved in artillery pieces that blew the river steamer's boilers, severely damaged the ferry, and killed and wounded many of the crewmen on both ships. The steamer ran aground on the bar and both ships were in danger of being sunk.

On the other side of the bar, Cushing brought the *Barney* as close as he dared and blazed away at the Confederate emplacements. He fought alongside his men through the hours before the tide changed. Every round of shot into the *Barney* sent long oak splinters—hell aboard a wooden ship—flying everywhere and burying themselves in the sailors' flesh.

In the end Cushing was able to knock out the Confederate batteries and lower the anchor "where I had fought all day." His ship had sustained severe damage. Three of his crew were dead. Five were wounded but still standing to the guns. Four others were mortally wounded unlikely to survive the night. Later, he wrote a long letter to his mother detailing the battle.

His proud mother presented the letter to the *Fredonian*, long the voice of the Republican Party in Central New Jersey. From there it was reprinted in a number of Northern newspapers. Later Union officers criticized his actions, saying that the Confederates were not trying to cross the river, they were merely trying to knock out the boats. However, Cushing answered them in the press, saying that if he had not held his position, the Southern army could easily have crossed.

Thereafter, fewer blockade runners attempted the run up the Roads. As their numbers as well as their successes dropped, thanks to Cushing and naval officers who followed his lead, the situation in the South worsened. The shortages that had appeared at the beginning of the war grew more acute as people had little means of planting crops and less of harvesting them. Every able-bodied black man who dared had taken the Underground Railroad to freedom and to work in the North where they were paid wages. Only a few cents a day were better than receiving nothing while starving in the South.

The military men of the South realized that fighting a defensive war was doomed to defeat. President Lincoln and the U.S. Congress were determined to fight to keep the Union together. If the South were going to win, they had to take the battle into the North. If the citizens were made to suffer as the Southerners were suffering, their outcries, their complaints, and their votes would surely influence the government and the president to decide to let the Southern states secede without further bloodshed.

This strategy had been agreed to by Jefferson Davis himself. After a relatively easy victory against superior federal forces at the Battle of

Chancellorsville, General Robert E. Lee made plans to take seventy-five thousand Confederate soldiers into Pennsylvania on June 3, 1863.

The push by Lee and his generals into Pennsylvania began and culminated in a battle that ended in a Confederate disaster. After three days of heavy fighting, it ended in a tragedy for the Cushing family as well. Alonzo, the brother whom William had missed at the railroad station in Washington, D.C., was killed at Gettysburg.

From that moment on Cushing fought with new purpose. Coincidentally, on June 3, 1863, Rear-Admiral Lee learned that the South had begun construction of a new ship—one designed to destroy the boats with which the North was slowly starving the South. Since the *Monitor* and the *Merrimac* had fought to the death in their battle in Hampton Roads, a dramatic change had occurred in shipbuilding.

This new ship was to be ironclad. She was to be a ram, harking back to the days of the Roman Empire when vessels powered by oars rammed each other amidships to sink their enemies. She would be flat-bottomed enabling her to move in relatively shallow water despite her weight. Her prow would be solid oak with iron plating. A slanting shield of railroad iron across her forecastle would be strong enough to turn the most powerful shells the North had in its arsenal. She would be steam powered and armed with two Brooke rifles.

While the U.S. Navy was alarmed at the progress the South was making, Welles' messages drew no response from Edwin Stanton, Lincoln's Secretary of War. Welles insisted that if the South were allowed to complete the proposed ship currently under construction in the Roanoke River, she could perform powerful land and water attacks on northern shipping. Welles asked Stanton to send the army in to burn her where she lay. Stanton refused. He considered this new vessel a navy problem and chose not to understand that nothing in the Northern navy could touch her.

The *Albemarle* was partially complete by April 1864, when she saw her first action. When she was called into combat to assist the Confederate army, her captain promised that she would come even though workmen were still on board. Frequently workmen were on board during the "shakedown cruise," but this voyage would be different. Her engine had not been tried, and the crew had had no drills. Still, the needs of the Confederacy were great.

By this time, Scott's Anaconda was no longer a trail of smoke from a brass pipe. It was a giant constrictor strangling the life out of the rebellious states.

For the past year, Cushing's response to his brother's death and the family's loss was to fight harder, to guard the rivers and shorelines zealously against Southern encroachment. Welles named his young protégé "the hero of the War." On November 9, 1864, he wrote a complimentary letter to the young hero, praising him in terms that can only be called effusive by the restrained standards of that day.

> To you and your brave comrades, therefore, belongs the exclusive credit which attaches to this daring achievement. The judgment, as well as the daring courage displayed, would do honor to any officer, and redounds to the credit of one of twenty-one years of age.
>
> The Department has presented your name to the President for a vote of thanks, that you may be promoted one grade, and your comrades, also, shall receive recognition.
>
> It is for yourself to determine, whether after entering upon so auspicious career, you shall, by careful study and self-discipline, be prepared for a wider sphere of usefulness, on the call of your country.

Cushing was very young to be promoted so highly. His achievements were the topic of everyone's conversations. And despite the formal tone of the letter, the Secretary of the Navy was fairly begging him to stay in the navy and serve his country.

On April 17, 1864, the *Albemarle* with Commander James W. Cooke in command started to move down the Roanoke River toward Albemarle Sound. The body of water was the one into which many blockade runners ducked for cover. The ram had been constructed in part to liberate it from federal hands.

In the meantime, the fort at Plymouth, North Carolina, at the head of the sound was under attacks from the Union navy. They had laid mines at the mouth of the river and sunk obstructions in the channel. Above all things, the blockade had to be maintained, and the monster must not be allowed to escape into the sound.

A fort in Union hands at Warren's Neck opened fire as the *Albemarle* passed, but the shots that struck her "sounded no louder than rocks" thrown against her ironclad shell. They made no more damage.

Two Union steamers, the *Miami* and the *Southfield*, were waiting to stop her. Their lieutenants had lashed their ships together with long spars and chains to form a barricade, but Commander Cooke steamed the *Albemarle* directly at them at full speed. Her oak prow side-swiped the *Miami* as he rammed the *Albemarle*'s iron beak ten feet amidships of the *Southfield*.

While the *Albemarle* reversed engine, she took hit after hit from the gunners of the *Miami*. The *Southfield* began to sink. Water poured into her side. As one party of the *Miami*'s crewmen desperately chopped through the spars and tried to detach the chains that threatened their boat too, the gunners were almost weeping with frustration as their shots ricocheted harmlessly off the monster's armored sides and deck. In the terrible final moment, the *Miami*'s commander Lieutenant Charles Flusser was killed by one of his own rebounding shells that tore him almost to pieces.

With her commander dead, the *Miami* managed to break free and retreat rather than lose the boat. The *Albemarle* picked up the survivors of the *Southfield* from the cold water before continuing down to Plymouth to lead the battle that ended with a Confederate victory—1,600 prisoners, twenty-five pieces of artillery, immense commissary stores, and two hundred tons of anthracite coal. Most important, the monstrous ship had gained free access to two of the richest counties in North Carolina.

Lieutenant Flusser had been a friend of Cushing's. Will wrote to his mother, "I shall never rest until I have avenged his death."

On May 5, the *Albemarle* set out across Pamlico Sound to the mouth of the Neuse River with a captured Union steamer and a floating battery (a series of cannons, rifles, or howitzers) puffing along behind her. Her destination was upriver—the great old port of New Bern, North Carolina. At the mouth of the river, Commander Cooke saw seven vessels arrayed against her. This fight was obviously an ambush.

He immediately signaled the steamer and the battery to head back to Plymouth. The battery disappeared over the horizon, but the steamer was too slow and was recaptured.

The Union battle plan called for the seven vessels to form into two lines and pass as close as possible to the ram without endangering their own paddle wheels. They were to pass her and travel around and around her in "a terrific grand waltz." Simultaneously, they were to concentrate their fire on the stern of the ram, at the same time being cautious not to hit their sister ships with their shot and shell.

The plan would never have worked—although some hits were scored on the initial pass—but the iron plates turned the hits back, and the *Albemarle*'s guns were formidable. Furthermore, as she got under way into the river, she quickly outdistanced her tormentors before they could turn to go in the opposite direction. Soon only one was actually in a position to continue the attack. The *Sassacus* managed to strike her amidships.

The Confederate ram heeled over but recovered. She was barely damaged while her attacker had sustained a hit in the boiler. As the scalded crew ran screaming out on the deck, the *Albemarle*'s crew met them with muskets and pistols. Even as she steamed away from the chaos, the Confederate crew continued to fire their small arms repeatedly at the *Sassacus*'s crew. As the little boat settled in the water, the *Albemarle*'s captain made the decision to turn back toward Plymouth rather than continue to New Bern alone.

Though the ram mission was not a success, the Union commander declared that she was "more formidable than . . . the *Merrimac*. She is too strong for us." He shook his head. "She is too strong for us."

The damage to Union morale was far worse. The Confederate navy had a ship that no one could sink. She was the South's "Goliath."

In the beginning of July when all else appeared to fail, Rear-Admiral Lee decided to send for "David."

"Get Lieutenant Cushing, the officer in command of the *Monticello*. Bring him to me as quick as you can. I've got some work for him."

Ready, willing, and able-bodied, Cushing was eager to volunteer to lead an expedition. He was sure the only way to sink the *Albemarle* would be to hit her below the waterline. He believed a torpedo would be the proper weapon. He would require eighty men and "a light-draft, rifle-proof, swift steam barge, fitted with a torpedo."

The device called a "torpedo" during the Civil War was actually what present-day warfare calls a "mine." It would be anchored to the bottom of a river where a ship would be likely to sail. It was unstable at best, containing a makeshift electrical circuit that frequently did not explode. The Confederates used torpedoes throughout the South. Admiral David Farragut declared his contempt for them August 5, 1864, as he won the Battle of Mobile Bay: "Damn the torpedoes! Full speed ahead."

Cushing insisted that he should be detailed to prepare his boats for the attempt. He proposed that a torpedo be attached to a 40-foot boom that would be lowered into the water as the little torpedo boat steamed forward at full speed. He would sink a ram with his little "ram" with an explosive in her nose. Of course, the chance of the torpedo boat being blown to bits at the same time was probable. If a second boat were allowed, Cushing suggested she be armed with howitzers and stand by to pick up survivors should any be in the water.

He was not referring to Confederate sailors from the *Albemarle*. So far as he was concerned, they could take care of themselves.

Finally, Cushing worked with Assistant Engineer George W. Melville to devise a complicated torpedo device from a new invention. Cushing later remarked that it "had many defects, and I would not again attempt to its use." When he tested it several times in the Hudson River, he found that it "could be made to work" if he had enough time to make sure that the forty-foot lanyard and trigger line were pulled at exactly the right moments.

Only he knew he really did not plan to use the torpedo unless he had to. He had in mind something much more dramatic. He actually hoped to surprise Goliath and take her by boarding her and piloting her out from under the Confederate guns.

In the middle of September, two picket boats were ready. They were not in the best of shape. Picket Boat Number One had a hole in the bottom and a damaged keel. Picket Boat Number Two had also had damage to her copper bottom. Their condition was proof positive of what his superiors thought of his plan. The naval personnel, one and all, believed the venture would fail and hated to consign top craft to destruction.

After repairs were made to Cushing's satisfaction, the boats set out from the Delaware River on September 25. All went as well as could be expected past Baltimore, but Number One's engines broke down at Annapolis. Number Two took her in tow. She was repaired, but then Number Two broke down. Through the ignorance of her captain and the bad luck of an unfavorable wind, she was captured by the Confederates, who burned her to the waterline.

Cushing could have screamed and torn his hair, but he continued with his preparations with only the sadly dilapidated Picket Boat Number One. The North badly needed a victory in the summer of 1864. June 3 saw Ulysses S. Grant make a costly mistake that cost the lives of seven thousand federal soldiers. A young soldier from Massachusetts wrote as a last entry in his diary, "June 3, 1864, Cold Harbor, Virginia. I was killed."

The diary's entry made news around the North. People were seriously depressed. They no longer had faith in the war. Many did not believe that reunification was the proper course for the United States. Horace Greeley wrote, "Mr. Lincoln is already beaten. He cannot be re-elected."

Yet, Grant and Phil Sheridan, and even George McClellan, who were being talked of to replace Lincoln as the Republican candidate, were winning victories. The sentiments in the North were changing.

Still the South had the *Albemarle*. Cushing had told himself and others that if he could destroy the monstrous ship, Lincoln would be reelected, and the Union cause would be assured. When Cushing told his mother about his plans and about the huge ship he was determined to destroy or die, she didn't understand. Her grief for Alonzo was still raw. She could not bear the thought that she might lose William.

She knew the facts as well as anyone. The *Albemarle* had destroyed nine ships and more than a thousand men by that time. How could the Navy? Welles? William? Any one man expect to destroy her?

She wanted to know why he must be the one. He told her there was no one else. And it was for the country. Finally, they prayed together finishing with the Lord's Prayer.

On October 10, Cushing arrived in Hampton Roads to take command of his remaining picket boat. To add to his lack of support, Admiral Lee was relieved of command on the twelfth. Admiral David D. Porter, his replacement, had no high opinion of Cushing.

Reluctantly, he agreed to Cushing's insistence that he be allowed to attack and sink the *Albemarle* if luck were with him. Privately, Porter believed that Cushing was so willing to proceed because he was in disfavor. Cushing had shown disrespect to the commander of the British ship *Hound* earlier in the summer. Since the British favored the South in hopes of a favorable balance of trade with the Confederate States of America, Cushing had let his feelings show.

Porter later changed his opinion of Cushing, but at the time he wrote, "I have no great confidence in his success."

Cushing set out in one boat on October 20, 1864, with six men, William L. Howorth, his ensign; Stotesbury, his engineer; Samuel Higgins, his fireman; and three men not even in the navy—Lorenzo Deming, Henry Wilkes, and Robert King. On the twenty-third when he arrived at Roanoke Island, he was shown a newspaper in which a plan closely resembling his had been printed. Also included was a story that such a suicide mission involving torpedoes had failed when the torpedoes had failed to explode.

What a "facer" he had been handed! The Confederate navy must now have some idea of his plan. If they could read, they had everything but the date. Still, he made a great show of telling the army commanders that he would push off the next morning for Beaufort, North Carolina. He also let it be known that he was taking two passengers on the trip.

While Confederate spies rushed vainly about seeking him and verifying the stories, he and his crew slipped away silently and steamed *up* the Pamlico Sound fifty miles to Plymouth where the Union Navy stood waiting for the *Albemarle* to come out of the river mouth. When he arrived, he met with Commander W. H. Macomb of the *Shamrock* to ask for volunteers. To Macomb's surprise, many men wanted to go. They had heard of Cushing and wanted to be part of the expedition. Some of their comrades offered the ones who were selected a whole month's pay to take their places.

At nine in the evening, he and his men climbed down into the boat.

"Lieutenant Cushing!"

He looked up to see a young, eager face above him.

"I'll pay you ten thousand dollars if you'll let me go along!"

Cushing laughed. "You haven't got it!"

"But I'd give it if I did."

Cushing could not refuse. "Who is that—is that Ensign Gay? If it is, you're on—I need another madman on this expedition."

Gay swung down the ladder laughing. "Acting Ensign Thomas S. Gay reporting, sir. The only ten-thousand-dollar ensign in the fleet."

After several starts and aborted attempts, finally, the boat moved up the sound. The plans to deliver the torpedo were extremely complicated with thin lines that might break or slip loose easily. Pertinent information from several sources was doubtful. The only thing going for the whole affair was the skill and luck of Cushing himself. When they arrived within striking distance, the rest of the way had to be sailed in absolute silence while they drove the torpedo under the monstrous ship.

In the end, commander Macomb had allowed a cutter to be towed down the river behind the pilot boat. Its purpose was to pick up survivors in the water if the torpedo should misfire.

At last they rounded a bend in the Roanoke River. A hundred yards away loomed the huge mass of the *Albemarle*. Cushing signaled to his crew to move straight for her. His plan to board the ship and take her was still in his mind when suddenly a dog began to bark. The Confederate sentinel awoke with a start.

The time for boarding had past.

"Ahead fast!" Cushing commanded. Behind him the cutter loosed her line. As her weight fell away, Cushing felt the boat's speed increase.

On board the *Albemarle*, the defenders sprang to attention, firing shots into the darkness on the hope that they would hit something.

Within fifty yards of the monster, Cushing began to worry about the darkness, but the Confederates had planned to have light to defend the ship. With a great whoosh, a huge bonfire blazed up on the shore. By its light Cushing could see that a semicircle of logs ringed the vessel. Their tops showed above the surface of the water.

The bonfire did not serve the Confederates well. Firing from light into darkness across the inky water, they had no idea that they would hit anything—or even if anything remained out there to shoot at. Taking advantage of the light, Cushing ran the boat up to the semicircle of logs, inspected them, then spun the wheel and ordered his master's mate to steer her away. When he judged he had taken her far enough, Cushing turned her again and gave the order to full speed. The pilot gaped at him in horror but obeyed the command.

Cushing knew he could not back off as he had planned when the torpedo exploded, but he did not hesitate. He had not come this far to plan a getaway. As the boat swept around, a charge of buckshot tore the back out of his coat. Had he been coming straight in, it would have killed him. Coolly, he ignored what might have been and held the lines of the howitzers and the torpedo.

Slings in both hands, David steamed straight for Goliath.

"What boat is that?" came the cry from the *Albemarle*.

"We'll let you know!" Cushing shouted.

His crew crouching around him called several less polite epithets.

Cushing ordered Gay to swing the boom around. At the same time Cushing pulled the lanyard attached to his left wrist. The howitzers let loose with a double dose of canister that exploded among the men standing firelit on the shore.

The torpedo boom grated into place. Cushing looked up to realize he was staring into the mouth of one of the ram's eight-inch guns not ten yards away. He did not blink; he did not flinch. Slowly, he counted to five allowing the torpedo to completely submerge. Slowly, for he dared not break the firing pin, he pulled the right hand line. The ball dropped on the pin. The torpedo exploded.

At the same time the *Albemarle* fired. Fortunately, the gun could not be sufficiently depressed, so most of the charge passed over the boat. But then the wave of water from the explosion of the torpedo struck the frail picket craft. She shattered against the logs. No chance at all remained to back her over and escape down the river.

"Men! Save yourselves!" Cushing screamed. He threw off his coat and shoes, revolver and sword, and dived into the water. Behind him as he swam down the river, he heard battle cries of "Cushing! Cushing!"

Quickly, he became exhausted with the effort of swimming. Only later did he discover that he had been wounded in the left hand sometime before or after he had fired the howitzers.

About half a mile down the river, he came across the Acting-Master's Mate Woodman. The man was losing strength even as Cushing tried to help him. Shortly, he gave out entirely and sank beneath the waters. Despite the icy cold, Cushing continued to swim down the current. Finally, out of sight of the chaos he had created, ignorant of whether or not he had accomplished his mission, he pulled himself up onto the muddy bank and collapsed.

When he regained consciousness, he discovered he was on the Confederate side of the river within sight of the fort on the outskirts of Plymouth. As he slowly became aware, he decided he was being mistaken for a corpse by unconcerned sentinels who walked the palisades beyond him. After several hours he decided to make a "crawl for it." Luckily, the mud he was covered in camouflaged him. He was able to get away and into the swamp.

Only after nearly twenty-four hours of hiding and traveling did he learn that he had succeeded. The *Albemarle* was sunk. He walked on for several hours until he finally found and stole a skiff. In it he paddled down the river. At last out in Albemarle Sound he came upon a Union gunboat *Valley City*. Her guns might have blown him out of the water had not the acting master recognized him. "My God, Cushing, is this you?"

"It's I."

"Is it done?"

"It's done."

Within an hour he was on his way to the flagship to report to Commander Macomb, who did not know whether or not Cushing had succeeded. All Macomb knew was that in the wake of the expedition, the Confederates had sunk schooners and other craft in the mouth of the Roanoke to prevent anything like that occurring again. As it turned out, their action was a classic example of too little, too late.

The U.S. Navy attacked Plymouth with full force, and within hours the *Shamrock* had planted a shell in the enemy's powder magazine. The town, the fort, and the wreck of the *Albemarle* were in the hands of Union forces. She lay on the bottom after attempts to raise her failed. Her iron was stripped off her, and the proud oak hull was left to rot on the bottom of the river.

Cushing's feelings of accomplishment were complete when he learned that most of his crew had survived. Confederate sailors had picked them out of the water primarily where they clung to the log barricade that had spelled the doom of their boat. Survivors, including the cocky Ensign Gay, were paroled a few months later from the notorious Libby Prison. Because of their short stay—all lived to tell their various versions of the tale.

With good news making headlines all over the country, Lincoln was reelected president of what he was now sure was going to remain the United States of America.

Though not fully recovered from his ordeal after the *Albemarle*, Cushing was called immediately. He was needed to lead a contingent to take Fort Fisher.

Only one great battle and one great fort remained in Confederate hands. General Lee had said he could not hold Richmond, if Wilmington, North Carolina, at the mouth of Cape Fear River was taken. On December 1, 1864, Cushing was named commander of the *Malvern*, Admiral Porter's flagship. She left Hampton Roads for Beaufort. Nothing stopped her. No Confederate ships steamed out to offer her battle. She sailed on a calm sea, her colors flying from her masthead for all the world as if she were taking a quiet cruise.

She was part of a flotilla of vessels in a show of strength. Everyone knew that this would be the last major naval battle of the war.

Fort Fisher had walls twenty-five-feet thick in places but was not well protected on the landward side. The Union also believed—correctly, as it turned out—that the occupiers did not have sufficient ammunition for a prolonged siege. They also believed that rather than surrender, the men in the fort were expecting the kind of attack that was planned and were ready to hold out to the last man.

Word had come down through spies that "*Albemarle*" Cushing was in the van. His name had become a word to scare children in the South. "Cushing will get you," had become a warning eliciting a shivery response.

Admiral Porter did not like Cushing and despised his antics. At the same time, he was sure he could do the same thing and draw for himself the attention, the publicity, and the acclaim that fell to this man. His idea was to put himself in a position to take the daring chances. With his future in mind, he assigned himself to Cushing's boat, the *Monticello*, and reassigned the man whom he regarded as a fool to captain the flagship *Malvern*. Only later did he realize that, technically, he had given Cushing the position of fleet commanding officer.

On Christmas Eve, the Union navy made an unsuccessful attack on Fort Fisher. Neither the *Monticello* nor the *Malvern* participated in any significant way. On the next day Cushing acted on the probability that the naval barrage had done some damage to the channel markers, which had not been accurately placed to begin with according to Union maps.

Surmising that they had probably been moved to lead Union ships into shoals and obstacles, Cushing took it upon himself to correct the problems with a few men in a small boat. Dressed in every bit of gold braid to which he was entitled (and then some), with his boat flying the flag of a commanding officer, he had his men making corrections at his direction in full view of the fort.

For fully ten minutes the Confederate guns were silent as the men gaped at the audacious behavior. At first, they were too amazed to do anything except stare at the "madman." Then they began their bombardment, filling the air with shells—firing ammunition which the Confederate defenders forgot was in short supply. Within sight and barely out of range of the Confederate guns, Cushing directed the re-placement of the markers. He also noted the underwater and shoreline defenses set up to destroy ships as they moved up the river to Wilmington.

One of his boats was hit, but the crew was picked up. No harm was done, except Cushing made a show of brushing at the water that splashed and soaked his uniform. His men almost immediately ceased to be afraid they would be killed and worked as he directed with a will. He was well satisfied with what had been done. The Confederates had wasted valuable irreplaceable ammunition on him and his little expeditionary force, and he had valuable current information to pass to the landing parties.

Even before Cushing and his men completed their mission, the guns of Fort Fisher fell silent. The defenders watched in something like awe as Cushing and his men steamed away. They had seen the legendary fighter—and he was everything they had heard and more.

Porter had watched in annoyance while Cushing carried out perfectly reasonable actions, which Porter would never have thought of and would not have carried out in any case. The next day Porter transferred himself back to the *Malvern* and reassigned Cushing his own boat. What the crews thought of these exchanges is unknown, but they can be supposed to have enjoyed the whole dance.

Back in his own light, fast craft, Cushing waited in anticipation for the Confederate navy to send out their warship *Chickamauga*, but they scuttled her instead. Disappointed, he remarked that she might "better have finished her career in a gallant action on the ocean" than rotting in the mud of the Cape Fear River.

On January 13, 1865, eight thousand assault troops were landed under cover of darkness. Many in the garrison at Fort Fisher had fallen ill and a devastating naval bombardment had begun earlier in the evening and was scheduled to last until the next day. Fort Fisher had no ammunition to waste answering the guns. They had to take their chances hunkered down behind the walls.

Though the army under General Alfred Terry was to take the place by storm, an assault column of sailors from the fleet were landed to assist the army. Of course, Cushing went ashore with forty men from the *Monticello*. He met up on the beach with sixty men from the *Malvern* led by an old friend from Annapolis, coincidentally named Porter. They both recognized a second classmate named Preston, who had the dangerous job of leading a detachment of "pioneers," men with shovels who were to go forward with the main body and dig trenches, two hundred feet behind the walls for the assaulting troops to fall back and take shelter in. Preston confided that he did not think he would survive the battle.

Cushing and his men had never been in an attack force before, but his excitement at getting to lead a real charge had buoyed them all up. He did not count the charge he had made at Fort Caswell as a proper engagement. He anticipated having the chance for hand-to-hand combat. In this he was doomed to disappointment.

Terry's army was to attack the western jutting angle of the fort at the same time that the sailors and marines were to attack the northeast angle. Cushing did not know that the sailors' target was the best defended point of Fort Fisher. The fort commandant Colonel William Lamb had deemed it the most vulnerable and had armed and garrisoned it accordingly. Terry probably knew its defensive strategy, but saw no reason to inform Cushing.

At three o'clock, every steam whistle in the fleet let out a deafening screech. The sailors rose in a body and tried to run across the beach. The soft sand grabbed at their ankles and the bright sunlight glaring down on the sand made their dark blue uniforms excellent targets.

The three friends charged together, Porter, the leader of the "pioneers," slightly forward with Cushing close beside him. Farther back was Preston.

The fort defenders opened fire with everything they had: muskets, rifles, and cannons. Before the withering fire, many sailors fell, but the columns went on. Fifty yards from the palisade, they staggered to a halt, milling around in confusion. Their numbers were decimated. Behind them their friends and comrades lay wounded and dying in the sand. They were under the big guns, but what should they do now? What could they do? The small arms fire was still coming as fast as the defenders could reload and fire. Porter grabbed a flag, waved it, and shouted for his men to follow him. As he reached the palisade, a sharpshooter shot him in the chest. He died minutes later.

Cushing turned to look back at Preston in time to see his other friend fall dead with a bullet in his head. The beach was covered with wounded and dead men. The firing from the fort ceased as the defenders tried to save their ammunition. A half-dozen official reports written by different officers describe Cushing's activity at this point in the battle. They commend his gallantry and, above all, his utter fearlessness.

Abandoning the charge, Cushing did what he could for the wounded. Those who would be drowned by the incoming tide, he dragged or ordered dragged to a relatively dry spot. Once they were taken care of, he gathered a group of unwounded men to make another charge at the palisade. General Terry saw him and ordered an end to the suicidal operation.

The sailor's charge had been so fierce that the western angle of the palisade had been all but abandoned. Terry had been able to get his own column into the fort. He wanted to reinforce it with reserves. He ordered Cushing and his sailors to the rear of the fort, to come inside and hold it so the Confederate general Braxton Bragg, known to be in the vicinity, could not come in.

The sailors held the wall all night long. When Bragg did not come, they returned to their ships the next morning. Cushing and Admiral Porter were both furiously angry. Nearly four hundred sailors and marines had been killed as a "diversionary tactic" to allow the army to go in the back door. Even the victory was not enough. The marines had not been told to pick off the sharpshooters on the palisade while the sailors charged with cutlasses and pistols.

Cushing pitched a raging fit. He had been detailed to lead a suicide charge that had never been expected to succeed. He had lost friends and crew members. The whole fiasco was the result of ignorance, poor planning, and lack of instruction. He felt betrayed as never before in his life. Still, he was a naval officer. He did not seek to leave the service.

One last story must be told. He was sent to drag the shoreline for mines and then to oversee the surrender of all the small encampments along the river before the final acts of the war were over. When that was done, he devised a trap for blockade runners using a disguised ship.

He had his men keep the signal lights that guided the blockade runners into the Cape Fear River and up to Wilmington. The *Charlotte* came up the river one evening and dropped anchor. The British captain and his five British passengers had just sat down for a candlelight champagne supper when Union forces boarded their ship and opened the door to the wardroom. Before them, a lieutenant commander of the U.S. Navy moved to at the head of the table. The candlelight gleamed on his brass buttons.

"Steward, another case of champagne," said Commander Cushing grinning. "Gentlemen, we will drink to the success of those who succeed."

They gaped at him in amazement as who he was and what his presence meant dawned on them. At last one of the passengers muttered, "Beastly luck!"

Cushing simply grinned.

Though he was praised and given a promotion and prize money of fifty-six thousand dollars, Cushing had sustained physical injuries that bothered him, handicapped him, and then incapacitated him for the rest of his life. He first began to have severe attacks of pain in his hip just after the sinking of the *Albemarle*. The diagnosis was "sciatica," an inflammation of the nerve, or any undetermined pain that could not be diagnosed by medical doctors in those days. He may have had a ruptured vertebral disc. Certainly, he had suffered enough shocks to have ruptured one or even two or three. The problem was probably much more serious, but there was nothing to be done, and he continued to suffer for the rest of his mercifully brief life.

Twentieth-century medical personnel studying the records have suggested the terrible pain and swift physical deterioration might have been caused by cancer or even tuberculosis of the bone. The disease took strange turns along toward the end leading to increasing problems. The only treatment was stronger and stronger morphine injections—to which he undoubtedly became addicted—as did almost everyone who had to take them for the chronic pain.

General Lee surrendered to General Grant at Appomattox Court House in April 1865.

After the Civil War, Cushing served in both the Pacific and Atlantic in command of the U.S.S. *Maumee*. In 1870, he married his sister's friend Katherine Louise Forbes. They had been engaged three years, but he had not been home long enough to marry.

He became aware of the shortness of life. He had already lost one brother at Gettysburg. His older brother Howard was killed May 5, 1871, fighting the Apache tribesmen of Cochise.

The U.S. Navy found various jobs for him, even gave him command of two different ships for brief periods of time. After all, he was *Albemarle* Cushing—the man who shortened the war and elected a president. His last command was the U.S.S. *Wyoming*, a third-rate screw steamer of the North Atlantic Squadron. Promoted to commander, he put his ship in harm's way when he boldly confronted Spanish authorities in Cuba to save the lives of many passengers and crew of the *Virginius*.

He never achieved a high rank. Though he was a national hero, he had never been promoted up through the ranks. Many of his superior officers resented his flair, his audacity, and his style. He did what they did not think of or dare to do.

He was at home in Washington, D.C., when his first daughter was born in 1873. He was given the post of Executive Officer of the Navy Yard. The post was not his choice, but his failing health made it impossible for him to return to command. He spent the summer pretending to be happy. The end of his career came in November 1874, just nine years after the sinking of the *Albemarle*, perhaps the greatest adventure of the Civil War.

He remained at home for another month, but he became impossible to care for. In 1874, he was removed to the Government Hospital for the Insane. His family visited him often, but he very seldom recognized them.

Commander Cushing died on his thirty-second birthday, December 17, 1874. His wife and mother were by his side.

He was buried at the U.S. Naval Cemetery in Annapolis, Maryland. His grave is topped by a large casket in white marble. On it is carved his cloak, his commander's hat, and his sword. On one side of the stone "Albemarle" is cut; on the other side is "Fort Fisher."

HISTORY'S ASSESSMENT

In his own time, the deeds of Cushing provide front-page stories for the newspapers who loved his flamboyant style, his daring, and his determination. The fact that he was so very young and from a family of warriors gained him much publicity and subsequent fame. Some of it caused problems for him later. Jealousy and resentment are always present in a system where promotions are part of a systematic process. When someone "skips some steps" or is considered an outsider because of his failure to educate himself in the proper away, he generally leaves some disgruntled peers and superiors vowing to give him a comeuppance.

Sadly, the deeds of Cushing are totally forgotten by the authors, playwrights, and movie producers of the entertainment industry. Even the history books fail to give him more than a passing mention—if they remember him at all. Almost all the great battles of the Civil War—Gettysburg, Bull Run, Savannah, and Vicksburg—were prolonged engagements on land with witnesses standing on every hill watching, taking notes, and even taking photographs. His adventures took place in command of small groups and generally in the dark.

In the annals of the U.S. Navy, however, he is one of their shining stars. Among the biographies of naval heroes, he is included in *Farragut and Our Naval Commanders* by J. T. Headley. The creative non-fiction biography *Lincoln's Commando* by Ralph J. Roske and Charles Van Doren details his life story.

Most important is the honor the navy has paid him in the subsequent centuries in the ways he would have considered most fitting.

A quarter of a century after Cushing's untimely death, the Navy christened a torpedo boat the U.S.S. *Cushing*. She was active from 1890 to 1920. She was in all ways a fitting tribute to the man who almost single-handedly sank the *Albemarle*.

In 1915, the U.S.S. *Cushing*, a destroyer, was commissioned. She was larger, faster, and better armed than the torpedo boat, but her mission and method of attack were the same as her little sister. She was to steam in close, hard, and fast, and launch her torpedoes into the much bigger battleships and cruisers and dart back out again. For five years the U.S. Navy had two ships bearing the name Cushing before the torpedo boat was retired. The destroyer saw service until 1936 when she was replaced by a new destroyer bearing the same name.

U.S.S. *Cushing* (DD-376) was launched December 31, 1935, by Miss Katherine Abell Cushing, Commander Cushing's daughter. In 1937, the destroyer joined the famous though futile search in the Hawaiian Islands and around Howland Island for Amelia Earhart, America's famous lost aviatrix. From there U.S.S. *Cushing* returned to the Pacific Coast of the United States where she cruised until December 17, 1941. Ready, able, and eager as her namesake, she escorted a convoy bound for Pearl Harbor ten days after the beginning of World War II.

On January 13, 1942, she sailed for Midway where she served on anti-submarine patrol. In August 1942, she departed San Francisco for Guadalcanal. Once there she was almost constantly at sea, escorting supply ships and fighting off ships of the Japanese flotilla.

On the night of November 12, she sighted enemy destroyers coming fast at three thousand yards. Closing with them, she fired her guns and launched her torpedoes. She was hit several times amidships and began to lose power. Still she fought on until she became a blazing "hell ship," her ammunition exploding and most of her gun turrets out of commission. At 2:30 a.m. the crew was forced to abandon ship. Her burning hulk was seen from Guadalcanal when she sank 3,500 yards southeast of Savo Island. Seventy of her crew were killed or missing. Later many of her wounded were picked up from the waters. By her heroic refusal to surrender but to keep fighting while still aflame, she had aided in saving Henderson Field from crippling bombardment by the Japanese task force. She was awarded three battle stars for service.

In naval history, she was one of the "Goldplaters," a high-tech destroyer with ultra new weaponry and a costly propulsion system. How proud her namesake would have been of her!

A fourth U.S.S. *Cushing* was launched in September 1943 as was the custom during wartime when a fighting ship was sunk. The Japanese must have believed a ghost had risen as the ship that they left blazing returned to attack and destroy. She saw service for the remainder of World War II and remained mainly in the Pacific for her long tour of duty.

The fifth U.S.S. *Cushing* was launched June 17, 1978. She was the largest of her Spruance destroyer class and the last ship in her class to be decommissioned. She is berthed at the Naval Inactive Ships Maintenance Facility in Pearl Harbor.

When and if the navy needs her, she will sail again.

In the Memorial Hall of the U.S. Naval Academy hangs a portrait of Commander Cushing in full uniform. Nearly all the other portraits in the hall are of admirals.

6

THE GRAY GHOST OF THE CONFEDERACY

John Singleton Mosby

THE SITUATION

On January 3, 1861, troops of the Georgia militia, acting under command of the governor, seized Fort Pulaski at the mouth of the Savannah River. Two weeks later it was transferred to the newly formed Confederate States of America. The taking and occupying of the property of the U.S. government could not be allowed. Northern artillery moved into place on Tybee Island, a mile away.

Commanded by Colonel Charles H. Olmstead, the militia within the fort opened fire with smoothbore mortars, which fell into the marshes where they did no damage. But when the northern rifled cannons—thirty-pounder Parrotts—answered, their shells crumbled the casemate wall. In one fell swoop, Northern technology had made obsolete every fort in the South.

Within the fort all was chaos. The whole of the parade ground was exposed. Judging from the position of the cannons and the unquestioned range of the guns, the next salvo would penetrate the powder magazine. Every man inside the fort might well have been killed.

Though he was haunted by his decision for decades, Colonel Olmstead ran up the white flag. In so doing, he knew he would spend the rest of the long war in a Northern prison—if he were not hanged for high treason. Still, he was convinced that he was doing the right thing. Surrender saved the lives of his men. To fight would have precipitated a slaughter.

Men with military training prophesied that the South had already lost the war. It could not win without the firepower to defeat the North. Sadly, "hot heads" paid no attention. Within two months Mississippi, Florida, Alabama, Georgia, Louisiana, and Texas had joined South Carolina to form the Confederate States of America.

Their determination stemmed in part from fear generated by the Census of 1860. It numbered the slave population at 3,954,000. Freed, their unschooled numbers would overwhelm all the institutions of the South, in particular the economy. The situation was beyond untenable. It was extreme.

On February 9, 1861, Jefferson Davis accepted the presidency of the new Confederate States of America.

On March 4, 1861, Abraham Lincoln became the sixteenth president of the United States of America.

The leading citizens of Virginia, the Old Dominion home of George Washington and Thomas Jefferson, negotiated with Lincoln to stay in the Union if he would promise not to invade the state. He refused to give such a promise. Instead he offered Robert E. Lee of Virginia command of the Union army. Lee agreed but with the provision that his home state remain in the Union.

On April 12, 1861, Confederate General Pierre G. T. Beauregard opened fire with fifty cannons on Fort Sumter in Charleston Harbor.

Five days later Lee was forced to decline Lincoln's commission when Virginia seceded from the Union, followed by Arkansas, Tennessee, and North Carolina. He had no choice but to assume command of the armies of the Confederate States of America, a loosely controlled group of eleven states with a population of 9 million people of whom nearly half were slaves.

The population of the remaining twenty-one United States of America was over 20 million. The South was not only outgunned. It was outnumbered four to one.

Immediately, Lincoln ordered a naval blockade. The South's economy depended upon exports of raw materials and imports of manufactured goods. The president's popularity took a dive with many people in the North because the blockade cut the Southern states from the Northern markets as well as the English and European ones.

On July 21, 1861, the Union Army met the Confederate Army at Bull Run, also called Manassas, just twenty-five miles south of Washington, D.C. Young John Singleton Mosby was with the Virginia Volunteers, an "uncongenial" group of men, who participated half-heartedly in the battle. His request for a transfer from the unit had not been granted because he was small and light. He weighed barely a hundred pounds and stood per-haps six inches above five feet. A horse could carry him easily and, if he were killed, he would be no great loss. Naturally, his commanding officer made him a scout.

Scouts had dangerous missions. Their jobs were to ride hell-for-leather among the various units of the battle carrying messages between the of-ficers while observing what was happening in the ranks as the battles ebbed and flowed. The general strategy of attack during the Civil War was a foregone conclusion. All of the officers on both sides of the conflict went to the same military academies. Both armies moved in three columns. In the frequently blinding smoke and dust of the battlefields, scouts were the only way for the officers commanding the columns to be sure they were shooting at the enemy and not at their own center between their flanks.

Casualties on both sides were high. Scouts did not last long, for they were the targets of sharpshooters whose purpose was to destroy the communications among the commanders of the various columns. Mosby would probably have remained a scout until he was killed had not his ac-tions under fire caught the eye of one of the generals.

Impressive as a leader of men standing against the Union charge was Confederate General Thomas J. Jackson, who that day earned the nick-name well known in American history. Citing him as an example, Briga-dier General Barnard Elliott Bee, Jr., exhorted his own troops to re-form their panicked lines by shouting, "There is Jackson standing like a stone wall. Let us determine to die here, and we will conquer. Follow me."

As the battle progressed, "Stonewall" and his brigade resisted the attack and, according to the story, chased the Union soldiers back to Washing-ton. Some historians credit neither Bee's attack nor Jackson's stand with the victory. In reality, they maintain that the Union lines broke and ran because the majority of the troops were men whose enlistment was up on July 21. They did not choose to die on the day that they could go home. Indeed, most felt they had signed up to put in their three months of ser-vice. Fighting and dying were not in their plans.

Jackson is reputed to have tried to argue with the other generals in his van. He maintained that the armies of the South should follow, fighting as they covered the distance to Washington, take the capital, capture Lincoln, and end the war on the first day of battle. Unfortunately, in 1861 Jackson did not have the influence that he was to garner over the next year.

Whatever the truth of that story might be, a legend was born that day and a tragic chapter in American history opened with a skirmish and rela-tively little bloodshed.

Stonewall Jackson was impressed with Mosby's scouting ability and pulled him out of the Virginia Volunteers. The young man was promoted to first lieutenant and assigned to the general's unit of cavalry scouts where Mosby's keen observations and clear reports helped the general develop attack strategies.

More and bloodier battles were fought for nearly a year and a half. The men of the United and the Confederate States of America were killing each other by the thousands. The longest line of cannon in the world at that time let forth a deafening roar from Peach Orchard at Shiloh. Shattered by the force, the peach blossoms fell like rain from the trees. Their petals covered the ground while twenty-three thousand American men—Confederate and federal—died.

At Second Bull Run, over 125,000 Americans fought until they were exhausted. The Confederacy drove the Union back to Washington again. At Antietam three weeks later, 26,000 American men and boys had died by nightfall. Inevitably, the South had not enough men and equipment to carry the battle to the North. Unfortunately, the North could find no general with Lee's acumen. Lincoln replaced five generals in 1862. Neither side could find the right combination to win. Exhaustion and attrition seemed the only way. Ill-equipped and ill-supplied, Southern soldiers faded to walking ghosts. Still, the South fought on even when all knew its "cause" was doomed.

Miserable and sorrowing, President Lincoln is reputed to have said upon his first meeting with Harriet Beecher Stowe, writer of *Uncle Tom's Cabin*, "So you're the little woman who caused this great war."

On January 1, 1863, Lincoln issued the Emancipation Proclamation freeing all slaves in all territories within the boundaries of the United States. So determined was he to preserve the Union that he called for black soldiers to enlist in the army. The call created much dissention among many officers and men who, though fighting for the Union, considered blacks savages. Yet, by doing so, Lincoln turned the war to preserve the nation into a "holy" war to free the slaves.

Eventually, the North was sure the South *must* surrender.

THE ACTION

In January 1863, twenty-nine-year-old Mosby was captured by Union cavalry and imprisoned in the Old Capitol Prison in Washington, D.C. For ten days he languished until prisoners were exchanged. Even in prison,

Mosby kept up his spying. He heard of an unusual buildup of shipping past Fort Monroe in Hampton Roads. Casual inquiries convinced him that thousands of troops were being transported up from North Carolina to reinforce Union General John Pope in Northern Virginia.

When he was released, instead of going home, he walked to army headquarters outside Richmond, a distance of approximately a hundred miles, to personally tell General Lee what he had seen and learned.

The young man's loyalty and intelligence were impressive. Men were brave; men were intelligent; men were loyal; but very few had all those qualities in such abundance, and fewer still had such a keen eye for military operations. Confederate Major General James Ewell Brown "Jeb" Stuart, with the approval of General Lee, detailed young Lieutenant Mosby into a command position and ordered him to choose fifteen men to become spies.

They became the foundation of the Forty-third Battalion Virginia Cavalry, a matchless body of guerillas. Quickly, they adopted many of the tactics of Robert Rogers as if they had memorized the Rules of Discipline. For the next twenty-eight months, they carried out their mission ranging up and down the Shenandoah Valley. Parts of it, particularly along the Blue Ridge, came to be known as Mosby's Confederacy.

They slipped through picket lines, observed troop movements, and carried messages. They rode into the very heart of Union encampments and rode back out again unscathed. They rustled valuable horses, hopefully those saddled and bridled, for leather was becoming scarce in the South. They raided wagon trains and Union outposts. They harried troop detachments. They raided headquarters and intercepted telegraphed messages in railroad stations.

They operated with superior courage, undiscouraged by the fact that their opponents had vastly superior resources and numbers. With an air of romance about them, they rode fast horses through the darkest nights. Like warriors from another age, they were brave, young, and handsome with a sense of fun. Despite the brutal warfare around them, they behaved with enthusiasm. Their youth had not been robbed from them completely.

Their leader, a slim, hard man with luminous blue eyes, was seldom still. Mosby would spend hours in the saddle scouting enemy lines. From the information gained, he was able to plan the raids for which he became famous. He knew where every building was, the corners and angles of every street, the corrals and the cattle barns, even the chicken coops where restless fowl could sound an alarm. According to his junior officers, his attacks were never spontaneous. Spontaneity cost lives. His mission was to bring everyone home alive.

During February, Mosby was almost constantly raiding camps and capturing prisoners. When the cold numbed their fingers, his men thrust their hands in their pockets and held the reins between their teeth. When the ride became too long, they dismounted and walked their horses to get the circulation back into their feet. A raid was a sudden rush of sound and movement in the darkness, horses galloping in, men snatched from their posts or from their beds, captured and borne off on the backs of their own valuable horses. Recruitment was easy. Many young Southerners wanted to join Mosby's Rangers for the adventure.

The older, more sober citizenry were not so enchanted. On February 4, 1863, Mosby received a petition from a committee of citizens of Middleburg, Virginia. They had been threatened by Colonel Percy Wyndham of the Fifth New Jersey Cavalry. When Mosby had attacked him and his troop as they trotted into town, Wyndham and his men had fled in confusion. Now embarrassed and the butt of jokes, Wyndham wanted revenge for Mosby's successful attack and the kidnapping of three of his troop. Wyndham threatened that he would burn the town if Mosby did not turn himself and his men in.

Mosby replied by letter to the citizens of Middleburg. In no uncertain terms, he informed them that his attacks had nothing to do with their town but were sanctioned acts of war. He could not compromise with "the Yankees." To give in to threats would be to destroy his effectiveness. Every Southern town would be threatened. He further stated that his men had never occupied Middleburg, and he saw no complicity between his acts and the town itself.

While he flatly refused the civilian requests, he did slacken his attacks in February. Six of his men were captured, however, when they went to a dancing party against Mosby's express orders. They were released on parole soon thereafter when they swore they would return to their farms and homes.

They promptly rejoined Mosby's troop.

One of the Rangers' most famous exploits occurred on another of their earliest raids. One of Mosby's volunteers played a big part in the raid. James "Big Yankee" Ames was a deserter from the Fifth New York Cavalry. He had left to join the Forty-third Virginia in February because he couldn't—in good conscience—fight a "war over a Negro." His protest was to join the South who wanted only to be allowed to exercise its "states' rights." His attitude reflected the way many Northerners felt. The cursed and expensive war had been going on for two years by that time.

Mosby's plan on this particular night was to steer his troop off the Little River Turnpike and into the Virginia countryside. Thereafter, they were to cover the twenty-five miles between Dover Mill and Fairfax Court House by midnight. The night of March 8, 1863, was pitch black; the roads and countryside were a sea of mud from the rain that kept falling steadily.

From time to time a sentry on a picket line would challenge them. "Halt! Who goes there?"

Ames would answer in his clipped Yankee speech, "Fifth New York Cavalry!"

The night was so impenetrable that quite a few of Mosby's men became disoriented. They took half an hour to find the trail again and catch up. As a result, the unit reached Fairfax two hours behind Mosby's schedule. There they learned that their operational intelligence was wrong. The Union colonel whom they were trying to capture was at the other end of town. Though they captured several soldiers on guard, their quarry would be dangerous to reach.

Furthermore, Mosby knew they needed to be moving rather than have dawn find them still behind enemy lines in sight of pickets who would give the alarm. The whole expedition was about to prove a disappointment.

Then one of the men brought in a telegraph operator who informed them that a "big fish" was headquartered in the brick house on the square. Brigadier General Edwin H. Stoughton, commander of the Vermont infantry brigade, was sleeping there. Quickly, Mosby mounted a squad.

At the door Big Yankee announced, "Fifth New York. With a dispatch for General Stoughton."

When the general's staff officer Lieutenant Prentiss answered the door, he was hustled inside at gunpoint.

Twenty-four-year-old Stoughton had a reputation for being a drinker and a womanizer. Empty champagne bottles lay about the room. In a nearby tent, he was known to keep a young woman named Annie Jones. She was listed as a major on his staff.

The four Southerners forced Prentiss to lead them up the stairs. Bold as brass, the men filed into the general's bedroom. Mosby reached over and shook the brigadier's shoulder. "General, did you ever hear of Mosby?"

Stoughton woke up groggily. "Yes. Have you caught the rascal?"

"No, but *he's* caught *you*," the lieutenant informed him. "I am Mosby. Stuart's cavalry has possession of the Court House. Be quick and dress."

Though Stoughton, a noted fop, dallied as he insisted that his uniform be just so, Mosby returned to the courthouse square with both the brigadier and his lieutenant. (The whereabouts of his "major" to this day remains unknown.)

Flushed with victory, the Gray Ghost decided that his men could rustle some Union horses and capture some other officers. In swift order, they collected Big Yankee's former commander, the captain of the Fifth New York, and R. B. Wardner, an Austrian baron. Neither seemed particularly upset about being taken prisoner.

A quick reconnoiter led them to the picket lines where they pulled up the ropes and started the mounts moving out of town. A man shouted from a second-story window, "Halt! Those horses need rest. I will not allow them to be taken out! What the devil is the matter?"

Ignoring him, they rode through the predawn mist, capturing pickets, guards, and small groups around campfires. Rounding up any lone soldier as well as any small isolated groups, the Rangers ordered them up on the rustled horses. Already a sizable troop, they continued to grow as they rode on their way.

At sunrise on a hill, Mosby looked back over his shoulder. Seven miles away were the Union tents, but no sign of pursuit. He and his twenty-nine men had captured a Union general, two captains, one lieutenant, thirty enlisted men, and fifty-eight horses. They had ridden into and out of a village garrisoned by Union troops with scarcely a hitch and were headed for home again. And no one knew they had been there because they had not fired a shot or started a fight.

Mosby himself termed it "an impossibility. One of those things a man can do only once in a lifetime."

And perhaps, more important, of the twenty-nine men who rode with him, each was satisfied that to this clever and intrepid man, they would give their unquestioned loyalty and devotion. If he couldn't bring them through alive, no one could.

Jeb Stuart laughed as he proclaimed the "Stoughton Raid . . . a feat unparalleled."

The armies around the South took heart at the news of Mosby's intrepidity.

It had the opposite effect on the Union camps and headquarters. Everywhere men on guard and in their tents felt their insecurity and vulnerability. If Mosby could do it once, he could and would do it again. Worse, other partisans less chivalrous and more lethal could do it too. In Washington, D.C., members of the president's guard and the cabinet came to believe that the president himself might be Mosby's next target. A detail was ordered to remove planks each night from the Chain Bridge that spanned the Potomac between the District of Columbia and the state of Virginia.

Lincoln's reaction was typical. He was not at all fearful for his own safety. He didn't even mind the loss of the general. But he shook his head about the horses. . . . He could make a better general in five minutes, but horses cost $125.00 apiece.

Lee promoted Mosby, listing the day of his advancement as the week *before* he made the Stoughton Raid. The additional seven days' increase in pay was the least he could offer as a reward. The newly minted captain immediately resumed his raiding with a strike against two cavalry outposts.

Mosby's own men observed that he never rested—"he rarely sat still ten minutes." He was metaphorically a centaur—half-man half-horse—who spent hours in the saddle scouting and preparing his next raid. With fabled Southern charm, he gleaned information from the civilians who were happy to talk with him. Small, wiry, and unprepossessing, he rode slightly slumped in the saddle. Although he was clean shaven for the campaigns, he never combed his hair but simply clapped his hat on, leaving wisps sticking out in all directions. He had a thin hatchet face with a hawk-like nose. His own men thought him unhandsome, as had "Swamp Fox" Marion's.

The entire length of the Shenandoah Valley, two hundred Union horsemen immediately set out to chase and capture Mosby and his men. The federal army labeled the Rangers "partisans," a term associated with a political party that may plot the overthrow of a rightful regime. As such, if captured, they could be executed rather than taken prisoner and paroled or exchanged.

The first unit of Union cavalry sent out to sight his troops set out in pursuit, slowly gaining ground. Mosby allowed them to come closer and then wheeled his column to lead a screaming, yelling charge directly at them. Unable to comprehend what was going on, the blue-coats scattered. Mosby and his men pursued the main body for five miles capturing thirty-six, killing five, and wounding a significant number of others. The following day, Mosby and his men added a twenty-five-man picket post to his captives.

Thereafter, the notion of capturing Mosby was not deemed a good one.

On May 1, 1863, at the battle of Chancellorsville, the Union army was defeated by Lee's much smaller force. Thirty thousand Americans died that day, and "Marse" Robert's good "right arm" was lost. Stonewall Jackson was mortally wounded when his own men accidentally shot him.

Despite the loss and perhaps made desperate by what he correctly saw as a deteriorating stalemate in the Confederacy, Lee amassed seventy-five thousand Confederate soldiers to launch his invasion. To take the battle into the North, he was convinced, was the only way to achieve any sort of peace with honor. The citizenry of the North must be made to feel the pain that the South was feeling. For his objective he selected Gettysburg, Pennsylvania.

On June 10, 1863, Mosby, by that time promoted to major, met with James William Foster, William L. Hunter, William Thomas Turner, and George H. Whitescarver in a stone house at Rector's Cross Roads, Virginia. Acting under authority granted him in letters issued by Lee and Stuart, Mosby officially created Company A, Forty-third Battalion of Virginia Cavalry. Foster was named company commander. Hunter, Turner, and Whitescarver became its first, second, and third lieutenants, respectively.

They were no longer guerrillas or spies, who could be summarily executed if captured. Mosby's officers and men were a fully formed company of Rangers, whose honorable traditions stretched back to the French and Indian and Revolutionary Wars. Unfortunately, while his successes continued and his casualties were light, so close-knit was the troop that every man was important to him. Indeed, he regarded each as a personal friend.

They were all stunned when Third Lieutenant Whitescarver was killed in action at Seneca Mills in Maryland on June 11, 1863—the very day after his promotion. Like all leaders of "bands of brothers," Mosby suffered with the death of every man. Whitescarver's death shook him to the core.

At the same time, the rest of the South was being brought to her knees.

Realizing the situation, in 1863, Lee set about to execute his ambitious plan to take the war to the North. Over a three-day period, July 1–3, the entire war hung in the balance and then turned, although not the way Lee had hoped. The results of the failure would become obvious only as time went on. Sadly, if Lee's officers had obeyed him at Gettysburg, the battle might have ended differently. Instead for the first time, Lee encountered procrastination, hesitation, and downright disobedience.

Lee's initial orders to General R. S. Ewell were disobeyed and the chance to overrun the Union troops on Cemetery Ridge was lost. General James Longstreet argued with Lee and simply refused to attack George G.

Meade. General Stuart's cavalry was led on a wild goose chase that accomplished nothing except to leave Lee without mounted troops.

On July 3, under the impression that the Union armies were short on ammunition, Lee gave the order to General George Pickett to launch a fresh assault on Cemetery Ridge. In so doing, Lee chose to ignore Longstreet's argument that "no 15,000 men ever arrayed for battle can take that position."

As Pickett's lines started marching up the hill, the grapeshot and rifle volleys tore holes in their advancing lines. To Lee's horror, he realized that the Union strategists had tricked him into believing that their cannons were almost out of ammunition. At the same time, the Union cavalry, led in part by young General George Armstrong Custer, repulsed Stuart's diversionary charge from the east.

Though Pickett's men reached the top of the ridge, they began to fall back almost immediately. The death toll was terrible. Finally, they retreated, leaving 7,500 men dead and wounded on the slope.

July 1 through 3, 1863, fifty-one thousand Americans died at Gettysburg.

The very next day, July 4, Vicksburg, the last Confederate stronghold on the Mississippi River, could hold out no longer. Though situated in what was believed to be an unassailable position on the bluffs, the town surrendered to General Ulysses S. Grant and the Army of the West. The South was split in two and, significantly, cut off from its supplies coming in through Galveston, Texas, and New Orleans, Louisiana.

While other Confederate generals became increasingly doubtful of success, no one among Mosby's Rangers even considered surrender. Their actions had been in large part successful. Mosby's philosophy was, "If you are going to fight, then be the attacker." His strategy was never to wait for the enemy to seek him out, but to take aggressive action. By raiding and harrying the enemy, he could force the Union to try to guard a hundred points and thus expend strength and resources.

Moreover, while Mosby kept a staff of nine to fifteen officers around him, his men, all Blue Ridge boys, went home to their families at night. They hid in plain sight behind their plows. They tended their flocks and worked in local mercantiles, smithies, and offices. In this way they supplied themselves, and he had no need of a quartermaster. When Mosby called, they disappeared into the night.

Still, hard, lean times began in earnest for the South, exacerbated by danger from some of their own. Impressed with Mosby's success, the

Confederacy sanctioned the creation of Ranger units without actually providing any rules or regulations for their formation.

Suddenly, the government had big problems on its hands. Month by month, lawless brigands grouped together throughout the South. They bore little or no resemblance to Mosby's disciplined hard-riding battalions of good citizen cavalrymen. Instead, loose bands of thieves, murderers, and plunderers posed as Ranger units while they raided, pillaged, and destroyed property belonging to families whose menfolk from age twelve to seventy had joined the armies of the cause.

The widowed women and orphaned children no longer knew what the cause was. They knew only that they were miserable and soon would be starving. The fall was coming on with little or no harvesting to be done because so few fields had been planted in the spring. Helpless and bereft, they were raided by destructive bands of outlaw Southerners posing as Ranger units. The Confederate government was flooded with complaints about their depredations. The peaceful agrarian life that the South had known was being destroyed, in this case by their own people.

On September 23, Mosby and four men rode into Fairfax County to execute another raid. Its purpose among other things was to dispel the rumor that Mosby had been killed. The target for his "return to life" was Governor Francis H. Pierpont of West Virginia, temporarily headquartered in Alexandria, Virginia. Fortunately for the governor, he was in Washington for the evening, but Mosby did take prisoner the military aide, Colonel D. H. Dulany. The colonel assumed that the men in Confederate uniforms were federal scouts in disguise. Only when he spotted the governor's son among them, did he realize that he was being escorted south by Mosby's Rangers.

Mosby's Alexandria raid was just one more tragic incident in the war that cost so many lives and so much treasure. If there can be said to be a good side to the raid, the rumor that Mosby was dead was dispelled, never to surface again during the remainder of the war.

The presence of young French Pierpont among his father's enemies drew into clear light the real horror of this American war—few were whole-hearted about it. Many had doubts and were left twisting in the wind. Northerners like Big Yankee joined and then changed sides for philosophical reasons. Young men like the governor's son might have joined as a sign of rebellion against their fathers' values as well as the aura of romance around Mosby's Rangers. Men captured by Mosby vaulted onto the backs of the stolen horses and rode away in his company without putting up much of a struggle or trying to escape.

Why?

Because they were Americans—who could see in everyman's face a comrade, a neighbor, or a friend even though they wore different uniforms. They spoke the same language although with regional accents. And perhaps—just perhaps—they hoped that someday "When the Cruel War Is Over," they would all be friends and families again.

Since neither the South nor the North had been prepared to house large numbers of prisoners, many ordinary soldiers were held for a time in local jails until they signed a parole and were released. Unfortunately, the South became infamous for its "house of horrors" at Andersonville in Georgia. Unable to feed its own people toward the end, nor willing to give up the prisoners that would presumably filter back into the battalions to return and fight, the South could not or would not prevent conditions at the camp from deteriorating. Thirteen thousand Union soldiers died at Andersonville.

Camp Chase in Columbus, Ohio, has over two thousand graves of Confederate soldiers.

As many as 9,400 were housed there at one time—and 25,000 prisoners passed through. The North could afford to parole and return Southerners. The South could not. This most un-civil of wars had no black or white, only shades of cold blue and mournful gray.

In the final days of September, Mosby conducted another raid, this time with Captain William R. "Billy" Smith at the head of the newly formed Company B. After the first attempt had to be aborted because of a howling rainstorm, the men took shelter in a private home to dry out. They assembled again the next day to reach Warrenton at dusk. Three miles past the town they approached a federal campsite. Security was so lax that they were able to dismount and walk all through the camp unchallenged. They counted approximately 250 Union soldiers, either asleep or oblivious to any intruders.

Smith then had the Rangers mount and led them in a shouting, yelling raid on the rebel camp. Though the raid was a total success, they were able to capture only six men and twenty-seven horses before the rest hightailed it for the woods. They themselves sustained no casualties.

As winter began to descend upon the Shenandoah Valley, Mosby wrote to Stuart, "I thought I could make things lively during the winter months." For the next two winters and the intervening summers, he and his nine-to-fifteen-man nucleus would "move with celerity . . . threatening many points on a line . . . to neutralize a hundred times its own number. The line must be stronger at every point than the attacking force, [otherwise] the line is broken." As he saw his military value, it "is not measured by the amount of property destroyed, or the number of men killed or captured, but by the number he keeps watching."

South of the Potomac River, west of the Blue Ridge, along the whole valley, "one of the loveliest countries in the world," Mosby continued to attack the defenses of Washington, D.C., and cut vital federal supply lines and communication links along the hundred-mile stretch that lay between it and the Confederate capital at Richmond, Virginia. It would be warfare predicated upon speed, mobility, and surprise. Although it had a certain glamour, those who rode at night knew they might be maimed or killed before the night was out.

The constant disruption of supply lines and disappearances of couriers drove Union commanders frantic with frustration. Worse was an incident perpetrated by Confederate guerrillas or more likely simply one of the many groups of pillagers who had become such a problem for Davis's government and were menacing not only Union units but Confederate farms and villages as well.

The situation in the South itself could not have been worse. With the men in arms and harvests small now going on four years, food was scarce. Only small plots kept families from starvation. Since Grant had taken Vicksburg, few supplies had crossed the Mississippi River. Texas, Louisiana, and Arkansas were effectively cut off. Northern soldiers frequently went out on foraging expeditions. The men of the South fighting in the South frequently stole supplies being shipped from the North for the federal troops. In retaliation, the men from the North then went out on foraging expeditions to steal food despite the danger of Southern sharpshooters and bushwhackers.

Determined to neutralize Mosby, if he could not be killed or captured, Phil Sheridan and his cavalry had moved into the Shenandoah Valley. At the very least, he hoped to destroy the good supplies in the valley and engage Mosby, whose troops still sustained very few casualties.

While Mosby was commissioning more men to carry out his highly successful missions, a quartermaster with Merritt's cavalry division voiced the complaints of every Northern soldier. "The feeling is becoming desperate. There is no safety in leaving the command. Even for short distances the bushwhackers fire on [us] on all occasions."

Each day brought another attack by a troop of Mosby's Rangers. Now he commanded six companies, with more recruits pouring in. Because of the skill and experience of his officers, he could send all six companies where he would, combining or dividing them into two or three attack forces. By extending his attack range, Mosby applied pressure along Sheridan's line of communications and harassed his patrols. Finally, Mosby's element of surprise, still employed to great advantage by his units, gave them the decisive edge in all the actions.

For Sheridan's men, Mosby and his Rangers were shadow warriors, galloping through the blue mists and fogs up and down the Blue Ridge, in Fairfax and Loudoun Counties in particular, and wreaking havoc wherever they went.

In September, a party of Union soldiers discovered the bodies of several members of the Fifth Michigan Cavalry. All had been shot or hanged. One had a ham tied to each leg and a note pinned to his body: "that was the way every Michigan man would be served caught out foraging."

Mosby's men were blamed.

On another road, a train of ambulances was alarmed by a group of horsemen, who galloped up claiming that Mosby's Rangers were about to attack. The ambulance drivers whipped up the horses, jolting the wounded men terribly as they tore down the rutted, dusty road. All was mass confusion. Again Mosby was blamed, although not a Ranger was ever seen.

Such incidents and stories fed fear and caused reprisals. The Shenandoah Valley shimmered in the heat of raids and battles as well as the heat of Indian summer.

Sheridan had originally brought his cavalry into the Shenandoah Valley to defeat the remains of the Southern army of General Jubal Early, an irascible man though an able general. When Sheridan was told to "clean out Mosby's gang," he believed he didn't have enough men to bring order to Mosby's Confederacy and overwhelm Early as well.

In early 1864, he requested the assistance of General George Crook's hundred-man force. Called the Legion of Honor, they came out of the newly created state of West Virginia and were assigned to Sheridan, who promptly requisitioned one hundred Spencer rifles. The Spencer was a seven-shot repeating rifle much improved over the Spencer carbine used everywhere by Union soldiers.

At the head of the legion was Captain Richard Blazer, who had piloted a steamboat on the Ohio River and claimed to have fought Indians in the West. Immediately, Blazer ordered the company into action impatient even to wait for the new arms and the special ammunition for them. He changed its name in all dispatches to "Blazer's Scouts." As they moved toward the Blue Ridge, they learned from a reliable source that Mosby "with a considerable force" was camped at Snickerville.

Eager to show his men to their best advantage, Blazer moved in that direction despite heavy rains making everything and everybody miserable. His report had been reasonably accurate except that the Rangers were not in Snickerville. They were in Snicker's Gap at the top of the mountain sleeping beneath the trees in the inclement weather.

A half a mile from Berryville, Major William E. Beardsley's Sixth New York Cavalry had better luck. Arriving at the Gold farmstead, they were informed of Confederate cavalry coming fast. Beardsley dismounted his skirmishers and opened the fire as the horsemen came into view.

Mosby's Ranger Company C and Company E split into two attack wings. Company C attacked from the road; Company E charged the field only to find a stubborn gate in their way. Meanwhile the Spencer repeaters opened up, firing at the skirmish line of Company E that was stalled at the fence. Two Rangers died before the third was able to open the gate.

The Rangers then ripped through into the field sending the New Yorkers fleeing to the rear.

Beardsley shouted, "Charge!" and his cavalry galloped forward. As Company E reeled back, Company C spilled in through a gap in the fence and hit the New Yorkers with everything they had. The New Yorkers, despite their superior firepower, were almost surrounded.

Beardsley ordered a quick retreat, promising that they would turn and fire from the trees, but they never had a chance. The Rangers relentlessly shoved the federals into a corner of field while shooting as fast as they could reload. Now thoroughly panicked, the terrified men might all have died there, had not one of their number finally managed to open another gate for some to escape.

The Rangers disarmed their prisoners and searched them for money and valuables, a custom practiced on both sides where pay was small and slow in coming. If a Yankee was slow to empty his pockets, a Ranger would point a gun at his head to convince him to hurry.

According to the regimental historian, Beardsley's New Yorkers lost forty-two men who were killed, wounded, or captured.

The Rangers lost four men with one wounded at the battle that came to be known as Gold Field.

On the other side of the Shenandoah River at Myer's Ford, Lieutenant Joseph Nelson assumed command while Mosby and a small squad of fifteen Rangers scouted to the north searching for Union troops. After the rain and constant riding, the chance to relax was like a gift. Nelson's seventy men tied their horses to trees, stretched out, smoked pipes, and generally relaxed in the warm afternoon.

Blazer's Scouts caught them unawares and opened fire with the Spencer repeaters. Blazer later reported that Mosby's Rangers "fought with a will, but the seven-shooters proved too much for them."

At Nelson's command, a knot of men gathered around him while the others escaped in all directions. He and his men held for thirty minutes taking their losses. Nelson himself was wounded and captured.

Myers' Ford was a signal defeat for Mosby. He had lost men in a defeat before, but he had always caused the enemy to lose more than he had. That day was different.

His men had been overwhelmed by the new technology. Christopher Spencer's new seven-shooter repeating rifle did for the Union army what Samuel Colt's six-shooter had done for the Texas Rangers during the Mexican-American War.

Despite his defeat, Mosby had seventy new recruits eager to join his battalion. Mosby's Rangers had grown so large that he instituted Company F. Their captain was Walter Frankland, the battalion's quartermaster. Frankland's best friend had been Whitescarver, who had been third lieutenant in Mosby's old Company A.

First Lieutenant in command was Ames, whose loyalty to Mosby was unquestioned. He had ridden with Mosby from the very first successful raid. Mosby regarded him as "one of the safest and best soldiers in our Command." As he looked at the men he was placing in positions of leadership, he could not have helped but think of those he had lost and thank heaven for those who remained with him with such unquestioning loyalty.

Meanwhile, the new Spencer repeaters were proving to be an overwhelming problem for the Confederacy. A hundred soldiers armed with seven-shooters could fire seven hundred times without reloading. Even if the rifle was captured, it was good only so long as the ammunition in the magazine lasted. It could not be loaded and fired with separate powder, percussion cap, and bullet. No Southerner had any weapons to compete with it in range and efficiency.

Mosby and two Rangers were scouting in the area of Centreville in Fairfax County when suddenly they were set upon by five troopers from the Thirteenth New York. The Rangers wheeled and galloped away, the cavalry in hot pursuit. Suddenly, Mosby wheeled his horse and opened fire with both of his Colts. He killed the mounts of the two leading cavalrymen and stopped the other three. In the exchange of shots, a bullet struck one of Mosby's revolvers and ricocheted into his groin.

Mosby managed to remain on his horse, and his two men led him away. A doctor looked at the wound and decided that he could not remove the bullet without doing irreparable harm. Mosby was carried to his father's temporary quarters in Amherst County where he was able to convalesce.

Though the federals sent a troop of men to try to capture their wounded foe, they waited almost a week to do so. By that time Mosby had healed sufficiently to be on his way. He carried the bullet inside him for the rest of his life.

Meanwhile, Sheridan could devote the larger number of his men to wage a campaign against Early from September 4 through 18. Unfortunately, his campaign seemed stalled. Maneuver and counter-maneuver ended with no real progress made.

Then Lincoln needed a Union victory. He needed one badly to bolster his run for his second term. Grant sent the order to Sheridan, "Go in." On September 19, Sheridan attacked Early at Winchester at dawn. Early's divisions became separated. When they regrouped, the two armies attacked each other in a bloody slugging, shoving, shooting fight. Sheridan's numbers prevailed in the end. Early's army fled southward.

Only Mosby's men of the Shenandoah Valley prevailed. More officers and men were captured. More horses were rustled. Union officers complained to Grant. Finally, their complaints were rewarded when Grant told Sheridan, "When any of Mosby's men are caught, hang them without trial."

On September 22, 1864, shortly after Sheridan had put Early's army to rout for the last time, 120 Rangers commanded by Captain Sam Chapman of Company E entered the Shenandoah Valley through Chester Gap east of Front Royal. He bivouacked for night between the gap and the town. His command heard gunfire toward the village of Milford, several miles south.

Chapman and several Rangers began a probe toward Milford the next morning. A few miles north of the town, they saw an ambulance train with a small mounted escort.

Chapman believed that the ambulances were moving back toward Winchester, where Sheridan had defeated Early so soundly. He and his men detoured around the train and rode ahead to alert the main body of his command. Chapman believed the Union cavalry was continuing southward. He based his attack plan on that surmise.

Dividing his force into two groups, he sent Captain Frankland with forty-five men on ahead to ambush. With his group of seventy-five, Chapman waited to engage the enemy. To his stunned surprise, directly behind the ambulances came an unbroken column of Union cavalrymen. They were headed straight for Frankland, who would attack as ordered without knowing he was seriously outnumbered.

Sending his men to fall back to Chester Gap, Chapman raced to warn Frankland. He found his friend on Prospect Hill and yelled, "Call off your men! You are attacking a brigade."

Frankland didn't understand. "Sam, we can't stop now. We've got them whipped!"

No sooner had he spoken than the Union cavalrymen surrounded the attacking Rangers. Seeing themselves outnumbered, but unwilling to surrender, the Rangers scattered in all directions.

Chapman and Frankland plunged into the midst of the cavalrymen, shouting to their men, leading them across the fields toward the gap. In the meantime, the other detachment of Rangers, rather than flee, refused to abandon their comrades. Led by Harry Hatcher, a fierce fighter, the two detachments linked up.

The cavalrymen trailing the ambulances had a score to settle with Mosby's Rangers. The Reserve Brigade of General Charles Russell Lowell, son of the famous New England poet, galloped around the ambulances and raced down the road. By the time the Confederates had linked up, the brigade was upon them.

At this point the Rangers knew they were outnumbered. It was every man for himself. Still they remained loyal to each other. If a man's horse was shot, another man took him up. Another man covered his friend's back and shot the federal cavalryman about to shoot him.

The vast majority of Rangers fought their way through, plunged into the woods, and scattered up the mountainside. Though some were wounded, no one was killed. In the mêlée, Union Lieutenant Charles McMaster was shot in the head. Before he died, he had enough strength to tell his friends that he had surrendered and was a prisoner when he was shot.

Reprisals came the same afternoon. Six Rangers who had been ridden down and captured were hanged.

Mosby later protested that there was no time to take prisoners, and the cavalryman had kept his pistol and sword rather than surrendering them. To this day the Union Cavalry report says one thing; Mosby's report insists upon another.

Two days after the event, Mosby learned of Lee's surrender at Appomattox Court House on April 9, 1865. He read it in the paper, the *Baltimore American*. He was not prepared to surrender so long as General Joseph E. Johnston's army was still in the field in North Carolina or until he received orders from Lee himself.

Believing that the long war was all but over on April 14, President and Mrs. Lincoln chose to attend a play, an uproarious comedy called "Our

American Cousin." At Ford's Theatre, during the third act John Wilkes Booth shot the president in the head. Though Lincoln lasted through the night, he never regained consciousness. He died at 7:22 the next morning.

While Lee never sent orders to Mosby, Johnston surrendered to Sherman near Durham, North Carolina, on April 18, 1865. With it, the last regular Confederate army laid down their guns.

Mosby recognized that his men were in a perilous position. Should the federals care to label his men as spies and partisans, they could be hanged for treason. Determined to get the very best terms that he possibly could, he corresponded at length with several federal officers.

Finally, after a lengthy correspondence, Mosby met face to face with Brigadier General George H. Chapman in a tavern in Millwood, Virginia. They had agreed to a cease-fire, and Mosby had come in under a white flag. Mosby sat at a table beside Chapman surrounded by fourteen Union and nineteen Confederate officers.

Chapman had changed his mind, or perhaps he had never intended to accord Mosby's Rangers the proper terms of surrender. In any case, he announced that he was not prepared to make any sort of terms, nor was he prepared to extend the cease-fire. From the outset, it was obvious that Chapman wanted Mosby punished as a spy and possibly executed. He demanded instant surrender. Mosby's men were to turn in their guns and their horses and remain in the area as if imprisoned until such a time as the peace was accorded. Mosby knew that Lee's troops had not been imprisoned. Instead, they had been allowed to turn over their guns and their horses, sign a parole, and go home. Mosby instantly refused. Then he and his men walked out.

Chapman hesitated, unable to bring himself to give the order that would result in bloodshed at close quarters. With the moment past and Mosby and his men still free and unpunished, Chapman then spoke to his commanding officer Henry Halleck, who telegraphed General Grant. Grant wired back, "If Mosby does not avail himself of the present truce, end it and hunt him and his men down. Guerrillas, after beating the armies of the enemy, will not be entitled to quarter."

A second meeting with Mosby was arranged. Chapman presented Grant's ultimatum.

At that point a young Ranger named Hern burst uninvited into the meeting room. "Colonel! The damned Yankees have got you in a trap: there is a thousand of them hid in the woods right here."

As Mosby rose, Hern cried, "Let's fight 'em, Colonel! We can whip 'em!"

Mosby placed his hand on his revolver. Looking directly into Chapman's eyes, he said, "If the truce no longer protects us, we are at your mercy, but we shall protect ourselves."

No one moved. In dead silence Mosby turned and walked out. Hern held the door while Mosby's men followed. Crossing to the horses, the colonel swung into the saddle. "Mount and follow me."

No one looked back as they galloped east toward the Blue Ridge Mountains disappearing in what had come to be known as Mosby's Confederacy.

Had one pistol been discharged, one of the witnesses among the federals present told later that he did not doubt that a bloody battle would have ensued. Most, if not all of the men in the room, would have died, for the Gray Ghost and his cohort would have fought to the death.

Instead, probably breathing private sighs of relief, Chapman and his men filed out of the tavern and watched them ride off. Not till much later did they come to know that they had witnessed a historic ride—the last sight of an organized contingent of Mosby's Rangers.

The following day, on April 21, 1865, in Salem, Virginia, the colonel summoned his men for the last muster. At noon he arrived. The regiment—all that remained—consisted of barely two hundred Rangers. Formally, he rode along the line, as if inspecting each man. Finally, he turned and faced them while his younger brother William read a prepared statement. It said in part:

> Soldiers!
>
> I have summoned you together for the last time. The vision we have cherished of a free and independent country, has vanished. . . . I am no longer your commander. I part from you with a just pride, in the fame of your achievements, and grateful recollections of your generous kindness to myself.
>
> Farewell.

Minutes later he waited at the edge of Rectortown Road to shake each man's hand as they departed. They rode away into the smoky haze of the Blue Ridge back to their families or whatever awaited them now that the cruel war was indeed over.

And so it was. Neither Mosby nor any of his men ever surrendered to anyone.

HISTORY'S ASSESSMENT

The Gray Ghost of the Confederacy was sharply criticized for later becoming an active Republican. Mosby felt secure in his choice. He maintained that working within the party in power was the best way to help the South.

Mosby's way was, as always, to become invaluable. He became campaign manager for Grant in his successful run for the presidency. Grant came to know Mosby and considered him a friend.

Unfortunately, his work made him unpopular in the South. He received death threats. His boyhood home was burned, and someone attempted to murder him. Grant kept him at his side in Washington during his term of office. At the end of Grant's term, Mosby was appointed U.S. Consul to Hong Kong where he lived from 1878 to 1885. He returned to serve in Washington, practicing law in various forms including as Assistant Attorney General in the Department of Justice from 1904 to 1910.

In 1895, he attended a reunion of Mosby's Rangers, who held them annually to raise funds for pensions and support of widows. His thoughts must have drifted back to the friends who had ridden beside him in battle and were no longer at his side: Whitescarver, Billy Smith, "Fighting Tom" Turner, Ames, and deaf Clay Adams. In his speech he mentioned some of their names and finally ended with the words, "Life cannot afford a more bitter cup than the one I drained . . . nor any higher reward of ambition that the one I received as Commander of the Forty-third Virginia Battalion of Cavalry."

He never considered himself a traitor to the United States of America but maintained staunchly that "A soldier fights for his country. The South was my country." He died in Washington, D.C., the capital of the country he had fought against, but where he worked for the latter part of his life.

The number of men who rode with Mosby will never be known. As the war years began to dim, more men probably claimed to have ridden with the Gray Ghost than actually did so. His legend grew as the four years along the Blue Ridge in the Shenandoah Valley softened in memory until they seemed a summer idyll instead of the bloody shambles they indeed were.

Possibly a total of 2,000 served at one time or another, with 35 to 40 percent casualties. Only 85 are known to have been killed, mortally wounded, or executed. At least a hundred men were wounded and recovered; 477 were captured. Sixteen are known to have died in captivity. The most significant figure is that only 25 members deserted. It is the one that sheds the most luster on the battalion. Mosby's style of leadership and his philosophy of command undoubtedly bred such loyalty. On the other hand, the certain type of man willing to commit himself to being a Ranger is not the type of man to desert once he has made the commitment.

Everywhere throughout the South where he rode and raided, he is remembered in stories, memorialized in buildings and monuments, and lauded in military circles to this very day. One man particularly influenced by Mosby was George S. Patton, himself destined to be a hero of World War II. When he was a boy in San Francisco, he listened and thrilled to the Gray Ghost's stories.

To this day America remembers him as a figure of romance and legend, a part of the past that has grown dear with reenactors everywhere celebrating the battles of the Civil War.

Likewise, the entertainment industry has embraced him as a romantic figure. In 1957–1958 CBS produced a television series *Gray Ghost* starring Tod Andrews as John Mosby. In 1967, a Disney television show titled *Willie and the Yank* was on the air. Actor Jack Ging portrayed John Mosby, and one episode, *The Mosby Raiders*, starred Kurt Russell.

Motorists can ride on John Mosby Highway, a section of U.S. 80 between Dulles Airport and Winchester, Virginia. Loudoun County, Virginia's, high school team is the "Raiders." Schools are named from him along the Shenandoah Valley. Biographers love to trace his life and tactics. To name only a few: *Ranger Mosby*, *Grey Ghosts and Rebel Raiders*, *Iron Scouts of the Confederacy*, and *Lee's Cavalrymen: A History of the Mounted Forces of the Army of Northern Virginia*.

What a tribute to America's spirit that she can remember and honor gallantry no matter who performs the acts!

7

THE TRAGEDY
OF WORLD WAR II

W orld War I lasted barely five years. Ten million soldiers were killed in action; 21 million were wounded. Another 8 million went missing. Possibly 10 million civilians were killed or died as a result of deprivations caused by shortages.

Let there be no argument!

No one can imagine the absolute hell-on-earth of World War I. Thousands of men died in many of the most awful ways invented by the merchants of death. War from the air with bombs being dropped indiscriminately on innocent civilians, poison gas (prohibited in 1925 by the Geneva Protocol) used purposefully and with torturous affect, and trench warfare where tens of thousands suffered and died in foul muddy water, surrounded by rats and their own body wastes.

Even more devastating were the ruins left across Europe. The old kings of Germany and Italy were unable to cope with the economic wreckage. Socialism and its more extreme form—communism—emerged as the old orders faltered and faded. While some people embraced collectivism enthusiastically, the majority gravitated to government by "strongmen."

After such a hellish catastrophe, the leaders of every nation on earth should have said, "Never again. Nothing will ever be solved this way. We must look elsewhere. We must find a better way."

With hopes of making World War I "the war to end all wars," the Great Powers created the League of Nations in an effort to function together and cooperate rather than compete. At its greatest extent the League contained fifty-eight member nations for the short period between September 1934 and February 1935. Its stated goal was disarmament. It met while back at home, the governments the delegates represented watched their economies fall into depressions and their own structures be replaced by radical groups with no thought of peace. No one trusted anyone else enough to disarm. No one could present a workable plan that would ensure peace. No one could agree on anything.

The first tragedy of World War II will always be that it happened.

In September 1921, Corporal Adolf Hitler was ordered to spy on a meeting of the German Workers' Party. The speech that night was on the elimination and overthrow of capitalism, but Hitler was impressed with neither the party nor the speech. He came away believing that a strong leader was the only hope for Germany. Not interested in recalling the Kaiser, he thought only of the creation of a new and superior government—a Nazi government. His creation was a call to the superior or super race of Germans, the lineal descendants of the tall, blond Teutonic races from whom the Vikings sprang. Since he was the father of this idea, he called himself *Der Fuehrer*, the leader.

Equally capable of resonating with the Italian people was Benito Mussolini's Fascism. Conceived and presented in 1922, it promised Italians that their national rebirth would be eminent when they recognized themselves as the "heirs of the Caesars," who had created the Roman Empire—the greatest empire the world had ever known—the empire that had lasted for a thousand years.

Though the temptation to take the name of Caesar must have been strong, Mussolini also called himself *Il Duce*, the leader. He began his new empire with the various semi-independent states dotting the Italian Peninsula. At the same time, he proposed to turn the woefully inadequate Italian army into the Roman legions. His eloquence as well as his charismatic personality inspired Italian men struggling and failing to make a living for their families. Never mind that Italy after World War I had neither the infrastructure nor the capital for the undertaking. Italians were suffering along with the rest of Europe in the grips of a crushing depression. They were ready for a new order.

On October 27, 1922, Mussolini and his "Blackshirts" staged a March on Rome. In quick order, they ousted the prime minister and "persuaded" King Victor Emmanuel III to hand over the government. Il Duce then "liberalized" the existing government laws and dismantled the unions. Later, Hitler's *Schutzstaffel* would copy Mussolini by changing from a small paramilitary unit of Brown Shirts (because brown cotton was cheap) to an elite force that served as his Praetorian Guard and later the Nazi Party's "Shield Squadron," SS. Both groups had as much or more influence and ability to inspire terror as the crippled German army. The Japanese resented the racial slurs that Westerners visited on them. They set about to elevate Shinto, their native religion, which promoted the Emperor Hirohito as the semidivine "Son of the Sun." Though they were his children, they were not allowed to look at his divine face.

In 1923, Mussolini invaded and conquered the Greek Island of Corfu in the Adriatic. The press trumpeted Il Duce's success to the Italian people. Greece was forced to accept the loss. The League of Nations barely murmured. Arrogantly, Mussolini remarked, "The League is well when sparrows shout, but no good at all when eagles fall out." With the Italian plebiscite behind him, over the next two years he quickly dismantled all the constitutional restraints on his power.

In 1925, Mussolini took over the tiny independent nation of Albania on his border and then Libya in North Africa. He delivered bombastic speeches about the Mare Nostrum, "Our Sea," as he called the Mediterranean. He took over another Greek island of Leros to build a huge Italian naval base there.

Though Japan had actually joined the Allies in World War I, its contribution had been slight. Still by 1926, its government and people suffered from the same economic depression that gripped the world. Internationally, "free trade" was in disrepute. Every nation maintained high tariffs to protect its specific products. In order to expand its economy, Japan sought to expand manufacturing and the military.

The cluster of small islands had no resources to do either. Industrialization was the key to building the Japanese nation while the warrior class—the replacements of the medieval Samurai—sought to strengthen their positions. Though Hirohito was the emperor, he had long been a divine symbol who reigned but did not rule. In 1931, "the warriors" invaded and took Manchuria.

The League made no significant comment. Only America objected, but not strenuously.

The people within the three countries were prime targets for leaders who could lead them out of their "cultural decline" brought on—so they were told—by inferior races not only outside their borders but also within. All leaders preached a "return to the people they once were" by promoting unity, strength, and purity. None of them had to look far for scapegoats. Jews, gypsies, Mongols, Slavs, Koreans, even Catholics and

Buddhists, as well as dozens of smaller ethnic groups dotted the European and Asian landscapes.

As European governments watched, some with approval, some with trepidation, Mussolini reiterated Italy's hold on Libya on the northern coast of Africa and invaded Ethiopia on the eastern coast. The invasion itself was a success, but the aftermath was a political nightmare that actually sent a wake-up call to the peoples of Europe.

The country's ruler fled rather than face imprisonment and probable death. He was Haile Selassie, Lord of Lords, King of Kings of Ethiopia, and Elect of God. He was an anointed king and the traditional lineal descendant of Solomon and Sheba. He ruled a kingdom even older than the Roman Empire. He held a place of highest regard in the ethos of European nations.

On June 30, 1936, he, who was referred to as the Lion of the Tribe of Judah, came to speak before the League of Nations. So high was their respect for him and what he represented that his speech prompted immediate action, especially when his speech reported the use of poison gas against his soldiers. This aggression must not be allowed to stand.

Suddenly, once suppressed reports of Il Duce's previous uses of phosgene and mustard gas against African civilians surfaced. Armies were being mobilized against him. Both Mussolini and Hitler saw the advantage of organizing a united effort, but neither could bring it about.

Half the world away, General Hideki Tojo became prime minister of Japan. Promptly, his armies invaded China in 1937. The general population of America became more incensed when the movie-going public saw newsreels of atrocities in Nanking, the capital at that time. By best estimate 370,000 men, women, and children were slaughtered by bullets, by bayonets, by bombs, by gas, even by burial alive. Though thousands of photographs and reels of camera footage have been circulated for seventy years, Japan has yet to acknowledge that it actually happened.

In 1938, Hitler began his efforts to engulf Europe into Nazi Germany. He demanded, annexed, and stole countries right and left while France and the United Kingdom tried to appease him. First, they allowed him to take back the Sudetenland from Czechoslovakia. He maintained that it had been illegally taken from Germany a decade before.

At the same time, he insisted that Mussolini strip the citizenship of Jews, who maintained an ancient and honorable community within the city of Rome. Italians were outraged. Pope Pius XII sent a letter of protest to Mussolini, who ignored the Holy Father. Since Italy was nearly 100 percent Catholic, Mussolini fell farther and farther from favor with the

Italian people who too late began to see their mistake. Italy and Germany formed the Axis Powers, a term coined by Il Duce, who was now a "good friend and equal" of Der Fuehrer.

Not until the invasion of Poland on September 1, 1939, did the United Kingdom (Britain, Australia, New Zealand, and Canada) and France honor their Triple Entente agreement and declare war on Germany.

Seeking a distraction from his transgression, Hitler suggested that Mussolini invade Yugoslavia while Der Fuehrer "reclaimed" Poland on September 28 and divided it with Generalissimo Joseph Stalin of Russia!

Stalin then began his own reclamation project. On September 29, 1939, while the League figuratively wrung its hands, the Union of Soviet Socialist Republics "reclaimed" Estonia. On October 5, Latvia; on October 10, Lithuania; and on November 30, Finland. *Finland?* The sovereign nation had *never* been part of the Soviet Union. The strongmen had gambled and now raked in countries like poker chips.

Before the League had time to catch its breath, Hitler took Denmark in an hour and Norway in a day—claiming that he had saved them both from a British invasion. *Blitzkreig* war had been invented and perfected. He marched into Belgium on his way to France. On May 10, the Netherlands was forced to surrender when Queen Wilhelmina escaped to England.

On June 5, 1940, the battle for France began. (Norway did not officially surrender until June 9, 1940, but her country had been in German hands for months.)

Like bowling pins, the small countries of Europe fell—the Netherlands, Belgium, Luxembourg. On June 10, Mussolini signed a pact with Germany.

In 1940, when the German army swept through Belgium and into France, both countries surrendered and made peace terms. While France was otherwise occupied, Japan seized the opportunity to invade French Indo-China (now Viet Nam, Cambodia, and Laos) and seize its huge rubber plantations. The American people might pity China, but France was the longtime friend from the days of our revolution. Sympathy was widespread.

Though urged by America's good friend, British Prime Minister Winston Churchill, President Franklin D. Roosevelt still sought to keep his country out of the direct conflict. The American public was not ready to become the world's policeman. He instead halted the sale of oil—which America was then exporting—and scrap iron to Japan.

The Japanese countered by attacking and taking control of the oil-rich Dutch East Indies (now Indonesia), since the Netherlands too had fallen to Germany. Only one problem existed in transporting that oil and rubber back to Japan. Only one possible barrier controlled that supply route—the American Protectorate of the Philippines.

After a series of fruitless negotiations, Japan staged a surprise attack on Pearl Harbor on December 7, 1941, thereby forcing America to declare war. The attacks from aircraft carriers destroyed the American battleships but failed to destroy America's own aircraft carriers. The Japanese very much regretted they had missed the opportunity to destroy the carriers— —but not so much as they would regret it later.

Simultaneously, they attacked the Philippines, Singapore, Hong Kong, Thailand, Wake, Guam, and Midway. At that time American oil fields were well developed and pumping steadily. The Japanese could not exist without it. Their next target would have been the western coastline of oil-rich California. On the same day, they took Singapore, England's strategic port on the Malay Peninsula. Then the Dutch East Indies (Indonesia), the Philippines, Guam, Borneo, Thailand, and Burma. Like malignant fleas hopping from island to island, the Japanese struck.

Coast watchers were set up all along the eastern coast of North America and the Gulf of Mexico and the western coast of America as German U-boats and Japanese one-man subs came in closer and closer.

Not until mid-1942 did the tide begin to turn. Then the battles fought in strange places like Bougainville, Guadalcanal, Pantelleria, Moulmein, Bengasi, and Cape Esperance made the front pages and newsreels for a day. Places like Myitkyina, Cisterna, and Pointe de Hoc hardly drew a sentence. They were so small and insignificant—and cost so many lives.

In the end, Mussolini was killed by partisans in Milan. Hitler shot himself in a bunker in Berlin. World War II officially ended with the signing of the peace treaty by Emperor Hirohito of Japan aboard the battleship U.S.S. *Missouri* in Tokyo Bay on September 2, 1945.

The magnitude of this shame of mankind can only be measured in lives it cost: 22 million young men and young women killed in action, fighting for their respective countries, and 40 million innocent civilians killed or died as the result of deprivations in less than four short years.

8

THE POINT
OF THE SPEAR
William Orlando Darby

THE SITUATION

In the spring of 1942, U.S. Army Chief of Staff, General George C. Marshall, ordered Colonel Lucian K. Truscott, Jr., to London to arrange for the British commando training of American soldiers. His first idea was to train them and send them back to their units where they would be leaders and initiators of action in other units.

No thought was given to actually maintaining special units of unique and highly skilled fighters. The creation of American Rangers was not the intent. Men with those particular battle skills had not been seen since the likes of John Singleton Mosby of the Confederacy during the Civil War. Mosby's Rangers, like Rogers' Rangers, before him were considered paramilitary groups. After some further discussion, the idea that America should have its own organization of this type took root and grew.

Truscott discussed the idea with Major General Dwight D. Eisenhower, Chief of Operations Division War Department General Staff. Truscott suggested "commando," but Eisenhower resisted the idea of offending the British. Winston Churchill himself was a hero of the Boer War where the term had originated to describe guerrillas. Eisenhower insisted that Truscott come up with a name unique to America rather than one associated with British special forces.

Harking back to American military history, Truscott decided that, in honor of Robert Rogers, America's first such paramilitary hero, the new unit would have the official designation of First Ranger Battalion.

In keeping with Rogers' burnished reputation, Truscott's next task was to find a special man to command this new unit. Major General Russell P. Hartle of the U.S. Army Northern Ireland Forces immediately realized he had just the man for the job. His aide-de-camp was Major William Orlando Darby, a tough-minded, courageous soldier.

Truscott took Hartle's recommendation, and Darby was given a free hand. His first move was to call for volunteers from any military unit then in Ireland. With this group he would assume the responsibility of organizing and training his battalion.

On June 8, Darby began the process of selecting men from the First Armored Division, Thirty-fourth Infantry Division. Over a ten-day period, he interviewed the 575 who had volunteered. Of that number, 104 were judged unacceptable and returned to their units. Darby eventually had to send six boards of officers on a recruiting tour to raise the additional volunteers.

His battalion, forever to be named after the man who would lead them, was activated on June 19, 1942. Twenty-nine officers and 488 enlisted men were divided along the same lines as Mosby's Rangers from the Civil War. They were comprised of a headquarters company and six line companies, two each of assault sections and a 60-mm mortar section.

Their light weaponry began with M-1 rifles, .30 caliber machine guns later replaced with Browning automatic rifles (BARs), .45 caliber submachine guns, and 60-mm mortars. The Rangers were to be—above all else—mobile.

From the beginning of their training in Scotland, Darby developed and implemented the buddy system, still in use today. Darby ordered pairs of men to eat, to perform details, and to train as a team. Training consisted of the most rigorous field tests—assaulting positions under directed live fire, swimming in ice-cold rivers, cliff climbing with full pack, and beach landings. In addition to basic soldiering skills, he ordered timed road marches and unarmed combat. All these and many more were conducted under the supervision of the highly trained British commandos.

So intense was the training that one Ranger drowned and three others were wounded. Only four hundred of the six hundred volunteers actually passed muster into the original unit.

More training and participation followed after a disastrous raid at Dieppe, France. Poor planning and reconnaissance as well as bad information cost the Allies dearly. Fifty Rangers sprinkled among the British commando units became the first American soldiers to fight the Germans on land in World War II. Unfortunately, the attack cost a Canadian Division 75 percent of its force killed, wounded, or captured within six hours. It was a national disaster for Canada. Ranger losses were two officers and four enlisted men killed, seven wounded, and four captured in the action—a high percentage, but not as terrible as the Canadian loss.

Darby was more determined than ever to have his Rangers even better trained and prepared. The rest of the force was moved on to Dundee, Scotland, for more training. At last on November 8, 1942, they were deemed ready to fight.

Operation Torch, a landing in North Africa, was planned to take and occupy Morocco, Tunisia, and Algeria. From there, units of the regular army would move across the northern Sahara. They would trap Erwin Rommel's Afrika Korps between the Americans in the west and the British in Egypt. Churchill believed that such a maneuver would give the Allies access to the southern coast of France and the western coast of Italy—the "soft underbelly of Europe."

The first landing by the Rangers under Darby was to be made at Arzew, east of Oran and west of Algiers, where the Atlas Mountains rise from the coast of the Mediterranean.

As Darby walked among his men on board the *Ulster Monarch*, the vessel from which they would disembark, a Catholic chaplain in the uniform of the British forces stood before an improvised altar ministering to their needs regardless of their creeds. Later when Darby was lying down in his cabin for a brief rest, Albert E. Basil, complete with green beret, knocked on his door.

The padre was distressed. "My name is not of the list to make the initial landing."

Darby tried to assure him that he shouldn't risk his life uselessly. "You'll be far more benefit tomorrow after the battle is over."

Basil begged to differ. "If I can bring one dying soldier's thoughts to God, I'll be accomplishing my personal mission."

Darby stared at the man, then agreed. "I guess you win, Chaplain. . . . You'll go in boat Number Five in my wave."

Later that evening, an insistent knocking dragged him off his cot again. A wild-eyed lieutenant thrust his way in the door. The man was one Darby had selected to lead the advance guard platoon against the main coastal battery positions. His face was chalky white. "My God, Colonel, I've drawn

THE POINT OF THE SPEAR

a blank. I can't seem to remember a thing. Please go over my job with me once more."

Just a few words and a critical ear and the young man remembered everything. He left much relieved. Darby, too, was relieved. He knew from that night onward that his men felt they could come to him with any problem. He was their commander, but he was also their mainstay.

That night, the landing boats hit their objective right on the nose. In the haze of mist and fog, visibility was limited to two hundred feet. Then as they came closer, the shape of the objective Cap Carbon loomed dark before them.

Darby and most of his group recognized it immediately from the maps and photographs they had studied. Still aching with suspense, they felt the keels of the boats grate over the sandbar. They ground to a stop, the ramps dropped with a bump, and the American Rangers leaped ashore on the continent of Africa.

Up the Cap they started, easily capturing an enemy sentry who wandered into their lines unaware. Like football players who had made the first tackle, they began to relax. The lieutenant who had panicked a short time before led his advance guard calmly and confidently, just as they had practiced the "plays." Noiselessly, they moved on toward the four big guns at Batterie du Nord.

During this invasion the Americans would actually be encountering and engaging troops of the French Foreign Legion in battle. Since June 5, 1940, when the French government had signed an armistice agreement with Germany, Marshall Philippe Pétain had been set up as the prime minister. Though a decorated hero of World War I, he collaborated fully with the invaders. The French army was placed under the control of German officers, and the French police and a newly created militia were set to rounding up the many Jews living in enclaves in their cities as well as other "undesirables."

No one knew whether the men of the Foreign Legion would be loyal to the old French Republic or the new Vichy Government, so-called because of its headquarters in the town of Vichy. The Americans' only choice was better safe than sorry. Any soldier they saw was made captive or eliminated as quietly as possible with a bayonet or a club.

As they proceeded the short distance overland to Arzew, the second Ranger group, Herman Dammer's force in five assault boats, were proceeding into Arzew harbor. To their surprise and elation, the harbor boom was open. The force proceeded right up to the docks. The only problems they encountered were caused by the low tide, which left the area slippery with slime.

While the Rangers were using wire cutters on some barbed wire around the docks, a sentinel came up. Before he could sound an alarm, a Ranger struck him from behind silencing him.

From the dock they poured through the opening in the wire, vaulted over a low parapet, fired a few quick shots, and captured sixty prisoners along with the all-important guns. The fight lasted fifteen minutes. In a triumphant voice Dammer reported to Darby by walkie-talkie radio, "I've captured my objective."

Gratified, Darby with Companies C, F, and E moved abreast along the coastal road toward Batterie du Nord. Company D manhandled the four 81-mm mortars five hundred yards to the rear along a ditch, which careful study of the aerial photographs had shown to be an ideal location to set them up.

At last they came to a barricade of concentric circles of barbed wire, eight feet high and fourteen feet deep. They began cutting the wire and were almost through when French machine guns opened. Several Rangers were trapped inside the wire barricade, but fortunately, the night was dark and they dropped prone.

Hastily, the mortars in the ditch opened fire behind them. When the lieutenant inside the barricade radioed back that the mortars were right on target, eighty 81-mm shells hit the French emplacements. The machine guns stopped.

Ranger riflemen sprang from their positions and went over the parapet, shouting and shooting. The Rangers carrying the Bangalore torpedoes rushed the big guns. They stuffed the four-foot sections of steel pipe crammed with explosives into the muzzles.

Below them a larger party, including Darby, burst through the main entrance to the battery.

The French soldiers had barricaded themselves in an underground powder magazine. When ordered to come out, they refused until hand grenades were pushed down the ventilators through another Bangalore torpedo. Sixty prisoners walked out with their hands in the air. Sixty prisoners winced and shuddered when the Bangalores atop the battery finished the guns and the ones in the ventilators blew up the powder magazine.

The First Division, five miles out to sea, would come in secure by knowing that nothing from the Batterie du Nord would hamper their landing. A slight delay occurred when Darby discovered that he had only green flares. The signal that the operation had been a success was to have been white flares. Finally, they managed to get their radio dried out enough to send the information to the British destroyer.

Within hours, the first action of Darby's Rangers had proved an unqualified success.

For two months thereafter, they remained at Arzew. Then reports came that Colonel General Hans-Jürgen von Arnim's Fifth Panzer Army forces were attempting to keep a corridor open along the coast for Field Marshal General Rommel's Afrika Korps. The Allied commanders required more information. The First Ranger Battalion was ordered to supply that information.

On February 1, 1943, thirty-two Douglas C-47s picked them up from Oran and landed them at Tébessa on the eastern border of Algeria from Tunisia. They were approximately 150 miles as the crow flies from Tunis, a major objective of the Allies in this campaign. The Germans bombed the airfield as the truckloads of Rangers rumbled away toward the front.

Their orders in this case were not to act as the point of spear, but rather to give the impression that they were a much larger, overwhelming force. To accomplish these diversionary raids, Darby devised night missions with fast movement accompanied by heavy firing of weapons. Their first objective was to keep the enemy occupied and off balance. A further objective was to take prisoners whose uniforms and documents would reveal the Italian and German troops moving into Tunisia. And, finally, they were to inflict heavy casualties on the enemy.

With some satisfaction Darby recorded they could "write their own ticket" so long as they did their jobs. They might have been Mosby's Rangers operating up and down the length of the Shenandoah Valley—but without the horses.

In order to operate efficiently, one technique that Darby had all his observers and reporters do was record in their logs *only* what they actually saw or heard. If they saw two German soldiers, they were not to interpret that their presence meant anything at all. If they heard shots fired, they were to record the number and insofar as they were able identify the arms. In this manner the details were absolutely accurate and told the Rangers exactly what to expect where. "Two 88-mm guns at the junction of Highway 410," told exactly what to expect. What those guns might signify was anybody's guess.

On February 11, Companies A, E, and F, and a battalion headquarters element all under Lieutenant Colonel Darby's command, conducted a night raid against Italian front-line positions near Sened. Half the battalion went out on the first raid; each Ranger, with his buddy. Each carried a

C ration, a canteen of water, and a shelter half. Transported twenty miles by truck, they made the last eight miles over rough terrain in the dark. Before dawn they rested less than four miles from their objective. The morning was spent in reconnaissance and further detailed planning.

Enemy aircraft zoomed overhead constantly.

Even though the Rangers were concealed by their shelters, Burnoose-clad Arabs wandered in. While they might have wanted merely to barter oranges for chewing gum and cigarettes, Darby didn't allow his men to take chances. They were put under guard until the main attack started out under cover of darkness the next evening.

Wearing knit caps instead of helmets, their faces coated with spit-soaked dirt, the Rangers crawled up the rocky hill. The Italians must have thought they were in an inaccessible place because they had posted no sentinels. The darkness was total but their precise movements paid off. Operating by time and distance, they spread out into a skirmish line, two hundred yards out.

Perhaps the approaching Rangers made a tiny sound. Perhaps the men guarding the objective sensed movement. Perhaps the sentries possessed a preternatural perception of approaching danger. Something alerted the Italians, who sprayed the hillside with tracers. Instead of returning fire and thereby confirming their presence, the Rangers continued to hug the hill and crawl upward on their bellies in silence. Miraculously, only one man panicked and started up. He was killed instantly—their only casualty.

Finally, fifty yards out, at Darby's command, they charged. Coming in low out of dark, they opened fire with machine guns and BARs. They tossed grenades and plunged into the lines of the terrified Italians, bayonets stabbing and slashing. In hand-to-hand combat in impenetrable darkness, the Italians couldn't begin to find their enemy. Likewise, unable to see the terrified faces of their foes, the Rangers were utterly ruthless.

The Italians came bursting out of their tents. Some tried to escape on motorbikes; some merely threw down their arms and screamed for mercy. A few with more presence of mind found their 50-mm antitank gun and began dropping shells. Some fell quite close to Darby's command post.

Darby called Captain Roy Murray, whose job it was to take out those very guns. The captain shouted into the walkie-talkie, "Objective reached, sir!"

"Well, when are you going to take out those blasted guns?"

At that moment a grenade took out the gun.

"Fifty millimeters reached and destroyed, sir," reported the captain.

The Italians were badly mauled. Many killed and as many more wounded. Eleven were captured by the "Black Death," as they called the Rangers.

Only one Ranger was killed and twenty were wounded, several of those only slightly. Darby's standing order to move fast with heavy firing of weapons and inflict heavy casualties had been obeyed to the letter.

One Ranger reported, "There was some pretty rough in-fighting there, but a man doesn't talk about what he does with a bayonet."

The next order of business was to pull back with only two and a half hours of darkness left before dawn and safety twelve miles away on foot. Darby created two columns—one fast, one slow. The fast column swung out at killing pace, reaching the waiting trucks before dawn.

The slow column waited for the first aid men and the doctor to give morphine to the two badly wounded men and sprinkle sulfa on everyone's wounds. Those with wounds that enabled them to walk were treated so as to reduce the shock and stop the bleeding. The medics were as hardened as the Rangers they cared for, so they moved right out with the slow column. No one expected Darby to stay with them, but no one was surprised when he did. No one seriously wounded expected to be carried on a stretcher, but Darby himself took turns carrying the stretchers alongside his men. No one questioned him. No one commented. But everyone among them took note.

The slow column marched the twelve miles to the French outpost, hid in the hills during the next day until jeeps and trucks came and carried them out the next night.

The action before, during, and after Sened made the Rangers' reputation for executing with fierce precision. Darby, four other Ranger officers, and nine enlisted men were decorated with the Silver Star for gallantry. Generals "Lou" Truscott and "Scrappy" Hartle must have congratulated themselves over and over again on their choice of the good ol' Arkansas boy to lead America's first warriors of World War II.

Unfortunately, the battle from North Africa was far from over. Field Marshall Rommel was not called the "Desert Fox" for nothing. He planned an attack that if successful would drive the Allied Forces—the Americans and the French defenders—back to Tébessa deep in Algeria. He could then turn east and force British General Bernard Montgomery's Eighth Army to retreat.

Von Arnim's Tenth and Twenty-first Panzer Divisions hit the Americans at Faid Pass. They drove back units of the American First Armored Division and continued toward Tébessa.

Darby's Rangers were ordered to spread out for two miles and hold the route. The mined road stretched below them. They held the heights of another pass—Kasserine. Behind them in the pass were a battalion of American infantry, two French batteries, and a regiment of Algerians with obsolete rifles. Despite their efforts, Rommel swept around the mined road and came upon the Allies from behind. The loss was considered one of the setbacks of the war.

The powers in Washington, D.C., were rocked back on their heels. On the same date a second Ranger Battalion completed their training and was assigned to the European theater.

General George S. Patton arrived in North Africa sent to replace General Lloyd Fredendall, who had proved himself to be ineffective. Darby was in the infirmary with a bad case of the flu that left him delirious, but his Rangers were ordered to serve as auxiliary troops to the First Division. Captain Dammer, who had been one of Darby's handpicked subordinates, took over until the colonel could get back on his feet.

Patton's orders were "Find 'em, attack 'em, destroy 'em."

Darby returned June 4, still not fully recovered but determined to go with his men. At a place called El Guettar, they were told that the entire Tunisian war hinged on the success of the Ranger company to get up those mountains to the enemy's rear.

Darby's Rangers numbered five hundred against a German force of about two thousand. The Rangers had been instructed to hold as long as possible, taking German and Italian prisoners by which their units could be identified. They were not to be committed to any fight from which they couldn't extricate themselves.

In darkness the Black Death strode out past the First Division troops. As they climbed the slope, they followed a gorge that led to their objective. Below them they could hear the First Division digging in along the macadam road. All the business of preparing for battle was going on below them. The town of El Guettar lay up ahead of them.

El Guettar, predicted to be the "most significant battle of the Tunisian War," was dark, silent, and empty. It proved to be a colossal piece of misinformation. No one complained. No one was hurt and most told each other to watch out next time. The Atlas Mountains were full of passes and draws where ambushes could take place.

The next pass was Djebel el Ank. With the reinforcement of an engineer battalion, they were to be the spearhead for the Twenty-sixth Regimental Combat Team. Under cover of darkness again, they crossed gorges, hills, and dry streambeds. They arrived and set up a camp on a plateau overlooking the plain.

Just at dawn on March 20, Darby remembered, "As if from the balcony of an opera house, we looked out across the plain to the south at black dots, which were evidently vehicles of the First Division advancing to the east." They came firing everything they had. Shells burst on the enemy positions.

At almost the same time, the German artillery spotted the Rangers' position on the plateau. At command the Rangers plunged over the edge of the plateau and started running down the slope. Screaming like wild Indians, their faces still black with dirt from their night advance, the Black Death went plunging down toward them, rifles held high, zigzagging and ducking for cover behind rocks and brush. Their objective was the Italian position.

In his book *We Led the Way*, Darby likened the charge down the slope of El Guettar to tactics employed by Rogers' Rangers. They relied on speed, surprise, and shock.

As they dashed closer, they heaved their grenades and fired their guns. Still yelling, they plunged into the lines stabbing and hacking with bayonets.

The Italians were completely overwhelmed. By noon, the Rangers had everything and everyone at Djebel el Ank under control. Hundreds of Italians were captured and scores were dead, their bodies strewn across the mountainside. The impregnable pass was in American hands. When Darby radioed, "The pass is cleared," the First Division, as well as the First Armored Division and Ninth Infantry Division, met the German and Italian combined forces in what became known as the Battle of El Guettar.

More important, it signaled the end of German and Italian occupation of North Africa.

Patton sent for Darby to offer him command of his own infantry regiment with the rank of full colonel.

Darby was reported to have said, "Nothing doing. You can keep your promotion and I'll keep my Rangers."

Turning down his offer did not keep Patton from awarding Darby the Distinguished Service Cross, second only to the Medal of Honor in the rank of American soldiers' honors.

Between the end of March and the first of May, Darby's Rangers bivouacked at Nemours, Algeria, close to the Moroccan border. There they had little to do except explore the historic town, swim in the Mediterranean, and loll in their tents. After so much heavy duty, the time was idyllic.

Meanwhile, British Prime Minister Churchill and American President Franklin D. Roosevelt met at the Casablanca Conference and conceived Operation Husky. While Roosevelt was willing for the Rangers to take part in the invasions of Sicily and Sardinia, he was reluctant to send the American army into Italy, which seemed on the brink of surrender.

Benito Mussolini was losing the popular support of the Italian people. Italian representatives from King Victor Emmanuel were sounding the Americans out as Italy itself sank deeper and deeper in depression fueled by hatred of the omnipresent Germans who treated them almost as if they were conquerors rather than allies.

According to Churchill's own words in *The Second World War, Vol. II*, he was deeply distressed at the idea that his good friend President Roosevelt might not order America to take part in the invasion of Italy. On May 25, 1943, immediately after the Casablanca Conference, he flew to Washington to stay at the White House and persuade his friend Roosevelt to let General Marshall come to Algiers.

Churchill knew that without the Americans the slog up the boot of Italy would exhaust the British and perhaps weaken their resolve. He could not expect help from the Russians. As he said, "They were fighting everyday on their enormous front, and their blood flowed in a torrent."

In desperation, Churchill asked Roosevelt how he could keep over a million and a half fine American troops along with all their terrific air and naval power idle for nearly a year. He was referring to the date that they both knew would be the most significant of the war. Still more than a year away, he was referring to D-Day, June 6, 1944. Roosevelt did not answer immediately.

Gela on Sicily's southern coast faced the Malta Channel. It was the narrowest part of the Mediterranean Sea and one of the important stretches of water in the world. From Gela the road to Messina ran somewhat over a hundred miles. And from Messina one could see the toe of the boot of Italy.

How many battalions would be required to take out its defenses? The word "Ranger" was implicit in the question.

When Darby was brought into the invasion plan for Sicily and asked that question, his reply was succinct: "Fifteen."

He was told he could add two new battalions to his First Battalion. They would be called the Ranger Force. And they would be formed with volunteers from other units in North Africa. He was given six weeks to find and train them.

"Dismissed, Colonel Darby!"

Since he was given no alternative, he took a few assistants and made a recruiting drive around Oran in eastern Algeria. They put up posters to appeal to "red-blooded Americans." They made speeches in local "hot spots." On May 17, they sent out a letter titled "Volunteers for Ranger Battalions" to all units through Headquarters, Atlantic Base Section. Requirements were as follows: white (since a policy of racial segregation throughout the military existed until 1947), five-feet-six or over, of normal weight, no older than thirty-five, in good physical shape, with excellent character references, and no higher in rank than private first class.

Darby and his other recruiters, among them newly promoted Major Dammer, Captain Roy Murray, and Staff Sergeant James Altieri, usually got one in ten from every group they spoke to—one hundred if they spoke to one thousand men. Evidently from the lack of enthusiasm, word had gone out about the rigorous training and the hazardous duty that went along with the pride and the glory.

Darby retained command of First Battalion, Dammer took command of Third Battalion, and Fourth Battalion was headed by Altieri, who was concerned about their status in the eyes of the military. "We were not a regiment, not a brigade, not even a combat team. We were now three sepa-rate battalions, each with its own commander, and yet we were all directly under the command of Colonel Darby (who hadn't been promoted to rank of Full Colonel)."

Even when Darby sought authorization for "Ranger Force" to be made a permanent regiment, the War Department denied his request. Somewhere, someone was clinging to the idea that those men who had volunteered—perhaps all of them—would eventually go back to their regular battalions.

Nevertheless with good spirit, the volunteers endured the training con-ducted by Rangers as battle seasoned as any men they had ever come in contact with. Castle climbs, six-hundred-foot slides down cliffs, landings opposed by machine guns fired over the heads, explosions on the beach ahead, blistering hot African sun, the works.

On June 19, 1943, they were officially activated. It was the anniversary of the formal creation of the First Ranger Battalion. Their commander Lieutenant Colonel Darby was thirty-two.

On July 9, at Patton's command, the Rangers came aboard transports in an armada of nearly five hundred ships bound for Sicily. At the general's command they were to attack "rapidly, ruthlessly, viciously, and without rest." In landing operations, "Retreat is impossible." It was "Patton's Manifesto Number One." They had begun to think of themselves with pride as the "point of the spear" for the troops of the regular army.

Darby remembered his recommendation that fifteen divisions would be necessary to take Gela. He didn't expect that he had been far wrong. The town was on a hill 150 feet above the shore. On the western flank sat a fort fifty feet above the town itself. The shore was a maze of wire obstacles and antipersonnel and antitank minefields. Besides three shore batteries, one battery of 77-mm field artillery, there were two mortar companies and twenty-five machine-gun nests inside concrete pillboxes camouflaged with vines and brush.

Accompanied by the tanks of the Hermann Goering Division, 350,000 men waited to drive half a million Allies back into the Mediterranean.

Bad weather was as disastrous as the waiting Axis forces. In a forty-mile-per-hour wind, Darby's men in their Landing Craft, Infantry (LCIs) bounced and pitched. Once they did make a landing, rendezvous proved to be extremely difficult.

The airborne drops were even more unsuccessful. Sixty-nine of the 144 gliders bearing British paratroopers crashed into the sea. Only twelve landed on target. American paratroopers—3,400 of them—dropped from their transports and scattered like leaves over a twenty-five-mile area southeast of the drop zone. Trying to link up in the dark with Italians and Germans also searching became extremely hazardous.

At 3:00 a.m., on July 10, Darby's LCIs headed into a beach swept by blue tracers and several huge searchlights. Nobody could possibly live on the sand. Then the LCI fired six rockets and blew up an ammunition dump. The explosion knocked out the defenses on that side of the beach and a block and a half of buildings. Several of the lights went out instantly. Seeing that they were forced into retreat, the Italians blew up the pier.

The LCIs landed and the Rangers charged up the sand. The first men were halfway up the beach before the first Ranger triggered a mine. The entire force realized they had run into the middle of a minefield. The machine guns opened up on them. With nowhere to go but forward, they kept running. Mines detonated, killing the men who tripped them and wounding their comrades close at hand. The charge might have faltered.

Then the point of the spear hardened. A machine gun swept the area, but Sergeant Randall Harris, one of Darby's original Ranger volunteers, pulled his cartridge belt tight over the deep gash left by the bullet wound in his side and led the rest of the company up a steep embankment onto a dirt road. Adrenaline pumping, he ran to the nearest pillbox protecting the machine gunners and tossed in a grenade.

With Harris showing the way, the team began to function. Following his example, his men leapfrogged along the road, taking out all seven pillboxes and effectively silencing their guns.

After the battle a lieutenant saw how badly the sergeant had been wounded and called for his men to take him to an aid station. "Hell, no!" Harris exclaimed. "I'm not helpless yet. Give me prisoners to guard, or something."

For his service to his country and his comrades, he was awarded the Distinguished Service Cross and a battlefield promotion to second lieutenant.

The next unit on the sand included Colonel Darby, who called for naval salvo from the U.S. cruiser *Savannah*. The big shells falling within the hillside fort effectively silenced their guns. The Rangers ran forward and Darby called to the ship, "Cease-fire!"

Behind the Rangers, supplies were landed on the beach—ammunition and food. Seagoing self-propelled trucks, known as DUKWs, moved back and forth between the flotilla and the sand.

Twenty German planes strafed the beach, machine guns chattering. One of the Rangers, Private Sherman Legg, actually downed one of them with his BAR. The rest continued out to sea to strafe the flotilla. Six Italian tanks came rumbling into town. The Rangers threw everything they had at them. They even climbed to the tops of buildings and dropped fifteen-pound blocks of TNT.

When Darby saw that nothing they had was effective against the armor, he hunted up the 37-mm antitank gun being used by Ranger Captain Charles Shunstrom. Darby hooked it on the rear of his jeep. Wheeling it into position, he opened fire. On his third shot, the tank burst into flames.

How could the situation get any worse?

After noon, the situation got worse.

Eighteen huge German Tiger tanks clanked into the center of Gela. Darby called for more fire from the *Savannah*. He ordered his Rangers to use chemical mortars and with the extra firepower of a 77-mm mortar; twelve tanks were blasted out of action.

Behind the tanks came a massed formation of Italian infantrymen. Darby ordered the mortars to hold their fire until the Italians were two thousand yards out, then to lay down several hundred 4.2 shells in a minute of concentrated firing. The Italian attack fell apart and ended with "every man for himself" fleeing ignominiously.

In the afternoon, the Rangers set up their command post in a restaurant where they found a liberal supply of cognac and champagne. A visiting staff officer immediately tried to commandeer their site. He was allowed to after a brisk argument. While it was going hot and heavy, the Rangers carried all the booze out the back door.

On July 12, General Patton came with the news that permission had been granted by General Omar Bradley to request that Darby be named to replace him. Patton asked Darby if he would like to take over the regiment.

"You mean I get a choice, General?" Darby asked.

"Take the regiment and I'll make you a full colonel in the morning," was the reply. Then Patton growled, "But I won't force your hand."

Darby's answer was that he would rather stay with his boys. Did Darby want to be available to take command of a Ranger regiment or did he refuse the battlefield promotion and new rank because of his loyalty to his men? He never explained himself since Patton did not ask.

The fighting continued for the better part of forty-eight more hours until finally the Italians seem to lose heart. The Germans withdrew leaving their ruined equipment behind. The battle for Gela had shown the determination of the Axis armies to keep the Allies off Italian soil and, furthermore, off the mainland of Europe, but in the end it had proved to be a portent of things to come.

The Ranger battalions fought their way across Sicily, skirmish after skirmish. In many cases, the Italians fled before them rather than fight. Late one afternoon, the Third Battalion rested in an olive grove north of the town of Porto Empedocle. In the rich golden light the three Ranger companies attacked in a line. None of them met any determined defense. After a short scrap 675 Italians and 91 Germans surrendered.

By this time, the Rangers were so far ahead of the main body of divisional troops that they were out of food. Though they still had rifle ammo, they no longer had any 60-mm mortar shells. A spotting plane from the U.S. Navy might have mistaken them for enemy troops. Their small radios could no longer reach headquarters units.

While the navy plane dropped leaflets in Italian and German, ordering them to surrender, the Rangers arranged oil barrels in the harbor waters to spell out "Yank" and "U.S. Army."

From Palermo, the march to Messina was a comparative cakewalk. Along the way they met people who told them they had seen "two Germans" or "yes, the Germans had ridden by."

The night Messina fell, the Rangers bivouacked in a cemetery. German batteries across the straits in Italy blasted away, some shells knocking caskets out of the walls. The smell of death was everywhere, but the Rangers slept right through it all. According to Darby, "Our clothes were in tatters, shoes worn thin, and most equipment ready for salvage. Only our weapons were in tiptop shape."

Sicily fell to the Allies in thirty-eight days. As Roosevelt had promised Churchill at the end of May, the Americans would go into Italy with the British. His promise was about to be fulfilled.

Darby's Rangers were headed for Italy.

The toe of the boot lay a few miles away across the strait of Messina, but the Allied commanders did not intend to fight their way nearly five hundred miles to Rome. Already targeted were the beaches of Sorrento west of Salerno and south of Naples. And a hundred miles farther north and barely twenty-five miles from Rome lay their eventual target—Anzio.

On August 1, all Ranger Battalions had been redesignated as Ranger Infantry Battalions. Darby attempted once again to obtain a regimental headquarters for the Ranger Force. Patton endorsed the request and forwarded it on to General of the Army Eisenhower. A month later the request was disapproved without comment.

In the meantime, Darby had been busy requisitioning some heavy equipment for his lightly armed Ranger Force. He requested and received four MC half-tracks equipped with 77-mm guns. These would be manned by former artillery men drawn from all the Ranger battalions and commanded by Captain Shunstrom, who was overrun with volunteers. He was well known because he was known to be where the "fighting was the hottest."

They named their new "rides" Ace of Diamonds, Ace of Spades, Ace of Clubs, and Ace of Hearts. Shunstrom named his brand new jeep The Joker.

In the meantime, although Bob Hope and his USO show visited the Rangers to entertain and lift their spirits, the enforced waiting brought its own problems. Dysentery swept the Ranger camp, and the heat and dampness led to an outbreak of malaria.

At the same time, word spread that Patton, who had been one of Darby's strongest advocates, had slapped not one but two soldiers whom he accused of malingering. His volatile temper and his intense sense of what a soldier must be, along with the tremendous strain, were presumed to have gotten the better of him. Even the soldiers whom he slapped would have uttered no complaints. Unfortunately, Drew Pearson, a Washington reporter famous for his muckraking column "Washington Merry-Go-Round," broke the story. Eisenhower and Roosevelt had no choice.

Relieved of duty, Patton was, nevertheless, kept in Sicily because the Germans feared him and spied upon him. He was never sent into any sort of battle situation (or any hospital) again. However, his influence continued to be felt. His presence or absence was a determining factor in many of the German preparations for actions their espionage had reported forthcoming.

Aware of what was happening, the Allied operations utilized him to deceive and confuse. Three days before D-Day, at a banquet in London, he yelled across the room to Eisenhower, "I'll see you in Calais!"

German troop movements in that direction were noted within hours, undoubtedly reducing some of the numbers that met the Allied invasion at Normandy on D-Day.

Operation Avalanche—the invasion of the Italian coast—began on September 9, 1943. The day before, many of the Rangers "suffering in hospital from malaria and dysentery," suddenly staged miraculous recoveries, throwing off their blankets, dragging on their clothes, and hobbling out the doors. With the whistles of the military police (MPs) blasting behind them, they climbed into the trucks and took off.

Ranger Force landed in advance of the Fifth Army at Maiori, twenty miles west of Salerno. Their incursion was a total surprise. By midmorning, moving light and fast, they had destroyed the coastal defenses and seized the town with its critical Chiunzi Pass. While they had done their part, the Fifth Army stalled on their beachhead. Ranger Force had to hold their position for two weeks instead of two days as originally ordered.

Though they were all volunteers, a sizable minority were not the hand-picked, conditioned, and well-trained men that had made up the original companies. They had had no training to tone their bodies for the forced marches, the meal and sleep deprivation, and the swimming through icy rivers that had fitted the original groups for their tasks.

General Patton's replacement, General Mark Clark, recommended augmenting the Rangers with motorized artillery and antitank units. About-to-be-promoted-to-full-Colonel Darby found himself in command of a regimental-sized force of 8,500 men. The enemy below him on the plain of Naples was "the most beautiful target" he'd ever seen.

While Germans and Italians engaged with British and Americans on the plain below, on the heights Shunstrom and his "*Aces*" played a game of "hit 'em and run." Standing in *The Joker*, Shunstrom would direct 75-

mm guns to fire on certain targets, then order them to "get the hell out" because the Germans sure to be in the act of retaliating, training their own artillery on the positions the *Aces* revealed.

For three weeks they played the deadly game, directing artillery fire and naval gunfire onto the main highway and keeping German units from reinforcing the men holding the majority of the Allied landing forces on the beaches. When the Allies broke, finally, out of the beachhead, the Germans had no choice but to retreat.

Darby led his force down the mountains in a rushing, tumbling scramble reminiscent of Roger's Rangers above Fort Ticonderoga on Lake George. With their enemy retreating before them, they charged on into Italy. On September 22, 1943, they joined the big push to Naples. "Despite every obstacle of nature and the enemy," the American and British divisions "had pushed on to their goal."

Casualties were high among the Allies. Fortunately, the Ranger Force with the advantage of the high ground counted only thirty killed, seventy-three wounded, and nine missing in action.

The ramparts of Adolf Hitler's Fortress Europe had begun to crumble, but not without taking a heavy toll on the Allies and the Ranger Force in particular. Enduring the bitter winter in the Apennines, they slogged past San Pectro, Venatro, and Cassino, sustaining losses that reached their peak at the end of November. By that time seventy men were killed, wounded, or missing.

The troops were stalled until the British made a successful amphibious landing at Termoli on the northeastern side of the Italian Peninsula. The realization that the Americans were to the south and the British to the east sent shudders through the Axis forces. They were in real danger of being cut off from any retreat and forced to fight to the death or surrender in the mountains south of Rome.

Despite the tactical danger, the Axis forces under Albert Kesselring were well entrenched, and resolute not to retreat. A sensible retreat was forever forestalled by Hitler's demonic denunciation of Field Marshall Rommel when he had met with *Der Fuehrer* in Berlin.

Rommel had presented facts.

Hitler chewed them up and spat them on the carpet. "I am sick of generals who want to retreat!" he screamed. "You do not win wars by retreating!"

Rommel had no choice but to keep any further facts to himself. Though Rommel was a tactical genius with tanks, Hitler put Field

Marshal Kesselring in command of the Third and Fifteenth Panzer Grenadier divisions, the Hermann Goering Division, and elements of the Twenty-sixth Panzer Divisions to be deployed immediately to Italy.

Among General Clark (Fifth Army), General Bernard Law Montgomery (Eighth Army), and British general Sir Harold Alexander, commanding the Fifteenth Army Group, it was decided to land at Anzio approximately fifty miles southeast of Rome as the crow flies.

In the words of Churchill, a successful landing would, "astonish the world. It will certainly frighten Kesselring." The only question was whether Kesselring had the sense to be frightened.

On December 11, Darby was promoted to full colonel and became officially a regimental commander.

For more than a month, the Allies had developed a plan for the amphibious Anzio landing. Darby spent that time training the new men among his seasoned troop. While they were imbued with the Ranger glamour and élan, they were sloppy. The diluted companies did not follow man for man the combat techniques that the colonel and his officers had developed over the years. Some of them made excessive noise during night action. On patrol they failed to reconnoiter likely ambush sites and to take required security precautions. Above all, many members moved rather than froze in place while flares were being fired. The minority was endangering the whole, but no time remained to sort them out.

On January 22, 1944, the 6615th Ranger Force (Provisional) reinforced by the 509th Parachute Infantry Battalion and H Company of an engineer regiment seized the port facilities and secured the beachhead. It was an easy task since they were met by an undermanned German coast-watching battalion, deployed to the port of Anzio for a rest.

In what could have been an ideal situation for a successful advance accompanied by lightning strikes into the German Winter Line, Major General John Lucas's VI Corps landed thirty-six thousand men and 3,200 vehicles overnight. Unfortunately, Lucas was no Patton. He managed to move inland only eleven miles in the next five days.

General Clark himself ordered Lucas to move faster.

In the meantime, acting as commander of the Third Infantry Division, General Truscott, the man who had recruited Darby, ordered the Rangers across the Line on January 30 to take and hold the town of Cisterna with its vital road junctions both highway and rail leading directly into Rome. The order stipulated "until relieved."

Darby suspected that Churchill's comment accompanied by Der Fuehrer's, both which were reported worldwide, had strengthened Kesselring's resolve. Churchill also was quoted in an interview conducted post-war in January 1946. Of Germany and the Germans, he said, "It was a halfway measure as an offensive that was your basic error."

Possibly more important was the fact that the law of averages had begun to catch up with the "old" Rangers. Howard Andre, the executive officer of F Company, was killed in action aiding the British at Carroceto, where they helped hold a line before pushing farther inland. In the same action Lieutenant Harris was seriously wounded for the third time. He was unable to protest as he was evacuated to the hospital ship.

Altieri found himself alone "at the top" of F Company.

Rain and sleet fell soaking the ground and then freezing. The *Luftwaffe* that was supposed to be finished flew unceasing raids, bombing and strafing. The German Panzers moved closer. The German artillery bombarded constantly. With so much equipment and so many troops on the beachhead, almost every shell hit somebody or something.

On the evening of January 29, the Rangers rolled their bedding and piled them on a tent canvas. They dropped their barracks bags in the same pile, leaving it in charge of several Ranger cooks and truck drivers. Their load lightened, they started out with the maps of "our march" that night.

The three groups were to infiltrate in a broad triangle—one company on the right, one on the left, and one in the middle—converging on Cisterna. Accompanying them were a tank-destroyer company and a cannon company as well as the Chemical Mortar Battalion. Behind them were supposed to be a regiment on the right, a tank battalion in the center, and another regiment on the left.

More or less at ease, the Rangers moved ahead past enemy machine-gun and mortar nests. Sometimes they passed close enough to hear orders being given in German.

On their left flank, the Fourth Battalion began to encounter difficulties: fire from houses and stone farm buildings, dug-in emplacements, a roadblock made by two damaged jeeps and an Italian truck. Six medium tanks came up to support them, but they were still slow—behind their appointed time to reach the town of Bella Isola, where they were supposed to set up communications.

Meanwhile, as the triangle narrowed, the First Battalion went into the lead in single file formation, followed by the Fourth. They had difficulty keeping quiet stumbling along in a drainage ditch, their equipment dragging and thumping noisily against the ditch's sides. Shortly before they had planned to arrive in Cisterna, the two battalions became separated. Then a runner from the rear came with the information that Third Battalion's commanding officer along with several of the men close to him had been killed by a shell from a tank that had suddenly appeared from the side.

About 7:00 a.m., the First Battalion broke radio silence. They were eight hundred yards south of Cisterna in an open field. Jack Dobson, the commanding officer, reported that they were taking fire.

Fourth Battalion reported dug-in-emplacements and enemy sniper resistance. Still outside Bella Isola they were nevertheless shooting mortars into the town.

First and Third Battalions were facing snipers and mortar troops holed up in farmhouses on either side of the Cisterna road. Three hundred yards from the town, they spotted two enemy tanks hidden in bushes on opposite sides of the road not fifty yards away. The well-trained Rangers immediately took out the tanks with rocket launchers.

The advance continued as the morning light grew stronger even though the Rangers began to realize that resistance was much stronger and better organized than their commanders had supposed. Within the next few minutes they realized the battle was lost. Sunrise doomed them.

They were surrounded. They saw one big building ahead with trees around it. From behind it, the muzzle of a cannon appeared. They thought it was their tank caught up to them, but it opened up on them. The Rangers attacked it with sticky grenades and bazooka. They shot and killed the crew as they tried to climb out of the turret.

Where was the army that was supposed to be coming up behind them? They were the "point," not the whole damned spear!

Other Rangers blew up the ammunition dump.

Their best efforts were too little. They were too few in number and too lightly armed even to defend themselves. Then ten more tanks appeared followed by German infantry armed with automatic weapons. The Rangers were trapped in an open field.

Their radio report told how they were surrounded and fighting for their lives. "Where was the division support from the flanks?"

All around Cisterna, the Germans closed in. Their artillery sent blistering fire into the battalions. Some of the Rangers attacked the tanks singlehanded, hurling themselves on the turrets, slapping on sticky grenades and sacrificing themselves for their comrades to blow the rolling cannons to hell.

Back at the headquarters, Darby listened helplessly as his men, his carefully selected and trained men—*his men*—were butchered. Finally when only a single officer commanded both battalions, he ordered the remaining men to close the gap at the rear of the circle and dig in. The call went out for reinforcements in the hope that the Third Division might reach them before they ran out of ammunition.

More and more Germans moved in pouring more and more shot and shell into the circle.

Still, the Rangers continued fighting. No thought of giving up. Distress calls reached the Third Division, trying gamely but tardily to reach Cisterna, but heavy odds kept an eleventh-hour rescue from happening.

One of the last words came from a sergeant who radioed, "Some of the fellows are giving up. Colonel, we are awfully sorry. They can't help it because we're running out of ammunition. But I ain't surrendering. They are coming into the building."

The radio went WHAM, WHAM—and then went dead.

The battle continued in pockets until 1:30 p.m. The First and Third had used up most of the ammunition knocking out fourteen tanks.

The end came when the Germans captured ten men of the Third Battalion. Out of ammunition they had no choice but to raise their hands in surrender. They were herded in front of the tanks in absolute defiance of the rules of the Geneva Convention and marched toward the last outposts of the remaining Rangers.

The battalion surgeon was shot as he cared for the wounded.

Eight Rangers led by Corporal Mosier were told by his company commander to "Take out and God bless you." The captain had two bandoliers of ammunition crossed over his tunic. As they ran he loaded up and commenced firing to cover their escape.

"We headed for the ditch," Mosier reported. "All this time the tracers were flying close enough to stop them with your hand. Along the ditch there were snipers all the way."

All night long the Fourth Battalion fought knowing that the First and Third were out of reach and probably gone. The next morning the Cannon Company made an attempt to get through the German ring with the remnants of the Fourth prepared to follow them. Four times the young captain in charge attempted to get through. Each time he was driven back with one or more of his half-tracks knocked out.

Not until January 31st did a regimental combat team fight its way up to the Fourth. Together they turned to attack the Germans taking 250 prisoners—150 of the First Parachute Division and one hundred of the Hermann Goering Panzer Division.

Trapped in a small pocket, some armed only with knives or bayonets, ammunition gone, their comrades dead or wounded, they lay in ditches, under ceaseless fire from the Panzer Grenadiers. Behind them were

the paratroopers. By mid-morning surrender was the alternative to annihilation. Darby himself heard the last words attributed to Lieutenant
Louie Martin of First Battalion just before his walkie-talkie went silent.
"They're closing in on us, Colonel. We're out of ammo—but they won't
get us cheap! Colonel . . . good luck!"

In agony he heard all the familiar voices of his men as they made no
excuses, offered no recriminations. Nothing but apologies for not succeeding against impossible odds. "Sorry, Colonel . . . Sorry . . . Sorry . . . Sorry."
When the last walkie-talkie went silent, he sent the rest of the men from
the room. According to his own account in his book *We Led the Way*, he
sent the men out of the room so they wouldn't see him weep.

On January 29 and 30, 1944, 743 Rangers died or were captured at
Cisterna.

Only six came back.

Darby's Rangers were no more. Those who returned were sent state-
side, including Darby, for a rest and to be hailed as heroes. For the some
four hundred who were taken prisoner, it was more than a year before
they were repatriated from Italian prison camps.

What went wrong at Anzio has been debated for more than sixty years.
While blame might be shifted from commanding officer to commanding officer, the number of theories indicates that many, many factors
came into play. Though blame undoubtedly can be laid on many of the
Americans, the historian must recognize the Germans' desperation as they
stiffened their resistance and moved everything they had into the battle to
drive their enemies back into the sea. Everyone, including Mussolini and
Hitler, knew that if the invaders were to be stopped, they must be stopped
on that beach.

No German sacrifice was deemed too great if it threw the Allies back
into the sea. No American or British sacrifice was deemed too great if it
established an unstoppable force on the Italian Peninsula.

To that end, the Allies had off-loaded twenty-one cargo ships and
landed 6,350 tons of matériel. By February 1, the port was fully occupied
and open. In a sense perhaps the three-day battle at Cisterna had provided
a cover for that operation. Rome was less than an hour away.

For several months as the war ground closer and closer to its ultimate
victory, Darby worked at a desk. Finally, he was sent back across the Atlantic on March 29, 1945, joining the command of Major General George
P. Hays. He was back in Italy again and was confident that the final bits of
the Italian operation were about to wrap up.

Civil society in Italy had fallen apart. On April 27, Mussolini and his mistress Clara Petacci attempted to flee to Germany. They were stopped by communist partisans who had every reason to despise the fascist dictator. Mussolini added to his own problems because he was recognized though he had tried to disguise himself. Being caught in a German uniform sealed his fate. He was a traitor.

The next day without benefit of trial, the two were summarily shot. She fell dying without a sound. *Il Duce* is reported to have torn open his shirt and shouted, "Shoot me in the chest!"

They did so. Twice.

The bodies were taken to Piazzale Loreto in Milan and hung from meat hooks in a gas station. Mussolini's corpse was suspended upside down as a further humiliation. Photographs of his body were seen all over the world including the newsreels in the movie houses in America.

On April 30, Hitler and his mistress Eva Braun committed suicide—she by a cyanide capsule, he by a bullet through his brain. The German commander in Italy announced that he would surrender all his forces unconditionally at noon on May 2, 1945.

On the same day Darby was riding back in a jeep from a conference that included an inspection of Mussolini's mansion. An incoming artillery shell exploded overhead. The driver was decapitated by flying shrapnel and half of the dozen men in the cavalcade were wounded.

Darby was slammed to the ground unconscious. The men carried him to a cot in a nearby building. Two medics came running, but two minutes later, he was pronounced dead. A piece of shrapnel no bigger than half a dime had arrowed between his ribs and into his heart.

He was already commissioned a brigadier general, though he had not received notification. He received the promotion posthumously, the only such instance in American history.

HISTORY'S ASSESSMENT

Fort Smith, Arkansas, has its William O. Darby Junior High School. Cisterna, Italy, dedicated its high school to him. Perhaps most important from Darby's point of view would be the fact that one of the three phases of Ranger School in Fort Benning, Georgia, is named Camp Darby.

The heroic story of *Darby's Rangers* became a film in 1958. It starred James Garner in the title role and was directed by William A. Wellman, who was famous for making gritty war films. The sad ending of the film probably contributed to its only moderate success.

Italian film director Dino De Laurentiis characterized Darby in his Technicolor epic film *Anzio* in 1968.

AUTHOR'S NOTE

In May 1944, William H. Baumer, a West Point classmate of Darby's, contacted the colonel while he was in the Operations Division of the War Department General Staff.

Baumer had exciting news. A publishing house was interested in the story of Darby's Rangers. Seizing the opportunity to create a written memory of his men, Darby and occasionally his executive officer, Dammer, came to Baumer's house in Washington and told the story of the Rangers in eight evenings.

Baumer had a stenographer in the next room taking down every word. In six weeks the manuscript was completed, but D-Day had passed. The publisher who had expressed an interest had decided that World War II books would be passé by the time he could rush the book into print.

Years later, Darby's sister insisted that Baumer take out the manuscript, supplement it, and try again to find a publisher. Willingly, Baumer wrote the introductory perspective for each chapter, but the majority of the twelve-chapter book is exactly as Darby told it through the tragic events in January of 1944. Presidio Press in California published it in 1980.

It is a brilliant account from the memories of the man who had it all fresh in his memory. The events from November 1942 through January 1944 scrolled out in front of him. The book itself is unique in military history because it was written "between the battles."

9

MARAUDERS IN THE JUNGLE

Frank Merrill

THE SITUATION

In 1937 the Japanese invaded China, setting off the Second Sino-Japanese War. China under Chiang Kai-Shek retaliated by bombing Japanese positions in what became known as The Battle of Shanghai. The battle was incredibly bloody by Western standards. The Chinese fought to the death, sacrificing their best troops against the Japanese and taking a toll of 122,000 of the invaders killed or wounded. At the same time, the Chinese government requested Western support. Adopting a strategically short-sighted stance, the West declined to intervene. The British Empire and America considered the war strictly an Asian problem.

Despite the best efforts of the poorly armed, poorly trained Chinese soldiers, Japanese troops were triumphant. Over the course of the following two months, they massacred Chinese prisoners of war and helpless civilians. The horrors that occurred during that period became known in world history as the Rape of Nanking. The actual numbers of victims vary according to Chinese or Japanese sources. Chinese sources accept three hundred thousand or more killed. The majority were unarmed civilians.

In the early twentieth century when global communications were limited and exceedingly slow, unaccompanied as it was by photographs and eyewitness commentaries by embedded reporters, the first Holocaust of

World War II was no cause for alarm. Unfortunately, only a small number of citizens in the Western world heard about it.

If its effect on Chinese society was terrifying, its effect on Japanese culture was profound. For the Japanese the massacre brought about a cultural revolution. It constituted a violation of the ancient Samurai code of *Bushido*. As such, it signaled a new type of ugly warfare to be waged without rules. The war in Asia would henceforth recognize no difference between combatant and unarmed or wounded prisoner. More horrible, the soldier was no different from the civilian.

For four more years, the British Empire and America hesitated to get involved. They hoped to be able to maintain neutrality by regarding the massacre as a local problem to be resolved between China and Japan.

The Western world also had problems of its own. For Britain, the war drums were already beating loudly on the European continent. For America, a two-ocean war cast a sinister shadow. Still Franklin D. Roosevelt and his advisors hoped for neutrality.

Their hope was blasted when on December 7, 1941, the Japanese Air Force destroyed most of the American fleet at Pearl Harbor. Simultaneously, the American islands of Wake, Guam, and Philippines were invaded. Their tiny garrisons outfitted with World War I equipment were caught flat-footed. On the same day, the Japanese attacked the British at Hong Kong. On December 10, two British battleships, *Prince of Wales* and *Repulse*, were sunk off Malaya. On February 15, 1942, Singapore surrendered.

The whole world reeled as bad news from the Pacific continued to make headlines in American newspapers. A few broadcasters related the news on the radio. To most of rural America it didn't seem real. Who had ever heard of the Strait of Malacca? All Burma lay unprotected except by British colonial garrisons. Who had ever heard of Burma? Moreover, many Burmese at first regarded the Japanese as liberators from their British oppressors and showed little interest in helping repel the invaders. The British Empire found itself fighting in a country where a man could not tell his friends from his foes.

For surely, the British had to fight. To get out while they could was never an option. Burma could not be allowed to fall. Strategically, it was the back door to India, the jewel in the British crown of colonies. They had an impressive army, but it was stretched far too thin to offer serious resistance in any one place.

For the Chinese, the Japanese must not be allowed to march over the Himalayas. Their mile-high crests must be held and defended. Burma was the back door to their wartime capital Chungking. A repetition of the Rape of Nanking could not be allowed to happen.

Time was the enemy. The Japanese knew it was their friend.

To maintain the freedom of Burma was given top priority by President Roosevelt, British Prime Minister Churchill, and Chinese Generalissimo Chiang Kai-Chek. All agreed the only hope was to garrison and hold Burma.

Even as they were meeting to devise strategy, Japanese armies were sweeping up the coast by sea and by land. Their armies took Moulmein, familiar to English readers in "The Road to Mandalay" by their first Nobel Prize–winning poet Rudyard Kipling. With British troops as well as Scots Highlanders, Gurkhas, and Sikhs still fighting their way through the jungle on the eastern side of the Sittang River, the British officers felt they had no choice but to blow the bridge immediately. The debacle turned tragic when soldiers tried to swim, to float on improvised rafts, and even to commandeer small crafts to reach safety on the other side. With Bushido banished from their culture, the Japanese machine gunned the helpless men in the water.

Before Allied plans could be formed, much less implemented, the whole of Burma was opened by Japanese access to the swift-rushing waterway and more important, the railroad that ran along beside it. Finally, besieged from north and south, despite heavy resistance, Rangoon, the port at the delta of the Sittang River and the Gulf of Martaban, fell. The railroad was in Japanese hands, as well as the road through the jungle and the airfield at Myitkyina (referred to as "Mitch" by Americans and British). Vital supplies could no longer be shipped in. At allied bases throughout India and China, motor-pool drivers were using their China, Burma, India (CBI) Theater of Operations credit cards—jerry cans fitted with siphon hoses.

Taking advantage of the desperate situation and recognizing weaknesses to be exploited, British-educated statesman Mohandas K. Gandhi seized the opportunity to free India from British subjugation. He called for "Civil Disobedience," a lesson he had learned from reading American transcendentalist Henry David Thoreau. Gandhi's followers were disobedient but hardly civil. They cut telephone and telegraph lines, looted towns, and dismantled railroads. They halted trains, pulled the Englishmen off them, and hacked them to death. Indian *sepoys*, infantry privates in the British Indian Army, who had become increasingly disillusioned with the rule of the Victorian Raj, made little effort to stop the murder and mayhem. Many willingly participated in it.

The whole world seemed to be going mad.

The only bright spot in the mess were the daredevils commanded by General Claire Chennault. Since April 1937, he had been assembling a group that became a legend—a world famous band of extremely colorful mercenaries that eventually became glorious heroes in spite of themselves. The Chinese people remained eternally grateful to America for decades. They were an American Volunteer Group (AVG) of maverick pilots whose commander, a Texas-born warrior, had acquired a fleet of Curtiss-Wright P-40 Tomahawks.

But why? Probably because no one else wanted them.

They were neither particularly fast nor easy to fly. A pilot taxiing for a takeoff had to keep weaving the plane back and forth across the flight line because the craft's nose pointed up at a slant that blocked his view straight ahead along the runway.

Fortunately, the heavily armored nose and fuselage straightened out parallel to the ground when the plane gathered speed and roared into the wild, blue yonder. As a matter of fact, the P-40 was better armored than most planes in the air over Southeast Asia. It was so well armored in fact that it could fly straight at a Japanese plane made of lightweight materials, open up with its nose cannon, and fly straight on through the resulting debris.

Some enterprising artist decorated the pointed nose of one of the planes with shark's teeth and eyes. The result was spectacular. Suddenly, the rather clumsy planes became the tiger sharks, and the Chinese newspapers went mad as the victories kept pouring in.

The symbol of China was the tiger. The planes captured the imagination and encouraged the people. They became the *Fei Wing*, translated as Flying Tigers. The Americans had come and brought the Chinese an air force they could be proud of.

The pay for these pilots, by the way, was a great incentive to their volunteering. They received $600 to $750 a month. Furthermore, each pilot understood that for every plane he destroyed he would receive a $500 bonus. In less than a year, the 50 planes of the AVG shot down 284 Japanese planes and destroyed 100 on the ground.

At the same time, the fight for Burma began all over again. Every crackbrained idea was open to discussion, anything that could delay and stymie the Japanese as they marched north through the country. Once the Japanese armies reached the end of track and airfield at Myitkyina, the way to China was simply a matter of marching into Chungking. To the north lay the heart of China, the valley of the Yangtze as well as the temporary headquarters of the Chinese government. Japanese progress would be virtually unimpeded on the 1,445-mile highway that wound over the tops of mountains higher than the Rockies except when it descended from those dizzying heights into rushing river gorges. It was the Burma Road.

If Burma fell, China would be attacked from both sea and land. If Burma fell, the Japanese could also send an army westward where the longtime British peace known as the Raj was already in danger of being destroyed from within when it was needed most.

THE ACTION

Saving Burma became the objective of the best military minds in the CBI. The only plan with a possibility of working seemed to be a guerrilla operation to be made up of volunteers who were eager to fight at command and willing to endure the on-the-job training. The plan had been suggested by Chennault for Generalissimo Chiang Kai-Chek. The Flying Tiger commander was listened to with great respect because he had the sponsorship of one of the most influential women in the world, Madame Chiang herself.

In April 1937, Chennault had retired from active duty and accepted her invitation for a three-month mission to make a survey of the fledgling Chinese Air Force. At that time she took over leadership of the Chinese Aeronautical Commission. True, her husband was the head of the army. However, by virtue of her father, the head of the powerful and incredibly rich Soong family, she had become the "general" at the head of the Chinese Air Force. Chennault was her greatest acquisition.

Thanks to Chennault, the Flying Tigers were exceedingly effective and their heroic pilots—among them "Pappy" Boyington and his Black Sheep Squadron, "Tex" Hill, "Bert" Christman, and "Red" Adair—were swiftly elevating themselves to legendary status.

Chennault's comrade in arms was General Joseph W. Stilwell, who fought the top brass as eagerly as he fought the enemy. His motto was the fractured Latin phrase *illegitimate non carborundum*, generally construed to mean "Don't let the bastards grind you down." He called Chiang "Peanut," although never to the Generalissimo's face. "Vinegar Joe" once remarked to British Admiral Lord Louis Mountbatten, "Gee, Admiral, I like working with you. You're the only Limey I ever met who wants to fight." He later came to despise Mountbatten and retracted one of the few complimentary statements he had uttered during the war.

With Chennault and Stilwell was British General Orde Wingate. A maverick not of the usual spit-and-polish British stripe, he was a perfect fit to sit at the table of *Alice in Wonderland*'s mad tea party. A famous eccentric born in India, son of a British officer, he prided himself on his bushy beard despite the jungle heat and his rather obvious toupee. The casual disrespect he showed for his fellow officers was rivaled only by Vinegar Joe. Educated in the "public" schools that were in fact private by American standards, he disregarded almost every rule including the ones for proper dress. Sometimes, he appeared for conferences in the nude except for his toupee and his pith helmet. While everyone deplored his tactics and despised his eccentric habits, he was the shrewdest tactician among them.

All of them—Chennault, Stillwell, and Orde—recognized the problems that stemmed from Generalissimo Chiang. Stilwell never used the multisyllabic word of his rank. He always referred to the man as Gi-mo except when he sneered and used the "long" version Gimme-more.

Time and again, the generals approached Chiang and requested that he make definite plans for the Chinese armed forces. They all knew that the Chinese army was riddled with graft and corruption. Generals were appointed by family background rather than knowledge of military science.

Unfortunately, Chiang could never rise beyond the desire for more and more men outfitted and armed by America. How they would be trained, who would lead them, and where they would be deployed if indeed they were ever to be more than paper divisions was never seriously discussed. Chiang was always vague when called upon for particulars.

Instead of cleaning up the corruption and replacing incompetent leadership with men more determined to fight for their country than wear a fancy uniform, the generalissimo concentrated his efforts on getting America and Great Britain to pour millions of dollars along with weaponry and equipment into his hands.

For all of China, the goal was to secure more and more American money as well as American weapons and machinery. When Chennault was demonstrating the possibilities of the P-40, all the Chinese officers watching were overwhelmed as they watched an American pilot take off climbing almost vertically, roar into a wide loop, spin, pull out of a screaming dive, and land the aircraft with dazzling skill. They immediately wanted one hundred planes.

Chennault tapped the flyer, who happened to be Tex Hill, on the chest. "You don't need a hundred planes," he said. "What you need are a hundred flyers like him."

Finally, Chennault, Stilwell, and Wingate hit upon a plan they named "Galahad," at the Englishman's insistence. Wingate was a voracious reader who loved the classics. He had named his own North African Special

Forces unit Gideon, after the Biblical warrior hero. Galahad after the perfect knight of Arthurian legend seemed a stretch, but in the light of what came after, perhaps it was apt.

The men were to be a special group patterned after Wingate's Long Range Penetration Group (LRPG). The mission they were to carry out was to be no longer than ninety days, and the targets were very specific. In January 1944 the Special Forces were to be sent in and then taken out April 1.

BIRTH OF MERRILL'S MARAUDERS

After marching for days through the nearly impassable Burmese jungle, a young volunteer named Benny Silverman groused, "Hey, Sarge, where the hell are we going?"

David Hurwitt, a radio specialist who had lost his stripes in an "AWOL moment," shrugged. "Why the hell are you asking me—why don't you ask the general?"

Expecting a laugh instead of an answer, the newly minted Ranger yelled up the line, "Hey, General! Where the fuck are we going? Sir!"

To the surprise of most, but to no surprise for a few officers, Brigadier General Merrill clenched his teeth around his pipe stem and marched back with a grin on his face. He glanced at Hurwitt's sleeve where the imprint of the chevrons remained.

Hurwitt snapped to attention. "I have been to Guadalcanal and New Georgia, sir."

Merrill nodded. Then he sat down in the middle of the trail, opened his map case, and drew out the contents. They were crumpled and smudged, but infinitely readable, at least what information was on them to read. Large areas were a maze of wrinkles indicating mountains. Several long wavy lines represented rivers. The maps showed the topography, which might or might not be accurate given mudslides and floods. They were noticeably lacking in place names. Rangoon, Mandalay, and Myitkyina were about all they showed.

Merrill then proceeded to tell them where they were going—the railhead at Walawbum—and what they were going to do when they got there—take it. And hold it! Against the Japanese Eighteenth Division, the conquerors of Singapore! The more he told, the whiter they all got. From him they learned that they were going to attack the Japanese headquarters in Burma.

Since the autumn of 1942, the American Army engineers had been building a two-way road and railroad southward from the province of Cassam in far eastern India over the Himalayas into Burma. It was called the Ledo Road and its eventual destination was a connection to China. One vital station along the way was the airfield at Myitkyina.

On later maps, circles with names like Broadway, Piccadilly, Blackpool, and Aberdeen would be added. Those would be bases of operations cleared in the deepest jungles for airfields and supply depots. Planes to transport wounded could be sent out from there and then flown back to hospitals in India. Of course, landing and taking off in jungles required that temporary fields be cleared. The flight itself was a hazard, since the pilots could easily miss the fields when they were given sometimes vague coordinates.

The Marauders were the first American army on the entire Asian continent. They knew nothing about these preparations, much less what was to come. And they were marching deep into the Burmese jungle where rain fell two to three inches in an hour, sometimes hour after hour—every day. High over the men's heads, the leaves, branches, and vines shut out almost all the light, like an ever-spreading living ceiling. Monkeys chattered from the canopy above, but the men seldom saw them. In the gloom on the jungle floor, the soldiers stumbled over roots and swatted at insects that buzzed incessantly.

Elephants and tigers roamed beneath the almost impenetrable canopy of monstrous trees. They seldom saw the wild animals, but they avoided the droppings of the elephants, huge balls of partially digested grasses mixed with smelly excrement. More terrible than any tiger or elephant attack was the constant attack of the leeches, the mites, and the mosquitoes—all of which carried potentially deadly diseases.

No American soldier had ever been expected to fight in this green hell before. They had volunteered and there was no backing out. No course except onward. Merrill had no problem telling them where and what and how.

After Merrill had done with his "briefing," he stood up and grinned again. "Okay, fellers?"

The troops gathered around him were scared to death. They had just enough strength to nod. With affable good humor, he raised his arm and headed them up. They were left to pass the word on to their comrades. He was the kind of man they would grow to love, and they followed where he led, even in the shadows of the jungles leading ever onward to the Burma Road.

Three brigades, no more than three thousand men had been extracted from forces all over the Pacific. They had been asked up front to volunteer for "a dangerous and hazardous mission." Ideally, they would have been "jungle trained" and in a "high state of physical ruggedness." They might have been close descendants of the men trained by Robert Rogers or led by Swamp Fox Marion. They would have gladly ridden with Ben McCulloch and the Gray Ghost, John Singleton Mosby. Under the name "Marauders" they would become noted for their ability to move swiftly over impassable terrain. The Marauders were composed of six combat teams of four hundred men each and a rear echelon logistic headquarters of six hundred men.

After Pearl Harbor when attacks on the American homeland seemed eminent to frightened citizens, the Japanese Americans living on the West Coast had been rudely rounded up almost without exception and transported to relocation camps in the interior. In most cases they did not have time to pack belongings beyond one suitcase or to make arrangements for their property and possessions.

They went to live in tarpaper shacks and tents in places that they had never heard of—small villages where even the amenities of running water and electricity were grudgingly supplied. From these impoverished conditions, the Marauders recruited fourteen Nisei, American-born and educated young men, who had returned to Japan for part of their education. They spoke the language like natives and more important they could understand and communicate in it. They were to be the translators, interrogators, and as it happened, spies.

Lacking military training, they were given a snap course along with several hundred other Americans of Japanese ancestry who eventually formed a battalion of volunteers that served with exceptional courage in Europe. That battalion also won fame as a group with indomitable courage and a memorable name—"Go for Broke."

Preliminary training for Marauders was secretly begun in the jungles of India starting in early November 1943. The fighting in Burma had been going on for two years when the Marauders were assembled in December 1943. At that time they were issued their orders: "Following breakfast this morning, the following named individuals will not eat any more meals except those which they prepare themselves. There will be no evasions of this order." Joe Rosbert, a chemical engineering student from Philadelphia, actually wrote his autobiography after the war, titled *Flying Tiger Joe's Adventure Story Cookbook.*

In January, they were moved to Burma. In February 2, 1944, 2,830 men were divided into three battalions of one thousand each, unimaginatively named First, Second, and Third Battalions, and designated A, B, and C. Though they were Stilwell's men, Wingate had trained them. They were perfect examples of the LRPGs that he had claimed would stand the best chance of winning the war.

As they moved out heading for the famous Burma Road, James Shepley of *Time* and *Life*, famous weekly magazines of the day, sang out, "There go Merrill's Marauders." Whether Wingate ever knew or cared is unknown. The members of the press, whether British or American, never referred to them as Galahad. The name remains this to this day—a name that has followed them to glory.

As part of their "on the job training and conditioning," they marched the final 130 miles to arrive they-knew-not-where on February 21, 1944. They went into combat February 24 against Japanese units. Supplies were flown in or transported on the ground from India by two quartermaster pack troops of seven hundred mules and horses.

These first Rangers on the Asian continent formed a seemingly endless line of American men, their faces chalky white under a full moon. They were dressed in dark green by coincidence or intent. The uniforms of the first Ranger contingent organized and led by Captain Rogers had also been issued distinctive green outfits. Everything was green: fatigue blouses, pants, undershirts, drawers, handkerchiefs, and matches for the cigarettes, which were mercifully white. Each soldier had been issued only the clothing on his back. Several wondered if they were supposed to wear it throughout the next three months. As a matter of fact some of them did.

As the course of the war began to turn for America, people were delighted with the name. It bespoke reckless "outlaw" courage to the world. Only on the requisition sheets for supplies were they designated the 5307th Composite unit.

The plan was to insert them into the jungles as a rear action support for the Chinese. When ordered to do so, they were to engage the Japanese army intent upon invading China from its southern border. Before that plan could be implemented, they would require on-the-job training. Vinegar Joe Stillwell knew just the man to command what would become a distinguished force.

Merrill was slightly under medium height. He wore glasses and smoked a pipe. He looked like someone's cheerful college professor. He was in fact a scholar who had been selected and elevated to brigadier general because he was fluent in Japanese. He had joined the regular army, been promoted through the ranks to sergeant, and then applied and been accepted to West Point, from which he graduated.

In 1944 when Galahad finally was implemented, Merrill had volunteered for the mission despite some health issues, which he kept to himself. He was immediately put in command. The plan as insisted upon by Generalissimo Chiang himself called for the Americans to be used to spearhead the Chinese units. Merrill immediately—and possibly in defiance of certain superior officers' plans—announced that Galahad, made up entirely of crack fighting men, would *not* be used to take fire for the Chinese. His exceptional band that he already thought of as heroes was to be used strategically to meet the enemy in small units, hurt him bad, and melt away into the jungle sustaining few if any casualties. The men were not shields for inferior fighters.

His reasoning was clear and unarguable. World War II had been going on for nearly three years. If the Chinese had been going to win it, they would have done so since they fought on their own turf and outnumbered their enemies by many thousands. Clearly, they had not the will, the training, or the leadership to win anything. Merrill refused to allow his men to be killed at the front of troops who would then retreat probably in full flight.

Of course, the new Rangers had to be trained too. Wherever they had come from, they had no training for what awaited them. And in their case much of it was going to be on-the-job training.

They had reported to Stilwell, who proposed that they march 140 miles through the jungle to their ultimate destination, the town of Walawbum. The march would toughen them. (Encountering and overcoming the problems of each day would be their on-the-job training.) Not far from there, the Ledo Road, running south from the Himalayas, met the Burma Road. They split into three battalion groups and entered the jungle by two-foot-wide game trails. As the Marauders traveled mainly at night, they could have nothing that would sound an alert in the darkness. Their food and ammunition as well as other supplies were carried by mules that had been "de-brayed." That is, their vocal chords had been severed.

Nine days and 109 sweaty miles later, they reached the reason for their march—the fabled Burma Road. A sixteen-foot wide winding ribbon built and maintained largely by coolie labor. One and all, the men looked at it in utter disbelief. This pockmarked ruin was what they were to defend and fight on.

Coolies had been little more than slaves when the road had first been conceived in the early nineteenth century. To lay the foundation for the

Burma Road, they carried hundreds of thousands of pounds of broken stone up to the mountaintops from quarries sometimes many miles away. The photographs of them carrying pairs of buckets or baskets hung from their necks by yokes had drawn worldwide sympathy once they were circulated. Later in response to diplomatic pressures their status rose to that of indentured servants who performed for several years and then could choose to stay with their master or go free.

Though the road was many years old, it was still much easier walking than what lay ahead. Some of the men might have looked back longingly as they turned aside and headed down into the jungle again. They encountered pythons twenty feet in length and kraits—six-inch-long snakes with nerve venom that could kill a man in minutes. Of course, tigers and elephants were less of a problem than they had been warned about. They never saw an elephant at all, although they stumbled over their huge droppings. When the mules caught a tiger's scent, they went crazy. Alarmed by their frantic rearing and plunging, everyone was alerted that a predator was about.

What they could not be alerted for were the leeches. In a jungle with rain every day, the creatures fell from the trees. A Marauder's uniform consisted of traditional long trousers, a long-sleeved shirt styled with breast pockets, thick socks, and thicker lace-up combat boots. Though most of his body was covered by thick serviceable material, if a man stepped off the trail, he would come back out of the bush with leeches hanging from any exposed skin and even down inside his shirt and up under the legs of his trousers.

The creatures were truly fearsome. The string-like beasts were little more than mouths that sucked blood until they became the size of sausages hanging off a man's body. Soldiers could not feel them attaching themselves to any exposed skin or dropping down from the trees to slip inside their clothes. Some men became frantic with revulsion and fear and pulled or tried to slap the little monsters off.

Serious mistake!

If a man ripped one off, the head almost always remained beneath his skin. There it would fester and rot sometimes infecting him all the way to the bone. The sores were hideous. The Burmese natives called the result Naga.

By trial and error the Marauders learned that a lighted cigarette touched to the leech's body would almost always make it drop off. Nerves of steel would allow a man to light a cigarette and use it and pass it on to his buddies while marching on without ever breaking stride. If a man was lucky, the spot would heal over and he wouldn't get an infection.

Men with vivid imaginations struggled to keep themselves under control. Otherwise, they'd start screaming and batting at the things. Probably some tears as well as sweat streaked their faces as they waited for a cigarette and imagined the loathsome body swelling with their blood.

Despite such terrors, the Marauders kept walking. Now they were completely enveloped by the jungle. They had no sense of direction except their compasses. They followed their leaders, whose maps were often unrevealing. The almost constant near-darkness beneath the canopy of trees was eerie.

The trailbreakers would pass the word back: "Big root here," "Big rock," "Elephant turd." Their knives kept swinging, cutting back the growth. The whole trek took on a surreal aspect. Some began to play with the idea that they would march on forever, they would never reach their destination, and no one would ever find them again.

On March 3 at dawn about fifteen miles from Walawbum, they spotted their first enemies. They had no way of knowing that Japanese General Shinichi Tanaka had been tracking their movements and was waiting for them. Suddenly, the column leader saw seven men trotting along a trail. The enemy sighted the Third Battalion at almost exactly the same time. The man in front raised a Nambu light machine gun.

"All hell broke loose. Many men fired, and five of the enemy were instantly killed."

That encounter was the first of several as they kept on marching toward Walawbum. Since they had given away their presence, they had no chance of sneaking up in the darkness. Still no enemy came out to engage them directly. A Marauder reconnaissance unit caught a unit of Japanese about to set up a machine gun. Again, the Americans "got the drop" on the group and killed three.

On the following day the Third Battalion suffered its first casualty—Private First Class Pete Leightner was cut down by machine-gun fire as he draped camouflage over what was to be his foxhole. While the machine gunner disappeared into the brush, the private's friends crawled forward and dragged his wounded body back behind their lines where they administered limited first aid. Thereafter, everyone took cover in their slit trenches waiting for the attack that was sure to come.

They didn't have long to wait. The enemy's tan uniforms and their helmets with twigs stuck up for camouflage were easy to spot in the intense green. The minute the Marauders had the range, they opened fire. The enemy hit the ground and began to chatter among themselves discussing plans to roust the Marauders out from cover.

Now was the time for the Marauders' secret weapons.

Each group contained two Japanese American Nisei soldiers. They were fluently bilingual and could understand the standard Japanese language as well as some dialects without any problems. One was Roy Matsumoto, who had volunteered from an internment camp in Jerome, Arkansas. Though he'd been born in California, other members of the company were cold and unfriendly when he first reported. They didn't know whether they could trust an "enemy alien." He proved to be such an asset and such an excellent soldier that he was later promoted to staff sergeant.

The other Nisei volunteer, Henry Gosho, became known as "Horizontal Hank" because he preferred to slither through the undergrowth to eavesdrop on the Japanese lines. In this case he lay concealed in his green uniform amidst all the intense green undergrowth.

There he could overhear the Japanese officers screaming orders. They had been told and universally believed that the Americans could not understand a word of their language.

When the Japanese first rushed forward to pursue the Marauders, Hank couldn't believe his ears. "I heard an officer giving firing orders exactly like those I had been taught when I was educated in Japan and took ROTC." He immediately passed the word to his platoon leader who gave the orders to deploy Marauder mortars to shell the enemy lines.

Matsumoto found he operated best when he climbed trees. He was all of five-foot-two and probably twenty pounds underweight. In his green uniform, a part of the thick overhead canopy, he was never successfully spotted. Though snipers fired at him again and again, he kept moving from branch to branch radioing information. Still, the Japanese had no fear that they were being overheard much less understood. They had underestimated their enemy—and the results for many were to be fatal.

Seconds later, Japanese mortar shells came whistling in from behind the enemy lines. They exploded in the trees above the heads of the Marauders, showering them with shrapnel, broken limbs, and flying wood splinters. While the main group of enemy advanced cautiously toward the center of the Marauder group, a second unit set up a flanking attack to move in from the left.

Across the Nambyu Hka River, the Americans' 81-mm mortar shells came screaming in on cue but unfortunately exploded too far behind the enemy to do any good. The Japanese took the misses as an encouraging sign. On command they began a series of banzai attacks, executed to overwhelm the enemy force.

Screaming "Banzai!" they charged into the face of the American's Browning automatic rifles (BARs) as well as machine-gun emplacements. The single word to them meant something like "May the Emperor live ten thousand years" and signified their willingness to die to ensure his long life. They would prove their loyalty and courage by charging into the face of the Marauders who answered each successive charge with merciless gunfire that cut the enemy down by the dozens.

Men dropped their guns and fell sprawling. At least a hundred men died while the Marauders lost one man and had seven wounded. Later after the smoke had cleared, Merrill wired that the attack had been a success.

Stilwell was ecstatic. In his diary he wrote, "FRANK MERRILL IS IN WALAWBUM!"

But Walawbum was far from secured. The Japanese staged a counterattack with six different banzai charges as well as mortars and field artillery.

At each charge the Japanese would scream "Banzai!" Their fanaticism was unlike anything the Americans had ever seen.

The Americans began to respond with "Fuuuck youuu!"

For the many untried troops new to the Asian continent, the battle was a nightmare. The Japanese mortars were well placed and scored hits, but the Americans were well dug in. Then Matsumoto, the Nisei interpreter of Second Battalion, spotted a Japanese communication wire in a treetop. He climbed up into the tree and began to listen in. From there he passed on information that the Japanese Eighteenth Division was spread too thin. He actually heard the Japanese commander begging General Shizuichi Tanaka for advice.

Tanaka had none to offer. Famous for his implacability, he would never have ordered a retreat in any case. Instead, he gave the instruction to fight to the end. Thirty-six hours later, the few survivors of the Eighteenth Division were withdrawn leaving their comrades' bodies strewn throughout the jungle. The loss of life had been terrible.

The Marauders climbed out of their foxholes. Matsumoto climbed down from his tree. They were all exhausted. They had eaten nothing and had very little water. While they were being resupplied, the Japanese started shelling the town. When they considered that they had "softened the Marauders' resistance," they began more banzai charges.

Again—a big mistake. Their own officers had no notion of the efficiency and the readiness of the men they were fighting. The Marauders had had time to set up their own machine guns and mortars from their foxholes.

As fast as they mowed the enemy down, another wave would come behind them. With no thought but victory or death, they kept coming, rushing forward to pick up machine guns and mortars from their comrades' dead hands, and carrying them a few feet, only to be shot themselves.

The Americans were about to be pinned down and they knew it. Still they held their lines. Then the order came to withdraw across the river. They had achieved their objective to distract the enemy from the main body moving into position to attack—Walawbum.

On March 9, 1942, the town fell. The combined forces of the Marauder battalions and a force of Chinese soldiers who had hurried down to join the fray had completely defeated the formidable Eighteenth Division. Only a few months earlier, they had been the victors to accept the British surrender of Singapore.

More than eight hundred Japanese soldiers, the best that Japan could send, died in five days at Walawbum. Even worse was the physical condition of the soldiers who survived. Later, the Allies learned that the enemy had been undersupplied. Many had had barely a handful of rice a day for a month, and then that too was exhausted.

Swiftly, the Marauders improvised litters out of bamboo poles and fatigue jackets. The understanding from the beginning was that no one wounded or dead would be left behind. With the Americans chest deep in water, bearing litters, unable to return fire, a Japanese team set up another Nambu machine gun to sweep the retreating soldiers.

On the opposite bank, Private First Class Norman Janis, a full-blooded Sioux, sighted along his rifle barrel.

One shot. "Chief" got the shooter in the head. Another one took his place.

One shot. The Sioux sharpshooter got him, too.

In the end he shot seven men, hitting everyone and killing each man instantly. With the party back across the river and melting into the jungle, the Japanese rushed forward, but their attempt to enter the water brought them in the line of fire from another well-entrenched Marauder unit.

In the meantime, another group had cleared enough area for a small plane to fly in, land, and take the wounded out, arriving and taking off in the midst of the battle. For the first time in the history of warfare, wounded men were airlifted while the propellers kept turning. The plane taxied around and headed back down the tiny runway, roared up, clearing the trees, and transported them back to hospitals where they could be cared for.

Their first casualties, Leightner and another man died during the flight, but the rest were brought out safely and treated by the best medics available. Leightner was the first of the Marauders to die in combat.

While the Americans were admirably supplied with food, ammunition, and backup of all kinds, the jungle was taking its toll in terrible ways that no one had foreseen or seemed to be able to change. The real killers of both Americans and Japanese were the alien character of the Burmese jungle south of the Tropic of Cancer. Equatorial heat, predatory animals, lack of rest, and the necessity of remaining in a state of constant alertness combined to produce physical symptoms that the human body could not overcome.

While only eight Marauders were killed and thirty-seven wounded in the five days at Walawbum, "miscellaneous sickness" cost the Marauders 109 men. Nineteen had died of malaria; eight had died of jungle fevers for which Western medicine had no names.

Even more tragic were the deaths of ten from what was listed as psychoneurosis, a result of the privations and horrors that beset them at every turn of the trail. Neuroses in young soldiers had often become evident in anxiety, depression, and distress in direct proportion to the hellish circumstances of the war and the jungle around them. Under more nearly normal civilian circumstances, they might have shown mild symptoms in their functions and relationships, but they would not have been incapacitated.

In their cases they never suffered a sense of loss of reality. Indeed, they suffered more because they could *not* lose themselves or forget where they were. Since ten died, it may be suspected that at least some of them committed suicide rather than go forward in their situation. Their deaths would have been given an acceptable name.

In the subsequent days, the Marauders came upon bodies of many, many Japanese soldiers who had committed suicide. Later as ammunition and food supplies ran low, companions would commit "double suicide." Two soldiers would put a grenade between them, embrace, and blow themselves up together.

On March 12, Stilwell ordered the Marauders on to their second mission. Vinegar Joe understood that they needed to move on while the Japanese were weak and they themselves were flushed with victory. They were to melt away into the jungle and surface to gain control of the town of Shaduzup (Shadu's Village, where the rivers join). From there they would control the Mogaung River Valley which in turn controlled the Japanese transport and supply hub in the city of Myitkyina. The Irrawaddy River is one of the great rivers of the world. It is just one of the Asian continent's several equivalents of the mighty Mississippi.

If Shaduzup fell, the Japanese Eighteenth, already significantly under-supplied with food and arms as well as replacements for the dead and wounded, would have no support whatsoever.

Although Merrill protested, Stilwell again ordered the Marauders be broken into three battalions. One would follow the trail; the other two would fan out in a line over the mountains and surround the Japanese-controlled town.

Hacking their way through the jungle, they met with less and less resistance and encountered fewer and fewer of the enemy. They did, however, find discarded equipment to "lighten the load." The enemy was in full retreat. Nevertheless, while the Marauders almost never had to fight, they themselves were not supermen. The effort expended in moving through the undergrowth was seriously undermining their strength.

They had been living, sweating, and fighting in the jungle for more than a month now. They were being used up hacking their way through forests of thick bamboo. The mules in some cases could not make the trail, so their packs were being broken up and distributed among the men, who already carried full packs on their backs. Unclean cooking and living conditions had left more than half of them with dysentery, which ravaged even the strongest in every battalion.

The mountainsides kept Stilwell's headquarters from hearing their radio calls for fresh supplies, and they were running out of food. They had two conditions: "one in which we felt unfed, the other in which we *were* unfed."

Every fourth or fifth day, the K rations were parachuted in. With each group sitting on the ground sorting through their packages, the members would try to trade among themselves for their favorite foods. Each ration box contained two hard biscuits, two soft biscuits, canned chicken, pork or egg yolks, a few fruit bars, a packet of lemonade for the canteen, and a pack of Wrigley's Spearmint gum. Included were everyone's favorites, cigarettes, and chocolate bars, called D rations (D standing for dysentery) because they were the only things some soldiers could digest without getting "the trots." Some men actually ripped their pants out at the seat, so they could relieve themselves more efficiently.

A week into the trip, the First Battalion encountered a patrol of Kachin Rangers led by OSS Lieutenant James L. Tilley. Their combined strength gave both units confidence. They kept moving until they were only a few miles from Shaduzup.

As they dug in to set up a preliminary fallback position in the night, they were fired upon. The Japanese had been waiting for them and were headed their way. The muzzle flashes from the Japanese rifle blazed in the darkness. Barrages kept falling. The forward Marauders were in danger of being overrun. Fears of a banzai attack that they might not be able to stave off were very real. Still they held.

Minutes later, they heard four large explosions up ahead in Shaduzup. In a few minutes another four explosions came again. Soon, the huts and buildings of the village were engulfed in smoke and flame.

Stilwell had ordered a light artillery unit with the Chinese 113th to track the Marauders. At the first sign of a battle beginning, they were to support the Marauders. In the darkness the Japanese began to retreat. In the light of dawn, the Marauder casualties were only eight. Another thirty-five men had been injured.

They were ecstatic at escaping so lightly when they were in danger of being overwhelmed minutes before. They were winning the battles and winning the war.

Dawn brought an end to their celebration. They learned that the Japanese had staged an end run and invaded India. Stilwell wrote in his diary, "This about ruins everything."

On top of the Japanese invasion, Chiang was proposing to halt any advances of his troops for the rainy season. Using his best diplomatic skills, Stilwell worked his damnedest to convince the Generalissimo and his father-in-law T. V. Soong that the Chinese armies were doing splendidly and that to pull them out would be tantamount to giving up the ground they had fought and died for.

Since this ground now consisted of all of northern Burma, the prospect of having to take it again convinced them to go on and drive for the airfield at Myitkyina.

Stilwell pulled out all stops for this attack, which would be the best chance of stopping any Japanese offensive into China as well as massing soldiers against them and driving them back toward Mandalay and eventually to Rangoon and out of Burma completely. Finally, Chiang agreed to an attack on Myitkyina *after* Stilwell convinced him that there was no way the Japanese could hold north Burma.

First, Wingate's men—Northern Kachin Levies and Detachment 101's Kachin Rangers—were dropped into position to drive south down the Irrawaddy River to Myitkyina. Behind them, on the trail they had broken, would come China's Y force unleashed by Chiang himself. After they cleared the Japanese out of towns and villages along the Burma Road, they would push south along the Irrawaddy to link up with the force coming north.

On March 15, the Second and Third Marauder Battalions started marching deep into the Kumon Range toward Myitkyina. Rather than fighting, they were inspecting the area for roads, trails, and communications sites. Another objective was to establish roadblocks that would stop Japanese supplies from moving north.

On March 18, they met up with Unit 101 of Vincent Curl and his army of three hundred Kachins. Myitkyina was the capital of the Kachin people who maintained a separate state from Burma even though they were strongly allied with it. The Kachin army itself numbered in the thousands and kept up a constant hit-and-run offensive against the Japanese. Just in time for morale and for renewal, the Kachins treated the nearly two thousand Marauders of the Second and Third Battalions to a feast. They roasted water buffalo over open fires. Villagers appeared out of the jungle and celebrated with music and dancing. Merrill was presented with a roasted goat all his very own. While the Kachins kept the rice beer flowing, the Marauders' medics treated all the sick villagers.

The next morning under orders from Stilwell, the Marauders returned to the fray. Second Battalion marched south accompanied by "Khaki" Combat Team from Third. Third Battalion separated and their "Orange" Combat Team remained behind to await the resupply airdrop.

The Second Battalion ran into trouble immediately. From their entrenched roadblock they were attacked with desperate ferocity by the Japanese. This time they heard no cries of "Banzai!" The first wave of Japanese soldiers rushed out of the tall grass. They were Japanese Marines, fully six feet tall in khaki uniforms. From twenty paces the Marauders opened fire. Still the officer in the lead kept charging. The Tommy gunner's weapon practically cut him in two. He fell forward with his head in the foxhole. The gunfire severed his sword.

So close were the opponents to each other that the Marauders could see the expressions on the faces of the men they killed—expressions of shock and disbelief—almost as if they did not understand that bullets could kill them. When one actually made it into a foxhole with an American, the two fought hand to hand, but the Japanese was easily pulled down and killed.

The carnage mounted as the day progressed. By the fourth wave, the Japanese charge was impeded by the bodies of their own dead. In one place, the Marauders counted seven bodies stacked on top of each other.

By the end of the day the unit commander had counted sixteen charges. Rather than risk his group running out of ammunition, he chose to keep his losses to two dead and a dozen wounded. He abandoned his roadblock and pulled the Second Battalion up into the mountains.

In the end the Second Battalion chose to occupy a village called Nhpum Ga. They were joined by the Third, which contained General Merrill and the Kachins. The Marauders were an offensive unit. This was going to be a defensive battle they were not equipped to fight. They had no heavy artillery and no tanks. They had nothing but light arms and the high ground. Sensing that this was going to be dicey at best, Merrill moved the Third farther into the mountains and established an airstrip in a rice field.

Meanwhile, the Japanese had encircled the mount and cut off the water supply from the spring just behind the village.

Beneath a constant barrage of 70- and 75-mm high-trajectory howitzers and light "knee mortars," 1,100 Marauders were stuck on the hilltop. The death toll of their mules and of their comrades began to mount.

They could account for the Japanese as they scaled the slopes. They had ammunition and were excellent shots, but the constant barrage wore on their nerves and what was left of their morale. They felt deserted, and most important, they had no water.

They sucked from the joints of the bamboo until the bamboo ran out. Then they drank mud from the elephant tracks and wallows. Of course, everyone developed dysentery. By the fifth day there was no water left at all. They went another full twenty-four hours before five hundred gallons of water in sausage-shaped plastic bottles were individually parachuted down by air transport from their logistics unit.

Because of the putrid dead all around them, the name Maggot Hill became the joke. But even jokes stopped when three Marauders back from recon patrol were shot by their own men. One subsequently died of his wounds.

After another week, Logistics learned that the Marauders were starving as well as thirsty. They fried chicken, boxed it, and filled an entire transport plane with the boxes. For the Marauders who had been living on muddy coffee and cigarettes for eight days, the meal was manna from heaven.

Through all this time, Matsumoto was the ears of Merrill's Marauders. He spent his nights crawling down the hillside, slithering through the vegetation to the edges of the Japanese trenches to listen to what was being said by the enemy soldiers, and more important what was being said by their officers.

At times he heard nothing more than the Japanese talking about going home, seeing their wives, embracing their children. They talked about the chickens they were going to raise on their little plots of land. He remembered he was lying so close to them, he could see "the flicker of stars in their eyes."

Finally, his nighttime vigil paid off. He heard a Japanese commander inform them that at dawn they would launch a full frontal attack. The commander explained that they would divide and launch themselves down the inclines on either side of a steep cliff where the Marauders wouldn't be able to defend themselves.

Matsumoto remembered that he was horrified as he realized that the Japanese would be able to slaughter the Marauders, who would have no opportunity to retreat from their exposed position. After the commander had left, Matsumoto pulled back and reported to Lieutenant Edward McLogan, whose platoon occupied the weak zone.

McLogan withdrew his men and booby-trapped the foxholes. Then he deployed them with their automatic weapons in a camouflaged position on a slope above the old position.

At dawn, the Japanese attacked. Cries of "Banzai!" and "Die! Joe! Die!" were almost lost in the explosions of thrown hand grenades. The attackers reached the foxholes and began to stab their bayonets into the dark holes. When they found nothing, they continued their charge up the hill. At fifteen yards, the Americans fired at command. Sixty Marauder BARs and machine guns mowed down the entire line of Japanese soldiers.

A second wave of Japanese cleared the jungle behind the first but dropped flat at the sight of their dead comrades.

Then Roy Matsumoto, the "enemy alien," screamed, "*Tosugekinini! Tokkan! Susume! Susume! SUSUME!*" (Prepare to advance! Advance! Charge! Charge! CHARGE!)

The second wave, obedient to command, rose to their feet and charged as their comrades had done into the teeth of the BARs and machine guns.

Fifty-four Japanese died, including two officers.

Despite this small success, the Marauders felt only depression. Their morale hit an all-time low when they learned that General Merrill's heart condition—aggravated by the month and a half of hard-living in jungle— had felled him. He had collapsed on the road. In the doctor's estimation, Merrill was too ill to be moved. The men erected a shelter over him until he could be evacuated to a base hospital. Despite his will, he was deemed so weak that Stilwell ordered him under protest to be transported to India. Colonel Charles N. Hunter was now in charge.

Word also reached them more by scuttlebutt than actual information that in the midst of the most important fighting for Burma, Wingate had been called back to India for a conference. The story they heard was one they cursed roundly and shook their heads.

He'd found himself thirsty and saw a vase on a nearby table. With his usual impatience and complete disregard for all the warnings of impure water, he tossed the flowers on the floor, turned the vase up, and drained it.

Within days, he had contracted typhoid fever. He was never able to recover from the disease. His body was stooped; his eyes, glazed. Still he tried to carry on his command responsibilities. On March 29, 1944, he was flying in a B-25 Mitchell bomber that crashed into a mountainside in Burma killing him and the other eleven men aboard.

On April 4, Colonel Hunter ordered Third Battalion to creep as close to the hill as possible. When all were in position, the men poured all available mortar rounds and howitzer shells into the entrenched Japanese. Under attack that seemed to come from all sides, the Japanese retreated when possible to higher ground, placing themselves within range of the guns of the Second Battalion.

At the same time, word came that the First Battalion was on forced march to add their numbers to the circle around the hill and the enemy trenches. The Japanese continued to hold out. What else could they do? Retreat with any sort of honor and without a heavy casualty count was impossible.

On April 7, the Third Battalion radioed that they were within five hundred yards of the hilltop, but the Japanese were between them and completely controlled the remaining distance to Nhpum Ga. The next afternoon the First Battalion arrived, making no secret of their armed advancement.

The Japanese realized that they had no chance except to slip away under cover of darkness. On April 9, 1944, they retreated, skirmishing only if they were threatened. As the Third and First Battalions pushed on up to relieve the Second, they found only "dead Japs everywhere." The defense of Nhpum Ga had cost the Marauders 59 dead and 314 wounded, but the mop-up parties found over four hundred dead Japanese.

Five hundred pounds of chloride of lime were air-dropped immediately. They covered the dead bodies of the soldiers and sweetened the air. Men with flame-throwers burned the bodies of the dead mules to kill the maggots. Unfortunately, the dead Marauders could not safely be carried away by airlift. Their bodies were buried in the center of the hilltop on which they died. Their dog tags were hung from the bamboo crosses erected over their graves.

Hunter arranged for new drops of uniforms, water, and rations in a ten-to-one ratio. He also ordered blood plasma and dysentery medicine.

Despite Hunter's efforts in their behalf, the Marauders without their general could count as well as anyone. They had started their march into the jungle on February 2. By April 9, Easter Sunday, they could count that they had only three weeks of duty left. Surely, in the light of the battles they had fought, the constant shelling they had endured, the hunger and privation that had depleted every reserve in their bodies, surely Nhpum Ga would be their last action. Surely they would be relieved and airlifted out. Surely replacements would be found.

A terrible rumor began to circulate when three high-ranking officers flew in to check on their physical condition. They learned at that time that Colonel Hunter had already detailed a survey party over the mountains toward Myitkyina. General Merrill was returning soon to lead them.

The grousing was high and morale was at an all time low. General Merrill had been lying on his back for nearly a month. They had been "used up" for that time. Likewise, their heroism, their valor, their unstinting performance of their duty had gone unrewarded with the trappings that they knew they deserved. Where were the promotions, the colors, the commendations, and the medals? In the Burmese jungles they seemed to be expendable.

Stilwell himself had called for an "End Run." It would be the killing stroke that would defeat the Japanese forces in northern Burma for good and all. As Stilwell's other forces pushed the enemy to retreat south toward the sea, the Marauders would be used "one more time" to take the airfield at Myitkyina. With their action, General Tanaka's Eighteenth Division, already depleted by the same conditions that the Marauders had suffered, would be forced to retreat, to pull back, out of Burma forever.

The Marauders were weak, sick, and dog-tired. Of their number, 1,500 had died mostly of jungle diseases and privations. Many fewer of that number had died in the fighting. They were great fighters, but they were used up. Just the mention of Stilwell's name brought forth streams of exhausted curses. They believed he didn't care about them and was more concerned about Chiang's Chinese fighters than about his own men. In this they were wrong—at least about Chiang's men. Stilwell cared about no one and nothing besides winning the war.

When Colonel Hunter suggested that his officers receive oak leaf clusters as rewards for exceptional work, Stilwell responded by telling Hunter that his men should "spend more time fighting and less time worrying about promotions."

By April 28, when the Marauders had had three weeks of rest, they were ordered to march over an unused trail that crossed over a 6,100-foot pass. At times they were forced to crawl on their hands and knees up the steep slopes. What passed for morale had been replaced by a what-the-hell-did-you-expect attitude—openly expressed anger that bubbled strong beneath the surface and kept the adrenaline flowing.

Matsumoto recalled, "It was unbelievable. Sometimes you'd be there, hanging on the mountainside, your hands clutching a root or small tree, which was all that kept you from sliding down the mountain. We were climbing straight up, like mountain climbers. But we were carrying lots of weight and, well, we were exhausted. But, somehow, we kept going."

More of the used-up mules died as well. When that happened, their packs were divided among the already burdened men. In a single day Third Battalion lost twenty mules. Rather than even try to divide their packs, they abandoned four thousand pounds of equipment in the jungle.

Morale sank to zero, and for the first time they began to pass by men who had fallen out on the trail. They couldn't go on, and their comrades couldn't carry them. There was no help.

Stilwell began to grow worried. On May 1, 1944, he wrote of his worries in his diary, "nothing can be done. The die is cast . . . but the nervous wear and tear [on himself] is terrible."

They attacked the airfield at Myitkyina on May 17, 1944. It was the only all-weather strip in northern Burma. Moving quickly, the Marauders were part of the force that surprised the Japanese and seized the airfield in a daring and brilliant daylight attack. Unfortunately, the assault against the town itself met heavy resistance and dragged on. For two and a half months, Stilwell was losing 130 men a day. General Marshall and President Roosevelt were being lobbied for his recall. Finally, bowing to pressure, Stilwell was to be replaced by General Albert Wedemeyer.

Vinegar Joe's comment was, "Good God—to be ousted in favor of Wedemeyer—that would be a disgrace."

On August 3, officers took stock and discovered that of the original group of 2,830 officers and men who set out on their first mission on February 7, only 1,310 had reached the objective at Myitkyina airfield. By the time the town was taken, only 200 of them were left on the line.

Merrill himself had been evacuated a few weeks earlier after yet another heart attack.

Having been promised relief, Marauders' morale and cohesion deteriorated as they remained on the line. Periods of rest and improved rations failed to maintain, much less restore strength and endurance. An inspector general reported "an almost complete breakdown of morale in the major portion of the unit." Physically and mentally exhausted, utterly worn out and depleted, this most heroic unit was relieved and consolidated on August 10, 1944, with the 475th Infantry Regiment.

HISTORY'S ASSESSMENT

The 475th was deactivated on March 21, 1956. This infantry regiment would serve as the forefather of today's 75th Ranger Regiment.

The 5307th Galahad Composite Unit was awarded the Distinguished Unit Citation. In 1966, the award was redesignated as the Presidential Unit Citation.

Matsumoto, the former "enemy alien," was awarded the Legion of Merit.

Wingate was buried where he lay until much later when his body was moved to Arlington Cemetery in accordance with the practice of burying the leader with the troops he commanded, in this case the Marauders.

When World War II ended, Stilwell stood on the deck of the U.S.S. *Missouri* to witness the signing of the peace treaty. The president receiving the surrender was not the man he had served. Roosevelt had died of a cerebral hemorrhage on April 12, 1945.

Stilwell himself died on October 11, 1946.

Major General Merrill served as Chief of Staff of the Tenth Army on Okinawa in 1945. He retired in 1948 due to ill health. He died of a heart attack at the age of fifty-two in 1955. He is considered to be one of America's greatest generals.

So completely did the assignment destroy the men who carried it out, that but for their unit name, courtesy of James Shepley, they might very well have disappeared from history. Only the name saved them with its alliteration and imaginative reference that spoke of daring, of toughness, of the will to fight, and of the determination to defeat the enemy at all costs. While their determination waned as their comrades in arms were killed or wounded and moved out into hospitals or died of jungle diseases, while the survivors' own mental turmoil almost laid them low, the name ensured their immortality. It captured the imagination of the public and carried their heroic sacrifices into history.

In five major and thirty minor engagements, they marched over one thousand miles through extremely dense and almost impenetrable jungles and defeated veteran soldiers of Japanese Eighteenth Division—conquerors of Singapore and Malaya.

The three battalions were immortalized post-war by a movie bearing their name *Merrill's Marauders*, starring handsome movie hero Jeff Chandler as Merrill. Probably for the sake of the budget, the movie was filmed in the Philippines in the dry season. The monsoon conditions under which the Rangers suffered such agonies are nowhere to be found. Likewise, the Japanese American who played so vital and gallant a role in the victories is replaced by a Filipino.

A better job is done by a series of comic books for boys and girls issued by DC Comics. Today DVDs, CDs, movie posters, and all sorts of memorabilia are sold on Amazon and eBay. Almost sixty years after Myitkyina, the history of the Rangers holds a special, honored place for Merrill and his gallant Marauders.

10

TAKE THE
HIGH GROUND

James Earl Rudder

THE SITUATION

June 5, 1944, was the day appointed to attack Adolf Hitler's defenses on the continent. He had grandly named them Atlantic Wall of Fortress Europe. Though it was never a wall except along the English Channel, it was a formidable obstacle.

On June 5, the weather was exceptionally foul. From Allied Headquarters in London, General Dwight D. Eisenhower delayed Operation Overlord for twenty-four hours. Thus, the date June 6, 1944, remains engraved in the collective memories of Americans, Englishmen, Frenchmen, as well as their willing Allies.

The Germans would just as soon forget it.

The entire 2,400-mile shoreline of the English Channel was open to a landing, but certain areas were deemed more suitable than others. *Der Fuehrer* had reasoned that the Normandy beachhead where the swift waters crashed endlessly over the sands and leaped up the walls of granite cliffs would be least likely to be the invasion site.

General Gerd von Rundstedt, Hitler's favorite commander, agreed with him. In addition to the steep cliffs, long areas had been fortified with concrete seawalls to prevent erosion of the beaches. In the unlikely event that the invaders could climb the cliffs despite the best efforts of the defenders, they would not be able to bring in any support equipment. The soldiers of the Third Reich would throw the whole pathetic effort back into the sea.

No. The consensus of the German High Command was that the Port of Calais, England, last toehold on the European continent lost in the sixteenth century and closest to their island nation, would be their target. Moreover, German spies in London had overheard a boastful remark uttered by no less formidable a personage than American General George S. Patton at a dinner party attended by General Eisenhower himself.

To further ensure that Europe would never be invaded, Hitler had ordered the building and maintaining of his Atlantic Wall, a wall that would maintain the Third Reich, like the Roman Empire, a nation that would endure for a thousand years. To maintain the impregnability of his Atlantic Wall, he had placed Field Marshall Erwin Rommel, the most respected and most talented of the military men at his command, in charge of the defense.

Even so, Der Fuehrer remained uneasy. While Hitler respected "The Desert Fox," Rommel had fallen out of favor since his defeat at El Alamein in North Africa. Despite Hitler's express orders, Rommel had retreated and then surrendered to save his men from annihilation.

Rommel was certain he had lost his battles in Africa initially because of Allied air superiority. He was correct in believing that the same air superiority would be employed against the defending German troops. Rommel was formidable when he had tanks at his disposal. If he was to stop the invasion on the beaches, he believed he needed to keep units of tanks as close to the front as possible, so they could move quickly into defensive positions when the invasion began. The moving artillery would kill and wound the invading Allied soldiers while destroying the vessels that brought them in. Within hours of heavy fighting, the Allies would run out of ammunition as well as other essential supplies. They would be forced to surrender or die.

His view had been contradicted by the commander currently in Hitler's favor. General von Rundstedt had been placed in charge of fortifying the 1,700 miles of French coastline. In the first place, von Rundstedt doubted that the British and Americans could land anything that would be effective. The Atlantic Wall with its bunkers and miles of naval cannon could easily blow the Allied ships away before they got close enough to land.

However, he did respect the firepower of the Royal and the American navies. They could and would destroy his tanks. He wanted to maintain the tanks near Paris where they could meet the oncoming Allied troops and cut them off from supplies at that point.

His tank commanders, of course, agreed with him. They were certainly in favor of remaining close to Paris. Most would have preferred to remain in the city itself with easy access to its delights and entertainments.

When Hitler was asked to decide, he vacillated and placed the tanks halfway between—too far back to be of use to Rommel and too far forward for von Rundstedt to execute a flank attack. Ten of the highly effective Panzer divisions were spread from Belgium to Bordeaux by order of Der Fuehrer. Rommel managed to have only one Panzer division at hand in Normandy. It would prove to be not nearly enough.

On hearing the reports of this distribution of resources, British Prime Minister Winston Churchill remarked that it was strange that the Germans had dispersed their most powerful weapon for counterattack when defense was most needed. And where was their most able and respected general when his cool head for strategy would have been invaluable?

Unfortunately for Rommel, he had been ordered summarily to Berlin to confer with Hitler several days before the actual D-Day landing. He was in no position to mount the counterattacks that he might have managed had he been at his command post.

The coast of Normandy, where the fifteenth-century English King, Henry V, had landed successfully to conduct his invasion in his quest for the French throne, became the target of the twentieth-century's invasion of liberation. There Allied armies would establish various beachheads code-named Omaha, Utah, Gold, Juno, and Sword. Allied forces involved in the battle besides the Americans were the British, the Free French, and the Canadians, as well as contingents from Poland, Belgium, Czechoslovakia, Greece, and the Netherlands.

Prelanding information superior to anything the German high command had ever imagined had been supplied by men and women of the French Resistance including—most amazingly—a *blind* piano tuner who had been allowed to wander around at will on top of Pointe du Hoc. The Germans did not bother him while he paced off the distances between gun emplacements, trenches, bunkers, and everything else he could measure with his even stride. The maps of the Allies were accurate to the square foot.

The Normandy site was chosen partly because it was *not* Calais and partly because of its location near the city of Caen where the initial base of operations could be located. Once the area was secured, the thinking was that Cherbourg, the deep water port to the northwest, could be taken to serve as the offloading dock for the thousands of men and machines that would pour into France and then into Germany. (Cherbourg proved to be a waste of effort. When the city did fall, the once great harbor was discovered to be in such neglected condition that it was of little strategic use.)

Crucial to the success of a Normandy landing was a promontory of rock thrusting into the ocean. When Lieutenant Colonel James Earl Rudder, a former football coach from John Tarleton Agricultural College in Stephenville in Central Texas, was told of his assignment—"to take a force of 200 men, land on a shingled shelf under the face of a 100-foot cliff, scale the cliff, and destroy an enemy battery of coastal guns"—he thought General Omar Bradley was joking. He told Bradley later, "I thought you were just trying to scare me."

Privately, Bradley observed, "Never has any commander been given a more desperate mission."

Some might have thought that it would take more than courage and determination to make such an assault. But not Rudder. The football coach believed that luck was and is merely the residue of excellent training. With that in mind, he had pushed his Second Ranger Battalion through intensive training maneuvers. They had attended the Scout and Raiders School in Fort Pierce, Florida, and Advanced Tactical Training at Fort Dix. They had undergone an intense training cycle run by the British Number 4 Commando. On the Scottish coast they had conducted amphibious invasions against a fortified beach defended by wire, beach obstacles, and anti-assault landing boat devices. They had learned infantry fighting with the British Assault Training Centre. They had toughened themselves through long marches and log-lifting drills.

Those lacking strength and stamina were reassigned to other battalions, and the word spread through the army ranks that these special Rangers were being groomed for something of great importance, as well as great risk. They were being trained for a dangerous mission. Cynics and perhaps those who had been rejected or reassigned referred to them as the "suicide squads."

But a special breed of men known in America since the time of Robert Rogers has found challenge irresistible. These men step forward eagerly into the teeth of death to dare and triumph or—if they must—give their all in the attempt. For them the most important thing is to do their duty and in so doing prove that they can be the "best."

Even the men who become chaplains to Rangers have a special attitude when they minister to the needs of the men who charge against the guns. Father Joe Lacy, the Fifth Battalion's Ranger Chaplain, exhorted them on the night before they boarded the transports. "When you land on the beach and you get in there, I don't want to see anybody kneeling down and praying," he warned them. "If I do, I'm gonna come up and boot you in the tail. You leave the praying to me. You do the fighting."

On the desperate morning when the Rangers fought, he moved about the shoreline. Careless of the machine guns, the mortars, the snipers, he hauled the dead, dying, and wounded from the water to protected positions where he could provide aid and comfort—

—or offer them their last rites.

The Rangers' first objective and one of the most important was Pointe du Hoc. It is a knife point of rock that extends out into the English Channel between the proposed landing sites of Omaha and Utah beaches. The Germans had armed it with six 155-mm cannons confiscated when France surrendered. Cast in Puteaux in 1917, they were of World War I manufacture but some of the best technology in the world and perfectly serviceable. With the idea of destroying these emplacements, the Allies had bombed the hell out of the knife point. The plan was to reduce Pointe du Hoc's sharp edges to rubble, flatten its bunkers and emplacements, and score direct hits on those terrible cannons.

How well the plan succeeded would be known when the Rangers climbed over the lip of the promontory. Till then the softening-up tacticians could only hope they had done enough.

On June 1, 1944, five days before the actual landing, the citizens of Weymouth less than 150 miles across the English Channel from Normandy turned out to cheer Task Force A—American Ranger Companies D, E, and F, Second Ranger Infantry Battalion—as they marched along the quay to board the transports H.M.S. *Ben Machree* and H.M.S. *Amsterdam* that would take them across. They were a pretty solemn uptight group of men. They knew they were going into hell.

Britain has a long history of sending her heroes into battle with the cheers of their loving, grateful families ringing in their ears. Even though it was 6:00 a.m., the school children were turned out to sing the national anthem and wave American flags. The townspeople lined the street to cheer and wish them well.

"Give 'em hell, Yank!" cried the British dockworkers.

Even though the mission was top secret, obviously the British people knew more about it than the Rangers themselves did. Likewise, newsreel photographers and correspondents were everywhere.

In the lead were Rudder and the battalion staff when Lieutenant Robert T. Edlin of Company A couldn't help but notice that the colonel was out of step. There's an old saying in the army that you don't tell a colonel "the time of day." In fact, you don't tell a colonel anything. You ask him. Politely.

What to do? What to do? The lieutenant didn't want the Rangers to look "rowdy dowdy" on parade.

When a superior sees a soldier out of step, he yells, "Everybody but Private Jones change step, *march!*"

There was only one solution—only one possibility. "Everybody but Colonel Rudder change step! *March!*"

The whole platoon changed step, and God knew they needed a laugh. Suddenly they were all snickering and laughing up and down the lines.

Later that morning before any of the three transports sailed, Rudder took the time to find the man who'd given the order to change step. Sizing him up severely, he asked, "Lieutenant Edlin, who told you to do that?"

Expecting that the colonel probably would only half kill him, Edlin answered right up. "Nobody, sir."

"My God," Rudder said, "you loosened things up for a minute. I even heard them laughing and joking and making fun of me." He wasn't upset. That was the kind of guy he was—the kind of a guy they were willing to follow into hell.

Lieutenant Colonel Rudder had taken particular care to meet with Company C—known forever as Charlie Company—to tell them they were going to be the first Rangers ashore. With Companies A and B they were ordered aboard the *Prince Charles.* He told them he expected that he would meet them when he with Companies D, E, and F met on the high ground behind the beaches and the promontory points.

As predicted, bad weather hung over the channel for several days. The conditions on the overcrowded transports were hellish. Almost everyone was seasick. Finally, General Eisenhower decided at 3:30 a.m. on June 6— bad weather be damned! He gave the command for Operation Overlord.

It was nothing monumental. Memorable for its simplicity.

"Okay, let's go."

The largest seaborne attack in history—over one hundred thousand American, British, and Canadian soldiers—had commenced.

THE ACTION

Shortly after 4:00 a.m. the intercom on the *Prince Charles* blared, "Hands to Operation Stations!"

While Companies A and B tried to continue sleeping, Charlie Company Rangers Second Ranger Infantry Battalion climbed aboard two landing craft assault (LCA) boats with their commanding officers, Lieutenants William Moody and Sidney Salomon leading the way. Thirty minutes later the boats were lowered into the icy, rolling waters of the English Channel. The Rangers had never before had full field equipment and a complete supply of ammunition on their bodies. They could scarcely move. Some had to stand. No one wanted to think about what could happen if the LCA was hit.

For an hour the boat wrestled its way through the waters.

Salomon stood in the bow practically all the way to shore. He looked for the familiar landmarks he had memorized on maps and aerial photographs, but the shore was merely dark and misty.

Then just before dawn, the sky turned red, and the thunder of guns erupted to the west at what he knew was Pointe du Hoc. Rockets opened up, arcing through the sky. The men watched as most of the rockets landed in the water. The distance had not been judged correctly.

Salomon shook his head. Those guys over there were going to have a hell of a time.

Two hundred yards from the shore, they still saw no sign of enemy opposition. As the thunder continued from Pointe du Hoc, nothing seemed alive on Pointe et Raz de la Percée, the site of the German radar installation, the eyes and ears of the German army, and their objective above Omaha Dog Green Beach. Several of the men broke into song. Today was Sergeant Walter Geldon's third wedding anniversary.

Nearer the two boats came.

As part of their action, Charlie Company was to destroy enemy gun positions located on the point. Allied tanks currently being landed would also shell them when the Rangers radioed their locations. They had been told there was a possibility that the radar station two miles farther west would be destroyed by bombardment and would be out of commission before they got there.

They could only hope.

Lieutenant Salomon was the first man off. He stepped from the ramp at a signal from the British naval officer. Current and rough water plus the wash from the boat immediately knocked him down. His sergeant, Oliver Reed, was hit by fire. He fell and was swept back under the ramp. Salomon caught him by the collar and got him back on his feet. The water was chest high.

Machine-gun fire from the German MG-42, the best automatic gun in the world at that time, never stopped. Rangers slumped in the surf, dead or dying without ever setting foot on the dry soil of France. Sergeant Geldon died with his feet still in the water. The ramp was blown off the second LCA by a direct hit that spun it half around in the water. Two more rounds hit it amidships and in the stern. It began to break up as the Rangers still able to function threw off their heavy gear and jumped into the water.

The Germans raked back and forth across the foaming surf with the Rangers trying to wade out of it.

Those at the water's edge started their dash for the cliff thirty yards away. A mortar shell hit behind Salomon, throwing shrapnel into his right shoulder. He fell face down and struggled to extricate his maps from beneath his field jacket and hand them off to Staff Sergeant Kennedy. The German machine gun sprayed sand in his eyes.

With a to-hell-with-this cry, he jumped up, almost knocking Kennedy down, and ran the rest of the way to the base of the cliff. Kennedy followed on his heels. They both fell to the sand and then rolled over and grinned at each other. Only a moment. Then they looked back toward the channel.

By the light of the rising sun, they saw the sand littered with bodies from the water's edge to the cliff base. Some men tried to crawl forward. Others lay too still with pools of blood forming under them and soaking into the soil they had come to liberate.

Meanwhile, Charlie Company's commander Captain Ralph Goranson was just learning that A Company had been practically wiped out. He gritted his teeth and ordered his adjutant to "get the word to Sid." The plan to take Vierville sur Mer was definitely out. The only thing they could hope for was to round up enough men still combat effective to take the radar installation.

They couldn't do that until they reached the top of the cliff. But how could they accomplish their mission? The Germans were throwing everything they had at them. Lieutenant William Moody, Sergeant Julius Belcher, and Otto Stevens were selected to carry toggle ropes to the top. But how could they climb a ninety-foot cliff? The last fifteen feet were straight up. While Charlie Company took aim at every German head that poked over the top, the three chinned themselves up hand over hand with their trench knives and secured toggle ropes to the barbed wire emplacement. Then they provided cover for those below. Every single man climbed faster than he had ever thought possible.

Lieutenant Moody was killed by a sniper as he led a team into the German trench system. It was horribly intact. Where was the destruction promised when the area had been bombed? Where was the air support? Only Salomon remained of the officers to lead the forces up to the radar installation at the top of Pointe et Raz de la Percée. With a white phosphorus grenade, Sergeant Belcher took it out. When the Germans tried to escape, he shot them coldly and mercilessly.

According to Salomon, when Charlie Company assembled after driving the Germans fleeing from their trenches, only nine men remained of the thirty-nine that had landed in the LCA. The price had been astronomical, but without radar, the Germans were blind to incoming planes and ships.

More important than the radar installation were the guns of Pointe du Hoc. The knifepoint of rock one hundred feet high thrust out into the churning sea was an absolutely essential target. One side of the blade looked out over Omaha Beach; one side, over Utah. A medieval castle of itself, the rock had an awesome amount of firepower installed on its crest. Heavy armament on the point could effectively destroy or drive back the landing craft on either or possibly both beaches.

Twenty-four hours before the scheduled landing, heavy bombers from the American Eighth Air Force and the British Bomber Command dropped everything they had on the two points and the five beaches. Cruisers and destroyers added their firepower to the fusillade. The Germans knew without a doubt the invasion was coming—and soon.

So much for a surprise attack.

Sounding an even clearer alarm, the battleship *Texas*, a veteran lady of World War I, opened up with dozens of fourteen-inch shells just before dawn. The sky to the west of Omaha Beach glowed with flashes and flares. Explosions, followed by dense clouds of smoke, deafened everyone underneath them. Charlie Company on Pointe et Raz de la Percée had watched the sky; they had heard the noise in their LCAs miles away. Altogether Pointe du Hoc had been hit by the equivalent power of Little Boy, the atomic bomb that was still to be dropped on Hiroshima, Japan, in August of 1945.

At 6:30 a.m. the guns of the *Texas* fell silent.

While LCAs were lowered into the channel, 225 Rangers of Companies D, E, and F, Second Ranger Battalion waited anxiously. One unknown Ranger is remembered for yelling, "All aboard the Hoboken Ferry!"

The LCAs pulled away from the side. Unfortunately, the English coxswain headed them toward the wrong point—Pointe et Raz de la Percée—the objective of Charlie Company three miles farther eastward.

Companies D, E, and F were supposed to land on the shingled beach at Pointe du Hoc.

Providentially, Rudder was in the lead boat. He had had an argument with Lieutenant General Clarence Huebner, the commanding officer in overall charge of the Omaha Beach landing. Huebner argued that Rudder was too valuable to risk. They could not afford to lose him "on the first round." Task Force B—Companies A and B—and Task Force C were going later supported by an amphibious tank platoon. Rudder was an exceptionally valuable officer and a warrior in the purest sense of the word. He was also as stubborn as he was fearless.

Rudder is recorded as replying, with just the slightest hint of a warning in his voice, "I'm sorry to have to disobey you, sir, but if I don't take it, *it may not go*." He had no idea how right he was although not for reason he thought.

As it happened, Rudder's presence may well have changed the entire course of the landing and the war as well. Recognizing they were heading for the wrong landing point, he ordered the English coxswain to come about, and the ten little LCAs with approximately twenty-five men in each boat headed back down the coastline. The water was dark blue-gray with waves ranging from two to four feet high. The breeze cut like a knife. A fall into the frigid water was a guarantee of hypothermia.

Slowly, laboriously, they retraced their wake, now bucking the riptide current. A minute in the English Channel that day was like an hour. In infinite discomfort heightened with fearful anticipation, they crept along.

Immediately, German emplacements all along the four kilometers opened fire. One boat overturned and sank. Twenty-five men ripped off their boots, ditched their 70-pound packs, and swam for their lives. Four drowned without ever setting foot on French soil. Some that were pulled from the water alive were too frozen to speak or walk. Even in June, the English Channel is not a place for swimmers. Evacuated later in the day, they could not rejoin their unit for nine days. Another boat was hit by a shell and sank with all aboard.

On the remaining LCAs, the Rangers were regretting the heavy breakfasts of pancakes, bacon, and eggs. The majority of them were in misery in the rough English Channel. One man recalled bailing water with his helmet, dodging bullets, and vomiting from seasickness all at the same time.

At last they reached their objective before the cliffs. An ominous silence settled. If any Germans were still alive atop Pointe du Hoc, they had had time to regroup.

As the gates dropped, the Rangers discovered the Germans were ready for them. The fire was withering. Worse and worse, the plan had been that if the Rangers landed and took possession of Pointe du Hoc, the code phrase "Praise the Lord" would be transmitted and reinforcements would be moved in. Because of their "detour," they had arrived at their beach objective thirty-five minutes late. If the message was not received by 7:00 a.m., the reinforcements from Companies A and B were to move on to Omaha Beach and proceed overland. In other words, if the code phrase was not delivered by the proper hour, there would be *no* reinforcements. By the time another company could be deployed, their help would probably arrive too late.

Arguably, the first man to step off an LCA was Lieutenant George Kerchner of Company D. "Okay, let's go!" he shouted and jumped into what he believed was water perhaps three feet deep. He disappeared with a splash. He was in literally over his head and struggling to come up. He had stepped into a shell hole. His men grimly stepped off to the right and left and waded ashore. Kerchner worked himself out and followed them.

At 7:10 "by the dawn's early light," the cold, wet, miserable Rangers with Rudder in the lead started up the beach. For the rest of his life, the colonel always maintained that if they had landed at 6:30, they could have taken the objective without firing a shot. As it was, he already knew "Praise the Lord" would arrive too late.

The landing force of 235 men was now reduced to 180. Before they had time to think, to regret, even to breathe, they turned to face the 80- to 100- even 120-foot cliffs. Even while the landing was being planned, one intelligence officer had told Rudder cynically, "It can't be done. Three old women with brooms could keep the Rangers from climbing that cliff."

But the Rangers didn't know that, didn't even have time to think about anything but attack. As their comrades started dropping beneath the hail of fire coming from the top, they quickly learned that plenty of Germans were still alive and killing. The massive amounts of explosives poured onto the top had failed to destroy the bunkers of steel-reinforced concrete.

When the bombardment ceased, the Germans had simply crawled out and concentrated on the Americans on the shingle. "Like shooting fish in a barrel." The fire from above was so intense that almost half of those remaining did not make it across the narrow beach unscathed.

"Beach" was the wrong word. The sharply slanted expanse was nothing more than rounded stones with slippery clay packed around them. Slipping and sliding, the Rangers struggled grimly away from the water while, a hundred feet above, the Germans did their best to kill them all.

They probably would have succeeded if help had not arrived all unexpected. The destroyers U.S.S. *Satterlee* and H.M.S. *Talybont* came in as close as they dared and opened fire to drive the Germans back from the edge. The "boys of Pointe du Hoc" never failed to credit the ships' guns with saving their lives. Otherwise, the entire battalion would have died in the water and at the foot of the cliffs.

The surviving Rangers ran for the protection of the cliff, which proved to be no protection. The shelling had crumbled the cliff edges, scattering debris in a steeply slanted pile to a height of twenty feet up the face. From the knife point above, the Germans were dropping concussion grenades, familiarly called "potato mashers," as well as firing their rifles and machine guns. Moreover, the tide was coming in. The rock shingle was only thirty-feet wide. At high tide it was underwater. If they didn't get up that cliff, they would soon be swept out into the channel to freeze and drown.

At that point, the LCAs that brought them in fired the rockets that propelled the Rangers' climbing ropes and ladders attached to grapnels. By that time many of the ropes were heavy with seawater sloshing about in the bottoms of the boats. What should have been the Rangers' lifelines didn't make the distance to the top. Grapnel after grapnel fell back several feet from the top or barely topped the rock lip without catching and fell back on the frustrated men.

Private First Class Harry W. Roberts of Company E fired a hand rocket about fifteen feet from the base of the cliff. It went over the top of the point and caught. He started climbing the sloping pile of clay debris, slipping and sliding as he went. Finally, he reached the sheer cliff face. When he was about twenty-five feet from the top, either the rope slipped or was cut. He fell crashing into the clay, tearing his hands and clothing. Someone else fired a hand rocket, and the determined Roberts shinned up that rope. Just under the cliff edge, he pulled himself into a small crater. When that rope too was cut from above, he tied it to a picket. As the next Ranger started up, the picket pulled out leaving Roberts marooned for several frightening minutes.

Other men who reached the cliff faces began to try to free-climb using their bayonets to pull themselves up, but for most the clay was too slick and unstable to hold their weight or make much progress through it. Eventually, one of the men from Colonel Rudder's boat, Tech/5 George J. Putzek of Company E, climbed over on the top of the cliff. He hooked the top rung of the ladder in his arm while the others climbed. He was seriously wounded, but his comrades made the top in seconds and relieved him.

Finally, four grapnels from LCAs actually made it over the top of the cliff. When the Germans ran forward to cut or toss them off, they ran back just as fast. Attached to each grapnel was a burning fuse that had been lighted just before the launch. The ruse worked when the Germans thought that the grapnel rig was about to explode and took cover.

With live ammo whistling all around them, the first Rangers finally made their climb up the cliff. Before he started upward, Lieutenant Kerchner, soaking wet and shivering until his teeth rattled, thought, "This whole thing is a big mistake. None of us are ever going to get up that cliff."

On one of the LCAs, Sergeant John Cripps of Company F saw not enough grapnels had made it over the top. In the best tradition of Rangers taking initiative, he dismounted the rockets from his boat and carried them ashore. Under German fire the entire time, he fired each rocket individually using a "hot-box." Miraculously, he managed to put all of his grapnel hooks over the lip of the cliff.

As the LCAs began to pull away, the vehicle (D), (amphibious) utility (U), all-wheel drive (K), two powered rear axles (W), that is, DUKWs, but familiarly called "Ducks," wallowed in. They were 2.5-ton cargo carriers. Each was thought to be especially important to the landing force because it was equipped with London Fire Brigade extension ladders. Unfortunately, the beach and the waves were so fierce that their commanders were unable to land in the high surf. One Duck sank; two ran aground. Only the fourth edged in and cranked its ladder upward.

No luck. It wouldn't reach the top in the crashing surf. No reinforcements could land from there.

Ranger bravery allowed it to serve a purpose. Scrambling up the bobbing, weaving tower went Staff Sergeant William Stivison of Company F. Ninety feet in the air brought him more or less at eye level with the German soldiers hovering near the grapnels, chunking "potato mashers," and taking aim at the Rangers laboring up the cliff. Armed with two British Lewis machine guns, Stivison blazed away while the ladder swayed, arced, and dipped beneath him.

The Germans dived for cover. Those who managed to fire at him missed because of the rise and fall of the ladder. Only when he ran out of ammo and the Duck threatened to overturn and founder, did Stivison climb down the ladder, grab his own Browning automatic rifle (BAR), and leap into the churning water.

And five minutes later, the first Rangers were over the top on Pointe du Hoc. In another fifteen minutes, all the men still alive and combat effective were in position to move forward.

Each man knew his mission and was determined to carry it out. They were alive to fight, to accomplish their mission, and determined that no one among those who had drowned, those who had been machine-gunned, those who had been concussed or blown to bits by "potato mashers" would have died in vain.

Colonel Rudder's craft landed with fifteen Company E Rangers, some radiomen, and Tech/4 Charles S. Parker, a *Stars and Stripes* photographer from 165th Signal Photo Company, snapping pictures as he waded ashore. With them was Lieutenant Colonel Thomas H. Trevor, a British commando. Just as he reached dry land, a German bullet hit his helmet, piercing the steel and wounding him in the head. The impact slammed the colonel to his knees and knocked his helmet off. Blood streaming over his face, he looked upward and screamed, "You dirty sons of bitches!"

After Rudder helped him over to the base of the cliff, Trevor had his wound treated by a medic and then walked back and forth on the beach, encouraging the men as they came ashore.

When the LCA of Company F last arrived at the shore, they had drifted almost a football field's length from their touchdown point. As they fired their rockets, the soaked ropes again failed to reach the top of the cliff. They were all scared nearly speechless at the thoughts of being left on the beach at the mercy of fire and explosions from above.

As the LCA turned back to nose in closer, their commander Captain Otto Masny shouted to the coxswain, "Don't fire those things until I give the word! We've got plenty of time."

To put teeth in Captain Masny's order, Lieutenant Richard A. Wintz pulled his pistol and pointed it at the Brit in charge. "You drop those gates or let those charges go before I give the order, and I'll put a bullet through your head."

The bottom of the LCA ran up onto the beachhead before the nose of their LCA dropped down against the sand.

Masny yelled, "Go!"

The sailor fired the rockets. *Stars and Stripes* correspondent Lt. G. K. Hodenfield fell over backward in the bottom of the boat, but they all charged ashore on relatively dry land rather than waded.

First Sergeant Len Lomell in Company D boat had started placing $100-bets on which LCA crew would be first up the cliffs. When he stepped off the LCA, he had also fallen in a hole. His guys pulled him out with his arms full of gear and "stuff," and together they ran for the ropes. He had also been shot, but so much adrenaline was pumping into him that he never noticed the wound in his right side until much later. So quickly and easily did they make the climb that he and many of the other men inter-viewed said the cliffs were less difficult than they had been led to expect.

Part of their recollection may be attributed to the shelling the cliffs had sustained that had created a pile of rubble some twenty feet high at their base. Instead of climbing, the Rangers could grasp the ropes and scramble up over the slope of shattered stone and clay. Of course, at any minute, they expected to see a German soldier behind the barrel of a machine gun taking aim.

Finally, at the top of the cliffs with the bright dawn sky and the smoke and the sea behind them, the men of Company D must have felt like *Stars and Stripes* correspondent and cartoonist Bill Mauldin's "dogface" cartoon character Willie. They "wuz all fugitives from th' law of averages." Colonel Rudder was able to radio "Praise the Lord" to headquarters at 7:30 a.m.—fifteen minutes too late. Companies A and B, Second Ranger Battalion and Fifth Ranger Battalion, had already moved on to assault Omaha at 7:15.

In front of the men of Companies D, E, and F lay what might have passed for a mountaintop in hell. The area was pockmarked with craters, holes small and large left by shells. It was littered with shattered stone that crackled and turned underfoot. Pointe du Hoc had been shot to pieces. The Rangers who had carefully memorized topographic maps of the whole area discovered they could not recognize a single marker.

They had no time to orient themselves. "Coach" Rudder's team had kicked off, and the big game was under way.

Though driven back by the guns of the *Satterlee* and the *Talybont*, the Germans were still tossing hasty shots at the ducking, dodging, running men who flung themselves over the cliff tops and dived for cover.

Sergeant Lomell led his men scampering from crater to crater and ob-stacle to obstacle, dodging fire as they advanced toward what they were pretty sure had to be the three casemated gun emplacements.

"We didn't stop," Lomell recalled. "We played it like a football game charging hard and low. We went into the shell craters for protection, because there were snipers and machine guns firing at us. We'd wait for the moment, and if the fire lifted, we were out of that crater and into the next one."

At the first casemate, the "team" found decoys—wooden telephone poles. The guns of Pointe du Hoc were not in their emplacements. Had the intelligence been wrong, or had the guns been hidden?

By this time, the Germans had begun to fall back as more Rangers made it to the top and engaged them.

Lomell reasoned that the guns must have been moved to an alternate position. Rather than waste time searching, he made the decision to go for the second objective. As he told his squad, they would hear the guns when they opened up. His team would have time enough to destroy them then.

A Ranger is trained to take the initiative. His secondary assignment after reaching the point and destroying the guns was to set up a roadblock along the hard surface road that linked the towns of Vierville on the west and Grandcamp les Bains on the east. In other words, Company D's secondary assignment was to take control of the road from Omaha to Utah beaches.

High command had determined that German troop movements back and forth across the narrow tower of stone must be prevented. Lomell and his eleven remaining men from Company D moved out until they came to the coastal road.

Before they could set up the ordered roadblocks left and right, they had to hide from forty to fifty German soldiers quick-marching in the direction of Omaha Beach. Undoubtedly, they were a contingent of reinforcements. The Rangers had gotten there too late to effectively intercept them.

They took no time to regret the initial failure. After the Germans had passed out of sight, they began to set their roadblocks. In the process they found a clue to their primary objective. They found heavy equipment tracks in what appeared to be a sunken road.

Lomell and his buddy Sergeant Jack Kuhn followed the tracks. "We came upon this vale, or this little draw, with camouflage all over it," Lomell told later. "Lo and behold, I peeked over this—just pure luck—over this hedgerow and there were the guns, all sitting in proper firing condition, the ammunition piled up neatly, everything at the ready."

The notorious guns of Pointe du Hoc!

Only five 155-mm cannons were pointed at Utah Beach rather than Omaha, but a couple or all of them could be easily moved into position to face Omaha. Their range was an estimated twenty-five thousand meters. Well-trained units could place fire along the fourteen-mile length of Omaha beach and the ten-mile length of Utah. Their bombardment would wreak havoc on Allied ground troops disembarking from their LCAs. Their covering fire would provide other German guns with the opportunity to blow up larger troop and equipment transports farther out to sea.

Lomell and Kuhn stared at them for a full minute. The guns on which the whole battle might hang were sitting all unguarded in a field. Their first mission, the entire reason for this desperate climb, was to destroy these monsters. Destroy them they would. Still, it had to be done quietly.

Through the green summer foliage, they could see about a hundred German soldiers who seemed to be in the midst of a meeting in a far corner of the field. They were more than enough to kill or capture every Ranger who had managed to make it off the beach.

Lomell took their two thermite grenades and ducked in under the camouflage netting. He placed each of the grenades in the elevating and traversing mechanisms of two of the guns.

The AN-M14 TH3 thermite grenades (about the size and shape of Campbell soup cans) were virtually silent when detonated. When placed on metal, these pyrotechnic devices generated four-thousand-degree (Fahrenheit) heat for thirty to forty-five seconds. They burned straight through the steel, melted the mechanisms, and made the guns immovable. The guns could still be fired, but only in their locked positions.

The Germans hadn't moved, so Lomell and Kuhn ran back down the road. They relieved all the men in their patrol of their remaining thermite grenades. Back they ran to the guns.

The Germans were still conferring.

Ducking low, they placed the other grenades, as many as they could, in the mechanisms on the other three guns, this time including the firing mechanisms. Within minutes, all five 155-mm cannons were useless. With his rifle butt Lomell smashed the gunsights—just to make sure.

As he and Kuhn started away, they were almost knocked off their feet by a gigantic explosion. As they struggled to regain their bearings, they thought that the *Texas* must have opened up again. Later they learned that another Ranger unit had blown up an ammunition dump nearby. Sergeant Frank Rupinski of Company E had stumbled across a huge stockpile of ammunition south of the gun battery. Using some of their own explosives, he had destroyed all German capability. Nothing was left to be fired from Pointe du Hoc.

It was not quite 8:30 a.m. In somewhat over an hour, the cliffs had been scaled; the high ground had been taken. The road between Omaha and Utah beaches had been interdicted. And incidentally, they had blown up an ammunition dump. The big guns had been put out of action. Ranger Companies D, E, and F had been the first American unit to achieve their military objectives.

But their reinforcements had never come. Unknown to Rudder, the rest of his battalion had been pulled away to be added to the chaos on "bloody Omaha." Could his boys who had achieved so much in such a short time hold what they had won?

Pointe du Hoc was a fortress in itself, albeit a shattered one. Its landward perimeter was heavily defended with machine-gun emplacements, barbed wire entanglements, and anti-personnel minefields. Still in action was a machine-gun emplacement that had caused so many casualties on the rocky beach below the point.

Rudder ordered Lieutenant "Dutch" Vermeer to eliminate it. He had no reason to believe that the ground between them wouldn't provide craters for them take cover in. Unfortunately, the shelling had not reached so far back. An open space nearly three hundred yards across stretched between them and the pesky machine gun.

Then as Vermeer prepared his company to move forward, a task he dreaded since it would mean the loss of so many men, Rudder countermanded his own order.

While Vermeer held, Rudder's communications officer Lieutenant James Eikner of Mississippi employed his backup trick one more time. Though they had lost all means of communication when Eikner had been shot (in the radio) coming ashore, the lieutenant had brought an old World War I signal lamp, the kind with shutters that the operator could close and open to send messages in Morse code. For several minutes, Eikner searched for dry cell batteries. Finally, he sent the colonel's order to the destroyer *Satterlee*. Antique communications or not, the message with the coordinates was crystal clear.

The destroyer trained its five-inch guns on the machine-gun position and blew it away with a direct hit.

Despite the support from the destroyers, the company was in a desperate position. Many were wounded, some severely. They were in short supply of everything. Most of their equipment had been unable to land, had been lost or destroyed, or had been damaged beyond usefulness. They were isolated, cut off from the sea. Many German guns were still operational although the men manning them were somehow unaware that Rudder's Rangers had taken the heights. Their attention and their guns were still trained on the beach where Company D had landed. The Rangers had no radio—no communication of any kind other than the old lantern. Most important, they had over 50 percent casualties.

Years later, Eikner would recall, "When we went into battle . . . there was no shaking of knees or weeping or praying. We knew what we were getting into. We knew everyone of us had volunteered for extra hazardous duty. . . . We were actually looking forward to accomplishing our mission."

By the time Company D was able to establish the blocking position on the road only twenty of its seventy Rangers who had made it out of the assault boats and up the cliffs were still combat effective. A battalion aid station had been established in a two-room concrete bunker, and the wounded were more than it could handle.

To cap the climax, the British cruiser H.M.S. *Glasgow* had fired a short marker round that had struck Rudder's command post. One of his men had been killed and another wounded. The colonel had been knocked senseless. When Rudder recovered consciousness only a short time later, he had gone hunting for snipers. He had been shot in the leg for his trouble. Because of them, movement above ground was pretty much impossible. The men hesitated to hunt the Germans in their own trenches, which they were sure contained ambushes and booby traps.

For the next forty-eight hours, the Rangers were on their own. Armed with little more than their BARs, 60-mm mortars, and various "liberated" German weaponry, the Rangers waited nervously for reinforcements from Omaha Beach.

When some of the men suggested their twice-wounded commanding officer might be evacuated, he flatly refused to consider it. He remained with his men and continued to direct the unit's defenses until they were all relieved.

Colonel Rudder's head was aching. His leg was hurting like a son-of-a-gun. His adjutant had managed to bring him a half a canteen cup of strong black coffee. He took a sip of coffee and asked Colonel Trevor his opinion of the operation thus far.

Trevor's head hurt as badly as Rudder's from the wound he'd received in the landing. He took a drag off his pipe. The British commando, a combat veteran who had seen action in Africa, shrugged. "Never have I been so convinced of anything that I will be either a prisoner of war or a casualty by morning."

Rudder refused even to consider that possibility. Vermeer said later, "He was the strength of the whole operation."

The Rangers of A and B companies, Second Ranger Battalion, had been ordered to move their landing site from Dog White Beach, the most heavily fortified, to Dog Green Beach. Along with the Fifth Ranger Battalion, they were to get up off the beach immediately and push through the Vierville Draw. They were to move past the inland fortifications at Pointe du Hoc, which was presumed to be in the hands of D, E, and F companies, and keep moving by the coastal road to Grandcamp les Bains.

Company C, Fifth Ranger Battalion, was preparing to land with assaulting units only two minutes after the initial landing of the A/116th Infantry, a historic unit known simply as The Regiment, the Virginia National Guard. Their mission was to cross the beach behind the dunes and secure the Vierville Draw. The landside entrance had been effectively blocked by Rudder and Company D up on Pointe du Hoc.

But every time an LCA let down its gate, the potential for tragedy was there. The historic regiment was virtually annihilated crossing the beach. They never made it to their objective.

Lieutenant Robert M. Brice commanding First Platoon had had no problems, no hits, and no near-drownings in the waves. He and his men were almost to shore before they got hung up on steel cables and other impassable obstacles, below water level. He ordered the ramp lowered and jumped into the water just over his knees. He struggled in the water, plunged forward, and became the first man from his craft to reach the beach. He turned and yelled, "Let's go!"

An explosion of machine-gun fire raked him across the chest. He was dead before he hit the sand.

Ranger Company C, Fifth Battalion, had been unable to see the carnage that was occurring up ahead. Because of those who had gone before, they felt rather confident that they would be able to walk ashore. In consternation they realized too late that they were off course. At 6:45 a.m. they were to assault a section of Omaha that had not been crossed. They hit it on the western edge, out of position and just west of the Vierville Draw.

As the first LCA dropped its ramp, it was immediately assailed by German fire and a few steps out into the water, the Rangers went under. The LCA had hit a sandbar some distance from the shore's edge. While they were drowning in their gear, the second LCA was hit three times with artillery fire.

The few who made it to the shoreline and struggled toward the bluff, hoping for some protection, were cut down. Dead Rangers lay everywhere: in the destroyed LCAs, floating in the water, rolling lifelessly in the surf, half in half out of the water. Sixty-eight men of Company C were reduced to thirty-one in a matter of minutes.

According to Churchill's best understanding of the situation written in his history of World War II years later, Omaha Beach had been recently taken over by a German division in full strength and on alert. For this unlucky chance, the landing might have been as respectively easy as the other four beaches. Unfortunately, "Bloody Omaha" remains in the American consciousness along with Gettysburg and Iwo Jima, where many thousands of men lost their lives in the space of a very few hours.

Bodies floated in the water and lay everywhere on the beach. Some of Ranger Company B ran across the beach to the comparative safety of a rock pile a hundred yards from the water's edge. Some took cover behind the concrete and steel obstacles thrusting up out of the surf to prevent the landings.

Company A had run aground a hundred yards from shore. They leaped into waist-deep icy water and were being shot down from German positions concealed on the beach. As medics tried to reach the hurt and wounded men on the beaches, they, too, were shot despite their Red Cross insignias.

By this time the German snipers cared nothing for the rules of the Geneva Convention.

Captain Joseph A. Rafferty, Headquarters Company A, started ashore, was wounded twice in the leg, and realized that they *had* to get off the beach. The sand was a killing field. He started yelling to his men, "Let's go! Come on, guys. Move it. Get the lead out. Get off the beach!"

Those still moving were grabbed by their collars and dragged toward the rock pile. Captain Rafferty kept yelling and rounding up his men until a mortar round struck him in the body and exploded.

Some of them made it on their own, crawling and in pain, blinded by the sand flying all around and in front of them.

Radio Technician Sergeant Gerard C. Rotthof, Company A, struggled manfully to get his sixty-pound SCR 284 ashore. His assistant radio man had gotten separated from him. The waves seemed to push him out rather than carry him in. As he was trying to walk the rail ties of one of the beach obstacles, an explosion tore his helmet off and half his nose away.

As he reached the beach, he was hit again in the back. The force threw him face down in the sand. He struggled but couldn't move under the weight of the radio. He was fully aware of how he must look to the German snipers. No helmet to protect his head, struggling with the damned heavy radio.

Private First Class Robert H. Cooley, also of Company A, dropped down beside him and helped Rotthof get the strap over his right shoulder. From there he managed to crawl to safety dragging his radio behind him.

The next thing he knew he was on an operating table where a doctor was saying, "I don't know what to do with this guy!"

Rotthof had a collapsed left lung. The top portion of his kidney was blown out. He had lost his nose. He received last rites twice—once in the field hospital and once in a hospital in South Carolina—but he survived.

Lieutenant Robert T. Edlin, A Company, who had ordered the First Platoon to change step to march with Colonel Rudder, was moving around the beach trying to help his wounded men to safety when a machine gun cut him down with holes in both legs. The bullet from the MG-42 made small holes not half an inch in diameter going in, but the exploded coming out, tearing two- to three-inch round holes and shredding the flesh around them.

Edlin tried to crawl forward, but his legs wouldn't move. His sergeant, William V. Klaus, crawled out into the open and helped his platoon leader to safety. Klaus himself was wounded and under the influence of morphine at the time.

It was now 7:45 a.m.

A few tanks had come ashore behind the Rangers and were firing at the German positions. One of the tanks got the machine gun that had killed and wounded so many including Lieutenant Edlin.

The battleship *Texas* rejoined the battle and was also firing her guns at the German emplacements above the beach.

The hell on Pointe du Hoc was as nothing compared to the hell below. The hell of desperation was Omaha. Every German soldier knew, for Rommel had told them, that the invasion must be stopped at the beaches. If the Allied armies gained a foothold, they would never give it up.

All the Allied soldiers knew that if they didn't take the beach this time, more of their fellows would have to come back and create this hell all over again. In B Company area, First Sergeant Manning Rubenstein and Headquarters Major Edgar Arnold were looking the situation over when one of their men Private First Class Robert R. Whitehead was shot in the back and killed by a sniper.

In a fury Rubenstein yelled to six Rangers standing nearest to them, "Go get that son of a bitch!"

He then stepped out to signal the tanks moving slowly forward, firing, then moving. A German sniper shot him through the jaw and throat. He was evacuated and survived, and received a battlefield commission. He fought with the Rangers till the end of the war.

Eighteen Rangers of Company B found the road that ran along the foot of the slope and moved forward several hundred yards toward the Vierville Draw. They didn't hesitate. Their numbers or the lack of them didn't bother them. They had a mission—an objective. They were headed for Pointe du Hoc ostensibly to join D, E, and F companies and eventually move east on the road to Grandcamp les Bains. They didn't consider waiting for Company A.

For all they knew there was no Company A by that time.

In the meantime, men from Company A, who had made it across the road with a few men from Company B, were working their way through vacation villas to assault the bluff. Germans were hiding in those villas but putting up a fight even as they retreated before superior firepower and fierce determination.

All knew when the tanks landed, the beach would be taken, but every yard of sand had to be paid for.

In the best form of massed attack, the survivors of A and B charged at the enemy's prepared defenses. They shouted. They screamed obscenities. They fired BARs and pistols. They tossed grenades. Angry and driven, they began to drive the defenders away from their cover. By this time the Germans were low on ammunition and awed by the determination of these men who kept coming and coming.

And coming.

The Germans fell back.

A machine-gun section from Company D, 116th Regimental Combat Team joined the Rangers.

Staff Sergeant William J. Courtney and Private First Class William E. Breher, First Platoon messengers, were the first to reach the hill. As their buddies joined them, they found the German trenches and the machine-gun emplacements and took them out.

Too late the Germans tried to catch the Americans in a cross-fire. Twenty more Rangers, the men of Company B, came storming up.

As the smoke began to clear and the firing slackened, the men of the Fifth Ranger Battalion gathered on the top of the bluff to the Rangers' east. The Second Battalion companies joined the Fifth.

And looked around them dazed, then amazed.

By God! They had taken the high ground. The Rangers had complete control of the Dog White section of Omaha Beach.

It was 8:30 a.m.

Only minutes before, after receiving negative reports and hearing only limited notices of success as the situation on the beach grew more dire, Lieutenant General Bradley was seriously considering redirecting the reinforcements to one of the other beaches. Over five thousand soldiers were trapped in the sand where blood pooled. Nearly 50 percent of them lay wounded or dead on the shore. Bodies lay sprawled where they had dropped when the enemy fire had cut them down. Body parts—headless torsos, arms, legs—rolled and floated lazily in the surf like so much flotsam after a terrific storm. Groups of frightened soldiers huddled under wrecked and otherwise inoperable vehicles that continued to draw fire whenever someone would stick a head or a shoulder around the corner to survey the heights.

Contributing to the noise and confusion, the tanks of the 741st Tank Battalion clanked up and down the beaches. They were putting up a stiff fight, firing and reloading, firing and reloading, despite the fact that they could not get over the shingle at the beach's edge and climb up the heights. The minutes before they had to "abandon ship" were numbered as the tide raced in, but still their commanders kept firing.

Late that evening, twenty-three more Rangers came up from the beach to the roadblocks established on the Grandcamp les Bains road atop Pointe du Hoc. They brought twenty prisoners of war, but the Germans gave them no trouble. During the afternoon of July 7, a landing craft was able to remove the wounded and the prisoners of war at the same time it brought in more reinforcements—another twenty Rangers from the Fifth Battalion from Omaha Beach.

Periodically, the fighting would resume atop Pointe du Hoc. Recognizing its strategic importance and not knowing that the guns had been destroyed, the Germans tried again and again to retake it.

Rudder's Rangers held out for forty-eight hours. They had fought nonstop for two days without relief. Only fifty men were still capable of fighting. Almost all of them were wounded in some way.

The first general officer on the beach was Brigadier General Norman D. Cota. His single star emblazoned on his helmet, he walked up and down the beach gathering the survivors of the ruined battalions for a push inward. Organizing a group of men, he led them through a mortar barrage across the beach and up the bluff. When the Germans immediately zeroed in on their ascension spot, he organized fire and maneuver teams that drove the enemy back.

From there he led his men along a dirt road running parallel to the beach to the town of Vierville. He secured it with the aid of a twenty-three-man patrol of Rangers that had joined him from the direction of Pointe du Hoc. Eventually, they linked up with the units on the top of the knifepoint and secured the heights.

Cota then moved down the Vierville Draw back to the beach. Knowing that the draw was heavily mined, his five-man team consisting of his aide and four riflemen managed to take five German prisoners. The men were "persuaded" to show them safe passage through the minefields, so everyone reached the beach safely.

Under constant machine and sniper fire, another "fugitive from the law of averages," Cota moved about the beachhead, ordering, encouraging, herding, and reorganizing units. Over and over again, he ordered them to one more effort.

"Don't die on the beaches! Die up on the bluff if you have to die! But get off the beaches or you're sure to die!"

In his traverse, he came across one of his son's West Point classmates. The captain was commander of a few men left from Fifth Ranger Battalion Headquarters Company. He put it to them: "You men are Rangers and I know you won't let me down."

They assured him they would not as they followed where he led.

Farther on down the beach he located the Ranger Battalion's Lieutenant Colonel Max Schneider. "What unit is this?" Cota demanded.

"We're Rangers, sir!"

With that, Cota yelled loud enough to be heard halfway down the beach, "Rangers! Lead the way off this beach before we're all killed!"

His exhortation has come down to be first the mantra of the Seventy-fifth Ranger Division and then the official motto of the Corps.

"Rangers Lead the Way!"

Corporal Gale Beccue of B Company shoved a bangalore torpedo under a tangle of barbed wire. The TNT exploded and blew a huge gap in the wire. The Rangers charged through the opening and tossed Lieutenant Francis W. "Bull" Dawson on top of a barrier seawall. Charging through more wire, Dawson destroyed a machine-gun nest and turned its own machine gun on the trenches of the defenders.

Led by the Rangers, Lieutenant Colonel Schneider deployed his battalion left and right and sent another unit four miles down the road to seize Vierville. By 9:30 a.m., Fifth Ranger Infantry Battalion linked up with the men of Companies D, E, and F at Pointe du Hoc.

Rangers had indeed led the way.

Officially, the battle of Pointe du Hoc was won on June 8 when an American flag was raised on the promontory and a bugler played sorrowful notes.

The reality was that the victory—an undeniable victory—had been won at the cost of nearly 70 percent of the Rangers who had stepped aboard the LCAs in the darkness of June 6. Still, they were a small number when compared to the number of lives they saved when they destroyed those guns.

Colonel Rudder and his Second Ranger Battalion took up a position in a field halfway between the Pointe and Grandcamp les Bains. They were off the main road in a swampy apple orchard. It was quiet. The trees were beginning to bud. It was paradise. They were left in the rear for the time being. They could relax. Those that were left to relax; 77 Rangers had been killed, 152 wounded, and 70 were still missing.

Rudder hoped and prayed that more would appear as the wounded in aid stations found their way back to consciousness and as the missing found their way back to their units. He never doubted for a minute the vital importance of the task he had set himself and his men. Though the sacrifice had been great, Fortress Europe was breached in one terrible day.

THE AFTERMATH

The Second Rangers received the Presidential Unit Citation for the successful accomplishment of their mission.

Historians and tacticians find speculation interesting and noteworthy. They love to theorize over this or that "supposed" mistake made in warfare. Such theories are money in the bank—the stuff of many successful books, theses and dissertations, articles and essays for military, news, and general men's magazines of all kinds. One prevailing theory is that taking Pointe du Hoc was a tragic mistake because so many lives were needlessly lost.

But how many more would have been needlessly lost if those five guns had been able to fire with ample ammunition, destroying the LCAs before they could land, hitting the British "swimming tanks" in the water with the crews aboard. Planes sent against them had failed to destroy the bunker from which they were moved, as Lomell and Kuhn discovered when they found the telephone poles sticking out of it. Even the power that would be accumulated in Little Boy had been insufficient. That they were pulled back and hidden would have made no difference. They were all on carriages. They could have been wheeled into position and loaded within minutes.

Unfortunately, what difference those five monstrous guns would have made on the beaches at Omaha and Utah can not be calculated. The guns were destroyed quickly, quietly, and efficiently with no loss of life. They were never fired. No amount of theorizing and calculating can prove a negative.

Some argue as well that D-Day itself should never have occurred because taking the high ground all along that beach cost thousands of lives. If not on the beaches of Normandy, then where? The insane chancellor of Germany would never have surrendered a single foot of soil so long as a single German soldier lived to defend it.

The toll of D-Day will never be known. Generally, it is believed that nearly five thousand Allies were killed or missing in action. Records were impossible to keep, to gather, and to collate. More than twice the number of Germans died defending the beach. Again that number will never be known. The fact that the attackers far outnumbered the defenders is incontrovertible.

At least four times that number of civilians died in France and Belgium from the bombing raids and German retaliation.

Many historians say that Pointe du Hoc was wasted effort. What sort of effort was *not* wasted on Bloody Omaha with the lack of preparation of the support elements? How many men died with no clear goal to strive for except to stop a bullet as they dashed up the beach? At least the Rangers of D, E, and F companies, Second Battalion had completed both their missions after scaling the cliffs of Pointe du Hoc. The Rangers of A and B had streamed through the Vierville Draw and taken the high ground above Omaha Beach. Company C had acquitted themselves gallantly, effectively taking out the radar station, though they had not gotten near the village of Vierville on Pointe et Raz de la Percée.

HISTORY'S ASSESSMENT

Countless historical as well as first person accounts have been written about D-Day. Biographies, autobiographies, and memoirs have been written detailing pieces of the overall event. This author's account came from half a dozen books as well as numerous personal "sorties" into materials available on the Internet in an effort to substantiate details that were often contradictory.

Research still goes on. Most recently, a research team visited Pointe du Hoc under sponsorship from the History Channel International to prepare a program on how the men of Companies D, E, and F found and destroyed the guns of Pointe du Hoc. It also covered the condition of the remaining German fortifications and the monument there dedicated by President Ronald Reagan on June 6, 1984, the fortieth anniversary of that "longest day." The investigators came from Texas A&M University, the Texas school where James A. Rudder served as president from 1959 until his death in 1960.

Even though Hollywood has used its magnificent scope of screen and sound and actors to brilliantly recreate visually some of what happened in such films as *Saving Private Ryan*, *Band of Brothers*, and *The Longest*

Day, in every case the impression becomes episodic and somewhat con-fused (as the battle itself was episodic and confused). In reading this chapter, hopefully, the reader will experience the episodic nature and the confusion that every Ranger landing all along that blood-soaked beach experienced that day. In selecting men and telling their stories, contradictions will of necessity appear, yet every man's story is the true one taking place at the same time on different parts of the beach. The wars fought by men marching toward each other in well-ordered lines are gone forever.

How can even men as talented as Darryl F. Zanuck and Steven Spiel-berg do justice to the efforts that brought about the deaths of an estimated ten thousand Allies, including the Free French, in less than twelve hours? How does one explain, with any feeling, the deaths of between four and nine thousand German soldiers? One wonders how such a discrep-ancy in the counting of casualties arose. Who was counting? When was the count made?

Even the attempt passes all understanding.

In my examination of a few books selected from an overpowering host of available material, I learned that for decades the people of France and Belgium have been turning up human remains in their fields, remains frequently accompanied by the guns, the helmets, the insignias, the belt buckles, and in some cases the dog tags that the men were wearing when they died. The artifacts tell their stories as well.

Historians themselves buckle under the sheer weight of materials to be looked at and the people to be interviewed. When Cornelius Ryan was writing his general history *The Longest Day*, he telephoned Lieutenant (by virtue of a battlefield commission) Lomell to interview him about the action on Pointe du Hoc. Lomell insisted that Ryan interview all the sur-vivors together (the football team, as it were). Ryan declined and left one of the most glorious stories of the war out of his book.

Consequently the three-hour movie produced and at least partially directed by Zanuck leaves those Ranger Companies D, E, and F standing befuddled in the bunker where the guns were supposed to be. One ac-tor says mournfully that they did it all for nothing. The audience never knows, can never know about Lomell and Kuhn as they found the guns and destroyed them single-handedly and in seconds. No Hollywood actor takes the part of Lieutenant Colonel Rudder, who ended the war one of America's most decorated soldiers. His honors included a Distinguished Service Cross, Legion of Merit, Silver Star, and French Legion of Honor with *Croix de guerre* and palm.

The author can only imagine what a scene would have been filmed of the Rudder's Rangers "football team" dodging, charging, and ducking in and out of the craters to escape German machine-gun fire. Almost beyond the Hollywood imagination would be Sergeant William Stivison (perhaps played by someone fiercely pugnacious such as Aldo Ray or Ernest Borgnine) mounted on his fire brigade ladder arcing back and forth above the rocky beach and the rolling waves while he emptied his machine guns into the Germans to cover his fellow Rangers as they scaled the point.

The audience would have been cheering rather than pitying a terrified Private John Steele played by Red Buttons dangling helplessly on his parachute from the church tower at Sainte Mère Église.

Later, Lomell was invited as a special guest of Spielberg's for the premiere of *Saving Private Ryan*. When interviewed, he said he was impressed with Spielberg's ability to create the chaos of war and the bloody chaos of D-Day. He opined that he had a lot of problems with the actors, including Hanks and his men, who were all much older than the soldiers had actually been. "We were all eighteen or nineteen years old; I was one of the old ones at twenty-four."

IN RETROSPECT

The following men of Second Ranger Battalion received the Distinguished Service Cross for the deeds recounted in this chapter.

Arnold, Edgar L., Captain and later Major
Belcher, Julius W., Sergeant
Courtney, William J., Sergeant
Goranson, Ralph E., Captain
Kerchner, George F., 2nd Lieutenant
Lomell, Leonard G., 1st Sergeant and later 2nd Lieutenant
Masny, Otto, Captain
Rudder, James E., Lieutenant Colonel and later Brigadier General

Others received this award, second only to the Medal of Honor, for bravery in combat. Some received it posthumously. Some men cited in this account may not be listed because a complete listing of Distinguished Service Cross awards is not available in any single army file.

11

FROM THE PUSAN PERIMETER TO THE CHONGCHON RIVER

Ralph Puckett

THE SITUATION

The entire nation of Korea, the "Land of Morning Calm," was formally annexed by the Empire of Japan in 1910. In so doing, the Japanese took over a body of land on the Asian continent somewhat smaller than their entire island chain, but with much more arable land. The islands that comprise Japan are a volcanic archipelago where relatively little farming is possible. Their conquest of Korea, a comparably fertile peninsula attached to the Asian continent, was one of political and economic ambition as well as desperation because their population was already outgrowing their islands.

With ruthless determination they forced the last ruling monarch of Korea to abdicate while his son was "married" to a Japanese noblewoman and "rewarded" with a Japanese peerage. From that time Japan governed the country through a high-ranking military officer whose title was governor general.

For forty years the Koreans suffered a Japanese "cold war" waged to destroy the Korean national identity. The assimilation began, naturally enough, with their schools. Gradually, Korean teachers were replaced by Japanese teachers. All printed material was restricted. Koreans could not publish their own newspapers or organize intellectual or cultural groups.

In 1930 as the government became more militaristic in Japan itself, so it did in Korea. The ministers in Tokyo decided that Korea would be totally assimilated when its young men were taken into the Japanese army. At first they were told to volunteer, but when an insufficient number did so, the rest were conscripted. None of the institutions of civilization was omitted in the assimilation effort. Besides education and government, all Koreans were to worship at Shinto shrines rather than exercise their own religious beliefs of Buddhism and Confucianism.

Enthralled by a dominating structure with warriors at its head, the Koreans could do little to protect themselves from their Japanese oppressors. Their economy was controlled to the extent that they suffered shortages almost from the beginning of the occupation. A majority of their agriculture was shipped to Japan, which saw Korea as a "rice-bowl" for the Japanese islands. In addition to growing a significant percentage of Japan's food, Korea's rich fishing industry was regulated by their rulers and eventually their major source of protein was in short supply when Japanese fisheries were allowed to fish in Korean waters without restrictions of any kind.

A manufacturing sector was created as Japan prepared to wage war on China with Koreans working in plants for less than living wages. In total, 84 percent of Korea's total output from its three major industries was being shipped to Japan. Food shortages were common in a country that had always had plenty. Economically deprived, the Koreans were unable to develop any sort of entrepreneurial class among themselves.

Beginning in 1937, all schools were to be taught in Japanese, and students overheard speaking Korean were punished. Two years later, Koreans were "encouraged" to adopt Japanese names. By the next year according to Japanese records, 84 percent of Korean families had done so.

Had the Japanese rule not ended with World War II, the total eradication of Korean language, culture, and religion would have been completed within another generation.

Sadly, 1945 did not see peace with a return to their old ways and a recreation of an independent country for Koreans. Though the Japanese were gone, their places were taken by even less benevolent Communists—first Soviet and then Chinese.

On June 25, 1950, about 4:00 a.m., an artillery and mortar barrage began across the thirty-eighth parallel. Five years of hostilities erupted into armed conflict between South Koreans and their neighboring fellow North Koreans, who had, by that time, been totally subjugated by the Communist rulers. It was the beginning of an action that ended only after literally millions of Korean soldiers and civilians as well as soldiers of ten other countries died for absolutely no purpose except perhaps for the nebulous ideal of a utopian classless society where nothing was owned and all worked for the good of all.

Approximately a century before, Karl Marx had conceived such a structure as a peaceful existence. He had written widely and popularly about it in his books *The Communist Manifesto* and *Das Capital*. The sticking point in his new society was that all other forms of government must be overthrown by violent means if necessary in order for pure communism to manifest itself. Whether the leaders of Russia or China actually believed such a utopia was possible will be the subject of debate so long as the governments they created exist. To this day no such society has ever evolved.

Both Russian and Chinese governments were intent on helping North Korea establish that society on a united peninsula. Technically, the Korean conflict was not classified as a war. Yet one can only wonder at the heartlessness of the leaders that drove the entity. Unfortunately, the Korean national heritage had been damaged to the extent that it was of little consequence or influence in their lives. Caught in conflict between the ideologies of communism and capitalism, the people were engulfed. They lived and died in the shadow of them.

The old warriors and politicians—most of them born and grown to manhood in the nineteenth century—became the instigators and perpetuators of what history books now refer to as the "Korean Conflict." Some were already relics in the twentieth century when they sought to make the peace after World War II. As such they were ill suited for their task. Kim Il-sung, Syngman Rhee, Douglas MacArthur, Chao Yong-kun, Mark Wayne Clark, Paik Sun-yup, Matthew Ridgway, Mao Zedong, Harry S. Truman, Joseph Stalin, and Dwight David Eisenhower were suited only to war. By 1950 most had not long to live.

Even the strongest willed and most determined men die but, given time, ideologies take root in large numbers of people and over time change and metastasize to accommodate their societies. The younger generations that grew up and actually faced the guns were the ones who died for those inherited principles. What does the world call an action dedicated to a chaotic destruction and reconstruction of a downtrodden people?

"Conflict" seems a mild word. What does one call such a phenomenon other than a war?

Three months after the surrender of Germany in World War II, the Soviet Union declared war on the Empire of Japan. These were cruel times: a country chose to enter a war almost won, to sacrifice young men unnecessarily, when they had just been through World War II where their losses were an estimated 10 million soldiers killed or missing.

With deadly purpose and the reluctant approval of the American military, they drove across the Manchurian border and into the northern portion of Korea. Their target was agreed upon. When they arrived at the thirty-eighth parallel, the Russian army was supposed to halt. The Americans were coming from the south. They were supposed to meet and—who knows?

Shake hands?

But before this meeting could happen (if indeed the possibility existed that it would ever happen), Lieutenant General Yoshio Kozuki, Secretary to the Japanese War Minister, radioed American Lieutenant General John R. Hodge that the Soviet Union had advanced past the agreed upon demarcation line into the city of Kaesong, lying just to the south. In fact, the mechanized army had gone farther and was only a few miles from Seoul, the capital.

The times were not just cruel. They were also strange. Certainly, Kozuki's call marked a new era in a time of war. A Japanese general calling his enemy counterpart for aid in fending off a more dangerous enemy. A conquering Russian army sweeping the length of the Korean Peninsula would have put Joseph Stalin in a position to demand the Soviet Union's inclusion at the peace table. They would be there to divide the spoils of the surrender and occupation of Japan once that war was won. The result might have seen the partition of Japan and the subsequent rape and pillage like the one that occurred in East Germany beginning in 1945. Not until 1990 did the eastern half of Germany finally succeed in emerging from behind the Iron Curtain and uniting with the rest of their sovereign nation. For thirty-five years while West Germany had taken its place among the most powerful in Europe, East Germany had suffered under the economically devastating Communist government of the Soviet Union.

In 1948, all Koreans welcomed their liberators, whether they were American or Soviet. However, when they tried to object to the reimposition of foreign rule, their objections did them little good north of the thirty-eighth parallel. An uneasy armistice existed for three years while the Soviet Union and America shared joint trusteeship over Korea while it rebuilt itself. By 1948, both countries had managed to establish ideologically different governments—a communist dictatorship in the north and a more or less democratic republic in the south.

America promoted democratic elections whereby Syngman Rhee was elected president of the Republic of South Korea. The Soviet Union created a Stalinist dictatorship governed by the *Juche* ideology of self-reliance. Kim Il-sung, Syngman Rhee's longtime opponent and sometime enemy, became the leader-for-life of the Democratic People's Republic of Korea.

After World War II the governments of several emerging countries found it politically correct to call themselves "democratic" even when their people had few or any rights—certainly not the right to vote freely for the men who invested themselves for life with the power to govern.

In 1948, as soon as America and the Soviet Union withdrew their forces from the two Koreas, tensions between the two nations accelerated. Border skirmishes were common. Kim Il-sung was determined to enjoin the two countries under his government with the intent of creating a Communist Korea to unite with Russia and China.

On June 25, 1950, the (North) Korean People's Army launched a surprise attack across the thirty-eighth parallel. Their intention was reunification.

Stepping up to the proverbial plate, something the defunct League of Nations had never dared to do, the five-year-old United Nations declared this an act of aggression against another sovereign power.

Officially, the world called it a conflict. What they had was a war.

THE ACTION

U.S. General of the Army Douglas MacArthur received the Medal of Honor for his service in the Philippines, in particular on the Bataan Peninsula, during World War II. The grateful Filipino government had named him Field Marshall of the Philippine Army. A recognizable figure, as few Americans had ever been in the East, he became the overseer of the occupation of Japan from 1945 to 1951. For those six years he protected Emperor Hirohito and the royal family while overseeing democratic changes in the government that set the country on the road to an amazingly successful democracy in the English style with a hereditary monarchy that reigns but does not rule.

With MacArthur's experience and the unequivocal admiration and respect of many Asian peoples, he was a natural choice to command the United Nations forces to defend South Korea.

The North Korean Army had begun sending small units to infiltrate and sabotage areas in the far southeastern tip of South Korea. The Pusan Perimeter was the southern boundary of this intrusion.

Warfare to defend against and destroy these sorties was the sort of warfare successfully waged by Ranger units, but the deadly Ranger groups that had so effectively and gallantly invaded and taken Pointe du Hoc and Pointe et Raz de la Percée on D-Day, Myitkyina in Burma, and Anzio and Cisterna in Italy no longer existed. Their very actions had left too many of their numbers on the beaches at Normandy, in the Burmese jungles, and on the roads and the fields in Italy. Because Rangers required specialization and an expensive and lengthy period of training, they had been deactivated in the drawdown from World War II.

When the need arose for such fighters, someone somewhere—probably several someones—muttered "oops!" Possibly a mistake had been made in estimating an army's needs. Rather than admit the mistake, they sought to rectify it even if the result might not be up to the high standards of the previous battalions.

The Eighth Army headquarters commanded Colonel John H. McGee, head of G3 Miscellaneous Division, to call for volunteers to fill the gap. He had seven weeks to select the personnel, organize, condition, and train the unit. Since they were all trained soldiers, they should be able to learn the "special stuff" in just a few weeks. And they were all in condition.

Based upon those assumptions, he foresaw no problems.

For reference, McGee had a single copy of the Table of Organization and Equipment used by Ranger companies during World War II.

And not much else.

The colonel flew from Korea to Japan in August 1950. When he called for volunteers and recommendations, he received names of enlisted men in plenty—but almost no officers came forward. Somewhat discouraged, he was looking around when two West Point graduates among the volunteers gave him a recommendation. Acting on their advice, he sought out a 1949 West Point graduate, Second Lieutenant Ralph Puckett, who was cooling his heels at the Replacement Depot. He had not yet seen action. But he enthusiastically volunteered because he "wanted to be the best."

While Puckett told McGee that he would be pleased to be a squad leader, a rifleman, anything, McGee told him that only one position remained to be filled. He would have to be the platoon leader. So Puckett, fresh out of Infantry Officer Basic Course and Airborne School, was immediately commissioned a captain of the 8213th Army Unit, the Eighth Army Ranger Company (8ARC) on August 25, 1950. His two classmates,

Second Lieutenant Charles Bunn and Second Lieutenant Barnard Cummings, Jr., who incidentally had recommended him to McGee, were named his platoon leaders.

McGee probably whistled softly with relief, "wiped his brow," and stepped way away to leave them to struggle and succeed—or probably fail.

Together the three friends interviewed volunteers. Demonstrated motivation proved to be the major discriminator. Were these men sufficiently motivated to "go the distance"?

When Puckett had gathered a more than sufficient number, he held a meeting. Before the meeting actually got under way, he made a general announcement that anyone not willing to volunteer for anything dangerous could leave the room immediately. Two-thirds of the recruits remained from which seventy-four enlisted soldiers made the final cut.

Immediately the men got to work preparing themselves to follow in the footsteps of Ranger units who had gone before. The five-man headquarters company with Captain Puckett at its head was organized first to handle details. Two 36-man platoons were organized. Each consisted of two assault sections, a special weapons section, and a headquarters element.

First among the details was conditioning. Most of the men selected were just average soldiers, most without much combat training or experience. Either they had been part of the replacement pool as yet unassigned or service personnel with little or no infantry training.

First, Puckett requisitioned equipment, most of which the men had hardly seen, much less become expert with: M-1 carbines and rifles, pistols, two M-1C sniper rifles, four light machine guns, two Browning automatic rifles (BARs), two 60-mm mortars, and two 3.5-inch bazookas. Armed but not knowing how to handle their equipment, they landed at Pusan on the southeastern tip of the Korean Peninsula on September 1, 1950. From there they were moved to Kijang, a small village north of Pusan, where they commenced training in a camp set up by Colonel McGee.

They were the first Ranger unit deployed to the Korean conflict, as well as the first Ranger unit scheduled to be trained and conditioned since 1944. They trained in a war zone. Their camp, located in an area where North Korean guerrillas were still active, was called "Ranger Hill."

In accordance with Rogers' Rules of Discipline for Rangers, their first activity was to establish a 360-degree defense perimeter. From there they moved to the requisite Ranger conditioning. In this case it involved the British commando training as well as other activities devised by William Orlando Darby and James Earl Rudder to prepare their units for the World War II invasion of Europe. It involved conditioning oneself beyond ordinary physical exhaustion, mental fatigue, and fear of physical injury. Adding to the stress under which they operated was the real fear that they might be hit by Communist sniper fire during the process.

After only five and a half weeks instead of the proposed seven, they were called into combat. Colonel McGee wanted to see if they were "ready on October 11." If they proved themselves, the training would be expanded to prepare other units. If they failed, the unit and the entire idea would be deactivated.

While they had been training, in the United Nations war room MacArthur had been preparing to wage a war the only way he knew how—the war to win. Though he was specifically forbidden to maintain anything but a defensive position, the old general was sure that the Korean Conflict would never be won unless the North Koreans were beaten so thoroughly that they would be convinced that they could never conquer South Korea.

As a precedent, he could point to the temporary surrender of Germany at the end of World War I only to reappear stronger and more determined than ever barely a generation later to wage World War II.

"It is fatal to enter any war without the will to win it," MacArthur declared as he commanded a combined force of army and marine troops in a daring and successful combined amphibious landing at Inchon, midway up the western side of the peninsula and deep behind North Korean lines although it was miles south of the thirty-eighth parallel. The daring move using American Marine and Canadian forces outflanked the North Koreans and forced their retreat northward.

MacArthur did not stop there. Waging running combat, he drove deep into North Korean territory, chasing them to the Yalu River, the border with China. In the course of the retreat, the ill-trained and ill-equipped North Korean troops were largely destroyed.

The Chinese foreign minister warned that if MacArthur crossed the Yalu, China would be forced into the war. MacArthur dismissed the threat as toothless. "The Chinese are not coming. The war is over."

While privately agreeing that he was a general to be reckoned with, Washington was alarmed by his lightning moves. Most important, he had done all this without seeking, much less waiting for, *permission*. President Truman had a rogue in his ranks.

Washington officials became more alarmed when the Chinese People's Liberation Army retaliated and proved MacArthur wrong (or perhaps called his bluff). Armed to the teeth, the army crossed the Yalu River into North Korea. At the same time Chinese foreign minister Zhou Enlai issued a warning that China would consider any further advance to the Yalu an act of war.

Though MacArthur did not actually take an army across the Yalu, he sent a letter to Representative Joe Martin, the Republican House Minority Leader from Massachusetts. In it he disagreed with Truman's policy of limitation. He also sent an ultimatum to the Chinese Army. The correspondence proved untimely. It interfered with and probably destroyed Truman's efforts to negotiate a cease-fire.

Truman had been a feisty captain of artillery in France during World War I. As President of the United States, a job he had not sought nor did he relish, he had given MacArthur orders, which his subordinate had disobeyed. Perhaps Franklin D. Roosevelt would have called for a conference. Perhaps Woodrow Wilson, the president during World War I, would have wrung his hands. But Truman was himself a military man. He understood authority and he understood rank. He brooked no insubordination by a man who was answerable to him. He always carried a copy of the Constitution in his pocket. "The President of the United States shall be Commander in Chief of the Army and Navy of the United States."

On April 11, 1951, Truman announced that MacArthur had violated the American principle that military commanders are subordinate to the president. Since MacArthur had seen fit to do so, Truman was herewith relieving him of command.

The national press reported that MacArthur had been fired. The stories as well as his poignant "old soldiers . . . fade away" address broadcast to the nation during a joint session of the Congress stirred national sympathy and controversy. Nevertheless, MacArthur's years of public service were over. He was succeeded by General Matthew Ridgway and later by General Mark Clark, who much later would sign an armistice.

Still the conflict remained to be resolved. The war remained to be won.

At that time, the United Nations decided to make a push northward across the thirty-eighth parallel—the very thing MacArthur had been chastised and removed for doing.

The new Ranger company was to be linked up with the Twenty-fifth Infantry Division, IX Corps. The division had long served in the Pacific theater. They called themselves "Tropic Thunder." Operating with them but separate from them, the Rangers joined the division to conduct mop-up operations of small pockets hiding in the mountains behind the advancing army. Those already carried out had been highly successful with more than 1,500 enemy soldiers either killed or captured.

The newly promoted Captain Puckett was informed that two companies, his Ranger and the Twenty-fifth Reconnaissance Company, were to link up at Taegu and to clear a sector around the village of Poun. Between October 11 and October 14 his two platoons conducted continuous day and night sweeps. Additionally, they set up ambush sites along roads that were suspected routes for the enemies to move back and forth.

Though this was their first test of combat, Puckett's patrols proved to be very good at what they were ordered to do. First Platoon captured a dozen enemy soldiers at one time. They further discovered and capitalized on the enemy's lack of stomach for a firefight.

During the "shakedown operation," Captain Puckett instructed everyone to learn by his mistakes. He rotated between the platoons to conduct debriefings after each engagement.

During one firefight, a fifteen-man North Korean patrol blundered upon the Rangers during a rest period. Like seasoned veterans, the Rangers went for their guns. Six enemy were shot and killed and one was made a prisoner before the rest ran for their lives.

By the end of October, the area was clear, and on November 3, the Rangers were ordered to close on Kaesong, a hair's breadth south of the thirty-eighth parallel. To this day Kaesong remains a subject of dispute. It had been the first town invaded by the army of the Democratic People's Republic of Korea (DPRK). Today the North Koreans assert that it was the "first town liberated by the Democratic People's Army." The people of South Korea for many years referred to it as the only "occupied" town south of the thirty-eighth parallel.

On November 14th, the Ranger Company led the way into North Korean territory for the advancing Task Force Johnson consisting of an Infantry Regiment and the Twenty-fifth Infantry Division's Reconnaissance Company. The Rangers were sent ahead to clear mines and patrol the flanks of the advancing army. Their section lay in a triangle bounded by the villages of Tongduchon-ni, Shiny-ri, and Uijonbu (mentioned briefly as the setting in the famous Richard Hooker novel *M*A*S*H*).

The weather was near-zero in the dark of night when they were ordered to march back to Kaesong. From there they were told they would be part of operational control (OPCON), a tank battalion under command of Colonel "Tom" Dolvin. Fortunately, as the temperature continued to drop, they were transported by trucks for that linkup.

All this moving around in seemingly aimless fashion made Captain Puckett, as well as the Rangers, wonder if anyone knew what to do with them. When the command for the tanks to move north was given, they were sent out five thousand yards ahead of the battalion on reconnaissance patrols. When they found no North Koreans and no North Koreans found them, they were moved into the center of the tanks rather than out on point. Eventually, all the Rangers were ordered to ride on the tanks to conserve their strength for the battles to come.

Again some wondered if anybody knew where anybody else was or what anybody else was doing. Was there any purpose to any of this? Was there any purpose to the war?

The Chinese Communists were retreating ahead of them. On the other side of the thirty-eighth parallel, they came across two American soldiers from the Eighth Cavalry Regiment, who in turn directed them back to another twenty-eight wounded Americans whom the Chinese had abandoned presumably because they would die without aid. Later that afternoon, another task force element found them all safe, though suffering badly from exposure.

Puckett's fifteen-man group including the captain was increased by the Eighth Army Ranger Company with three commissioned officers, sixty enlisted men, and ten Republic of Korea (ROK) soldiers. Reinforced, they moved up on their objective Hill 222.

At that time, the battle was joined. The first Ranger killed in action in Korea was Private First Class Joseph Romero. He led his fellows in a rush across a rice paddy. Though he was seriously wounded, he continued to fire his weapon, covering his buddies, until he died.

The Rangers had no time to mourn their loss. They were in combat with tasks to perform. They swept and cleared a triangular area bounded by small villages where they met no resistance. On the next day, the 14th, they were ordered to clear mines and provide flank security for an armored convoy.

So far they had had little use for their grueling Ranger training. Indeed, as the days passed, they began to wonder if they were going to see action that would challenge them. On the twenty-fifth of November, that all changed.

They were over a hundred miles into North Korea, approaching a hill that overlooked the Chongchon River. They began to encounter heavier Chinese Communist resistance as they approached Hill 205. Heavy fire by mortars, machine guns, and small arms came from both flanks.

The tanks on which they had hitched a ride halted and "buttoned-up." While they were securing themselves, the men in the tanks were not firing on the enemy positions. As the Rangers started across a frozen rice paddy, they were pinned down by withering fire. At that point Puckett discovered he couldn't call for or direct artillery fire. The phone call box on the closest tank wouldn't open because it was encased in ice.

Quick as thought, Puckett leaped on top of the tank, exposing himself to enemy fire and slammed the butt of his M-1 rifle onto the hatch. When the tank commander (TC) finally cracked the opening, he had to face Puckett's wrath.

Puckett berated the TC for not providing his men artillery support. The TC cowered back. At the same time, he argued that they had to be careful not to draw fire from the North Korean artillery because they had only a couple of inches of armor plate.

Captain Puckett angrily reminded him that he and his Rangers had only an eighth of an inch of cloth. They needed artillery support—now!

The tanker ordered his crew to fire while he phoned other tanks to do the same.

While the enemy ducked, Puckett called up air support to attack the high ground from which the enemy was directing the most fire. Though they were in danger, they managed to take Hill 205. In the course of the fierce battle, they had sustained six American and three ROK casualties. Though they were still drawing enemy fire from another hill in the vicinity, Puckett reorganized and set up a 360-degree perimeter with groups zeroed-in on likely approaches where the enemy might try to overrun them.

In a brief breathing space, Puckett decided the tactical situation was even worse than he had first imagined. Based on his study of map overlays when—though still under fire—he had a few minutes to survey them, he did not like what he saw. His company was sitting on the very top of Hill 205 with both flanks exposed. Moreover, they were several kilometers from the nearest friendly units.

His position was not one he would have chosen either to defend or from which to launch an attack, but it was the one he was ordered to take and hold. Battle weary with wounded-in-action among them, the Rangers dug into the frozen ground as the temperature continued to drop. In the icy darkness they listened to a firefight going on in the distance without knowing that the Chinese communist forces were overwhelming a platoon of ROKs.

For an hour they were left alone. They took advantage of the respite to dig deeper into the frozen earth and rock. Then a mortar barrage began and with it the onset of a sequence of Chinese attacks dedicated to over-whelming their position. Almost before the last explosions had ceased, whistles began to blow in the darkness; bugles trumpeted their notes.

Preceded by a storm of hand grenades, the Chinese army charged. The noise almost drowned out the shouted commands of their officers.

The Rangers immediately hurled their own grenades into the midst of the noise. They fired their weapons into the darkness, here and there getting targets from the flashes from the Communist guns. Puckett himself used his flares to illuminate the sides of the hill. Fortunately, two sides were quite steep, so the climbers couldn't charge firing as they came.

More Rangers fell. Puckett himself was wounded by shrapnel in his thigh. They had no artillery support. The tank company in position at the rear of the base of the hill was unable to get off a single effective shot.

On four separate occasions an attacking party of Chinese penetrated the perimeter that night. Bayonets fixed, adrenaline pumping, the Rangers braced themselves and met the lunging, screaming silhouettes at the edge of their foxholes. Puckett never stopped moving from foxhole to foxhole on his belly if he had to. From group to group, he moved, encouraging, steadying, injecting himself into their defenses, reminding them who they were.

They were Rangers. They were the best. He told them they were. They believed him and always drove their attackers back.

As the Rangers began to get low on ammunition, Puckett made the decision to call in long-range artillery fire "danger close," that is, well inside the recommended edge of six hundred meters for covering fire.

At 2:30 a.m. the sixth and final attack came. A battalion-sized force came charging up Puckett's exposed right flank. With wounded Rangers fighting beside their buddies, their ammunition running low, they had no answer for the overwhelming force estimated to be six hundred maniacs flinging itself up the hill against a mere sixty-seven Americans. Within seconds, they breached the Second Platoon's sector.

Puckett was on his knees in a foxhole, continuing to radio for artillery support.

Captain Gordon Sumner, the artillery liaison officer, replied that his battery was firing at another target.

In the meantime Sergeant John Diliberto organized his men for a withdrawal. In keeping with the Ranger tactic of leaving no man behind, he dragged two members of his wounded platoon away from the exposed position where they had fallen. Without regard for his personal safety he rescued them as the enemy overwhelmed the defense perimeter.

As Puckett waited for the artillery support, a tremendous blow struck him. A mortar round had detonated *in* his foxhole. His feet, legs, buttocks, and arm went numb. He dragged himself out of the foxhole but couldn't move after that one effort. A moment later a second round came in. Corporal James Beatty was wounded.

Puckett barely had time to realize that his longtime friend First Lieutenant Barnard Cummings, who had been with him since West Point, had died at his side.

Puckett turned his head enough to see three Chinese soldiers barely fifteen yards away bayoneting some of his wounded Rangers.

At that moment Private First Class Bill Judy ran to his colonel's side.

Puckett told him he couldn't move and ordered him to leave. Judy ran to other Rangers telling them to get help.

Private First Class David L. Pollock and Private First Class Billy G. Walls immediately charged up the hill and shot the three Chinese who were, by that time, less than ten yards away.

Walls came over and asked how the colonel was. Puckett later wrote that he thought that was the dumbest question he'd ever heard, but he didn't say that to Walls. Instead, he said, "I'm hurt bad. I can't move. Leave me behind."

Ignoring the command, Walls picked Puckett up in his arms and started staggering down the mountain. He made it forty yards before he had to apologize. "Sir, you're too heavy! I can't carry you any further!"

Then Walls and Pollock each took one of Puckett's arms and started dragging him unceremoniously down the hill on his butt. They dragged him two hundred yards to safety with no thought of their own lives.

At one point Walls asked, "Are you all right, Captain?"

To which Puckett replied, "Yes, I am all right! I'm a Ranger!"

The gallantry of these two enlisted men shows how much Puckett's men loved him and how they lived the as-yet-unwritten Ranger Creed: "I will never leave a fallen comrade to fall into the hands of the enemy."

They were each awarded the Silver Star for gallantry.

(And Puckett never so much as said a word to them for disobeying a direct order and saving his life.)

The Rangers on Hill 205 were done. Their only reasonable move was to gather their wounded and retreat. Overwhelming numbers of Chinese soldiers, spurred to fury after seeing their own comrades die, came charging from foxhole to foxhole bayoneting the wounded inside.

Panic would have been easy. Much harder for the defenders was the effort required to gather up their own wounded while fighting an action and retreating down the hill.

At the bottom of the hill, Puckett was placed on the back of a tank that carried him out of the immediate area. Soon he was medevacced to the task force's aid station.

Back on the hill, Ranger Merle Simpson escaped to Private First Class Harland Morrissey's squad and screamed a warning about the overwhelming advance as the Chinese came over the crest of the hilltop. Four brave Rangers—Sumner Kubinak, Librado Luna, Alvin Tadlock, and Ernest Nowlin—sacrificed their lives to lay down covering fire so that their comrades could get off the hill. Three others—Private First Class Harry Miyata, Private First Class Roger E. Hittle, and Private First Class Robert N. Jones—also laid down covering fire for their comrades and lost their lives in the same engagement. These seven men were each awarded posthumously the Bronze Star for Valor.

Later, Intelligence reported that the Rangers were on point to meet an advancing army group that was the leading wave of half a million Chinese soldiers.

On December 5, 1950, Captain John P. Vann assumed command of the Rangers. He had served in the G4 (Logistics) section. His first task was to increase the number of Rangers and to equip them. They were increased to five officers and 107 enlisted men divided into three platoons. First Lieutenant Bunn began their training immediately,

Because of the extreme severity of his wounds, Captain Puckett was hospitalized for twelve months until November 1951. He received the Distinguished Service Cross for his service during the Korean War. After he recovered from his wounds, he took command of Camp Frank D. Merrill Mountain Ranger Division of the Ranger Department in Dahlonega, Georgia.

The Seventy-fifth Ranger Infantry Regiment (Airborne) was organized on January 1, 1969. Fifteen separate Ranger companies were formed during this reorganization. Thirteen served in Viet Nam until they were inactivated in 1972. Puckett served as a battalion commander in that conflict. Twenty years later, stationed in his last post, he was asked to draw on his experiences facing a fanatical enemy under extremely difficult conditions. A thoughtful and analytical man, he was able to suggest improvements especially when he had seen that violations of fundamentals resulted in unnecessary casualties. In particular, he was a stickler for safety.

His attitude, which prevails to this day, is that Rangers are exceptionally valuable men. Not a single one of them should be injured or lost if his Ranger training could in some way prevent it. One of Puckett's most important dicta is that Rangers (and all soldiers) should move to a higher level of training to the limit of their physical and professional capabilities. Stress and overcoming it should be a part of their lives. One of his most asked questions was, "What happens if a company is facing annihilation?"

He was inducted into the Ranger Hall of Fame in 1992. In 1996, he was selected by the Secretary of the Army to be Honorary Colonel of the Seventy-fifth Ranger Regiment (HCOR). Duties of this post included spending time with the Rangers, learning their states of mind. He was also asked to observe their training and make recommendations. When his two-year term was finished he was asked to remain to further advise and recommend. His time with HCOR turned into eleven years during which time, he went everywhere, observed all sorts of operations, special testing, and evaluation exercises conducted at the three Ranger training camps.

During his time at HCOR he wrote *Words for Warriors: A Professional Soldier's Notebook*, his collection of advice, observations, and autobiographical material intended for the Rangers who will come after him. It was published in 2007.

Puckett recalled an operation he was observing. The Rangers who were being "fired upon" were supposed to "fall dead." Their "opposition" was then to run forward and relieve them of any valuable equipment and supplies before "moving on."

Puckett remained on his knees until a Ranger captain came running over yelling, "Get down!"

Puckett went down but still kept his head up. The captain yelled again, then yelled to his leader, "Hey, Joe, this guy won't get down!"

Joe yelled back, "Put your knee in his back and make him go down!"

Puckett protested, "I'm administrative."

The captain was having none of that excuse. "Who are you?" he yelled.

"I'm Colonel Puckett."

The captain then yelled, "Oh, my God! It's Colonel Puckett!" As embarrassed as he had ever been in his life, the captain ran away.

Colonel Puckett never asked who had challenged him. He thought the whole thing was funny. Evidently, everyone else did too.

The next night at a general meeting when the room was ordered to rise at Puckett's entrance, all the other captains turned around and yelled, "Colonel Puckett, it was Captain Gray!"

Gray, the intelligence officer for the Third Battalion, turned bright red with embarrassment while everyone else laughed.

The story says everything that needs be said about how admired, respected, and liked Puckett is. He is an extraordinary man—the sort of man who could lead and advise battalions of some of the world's greatest warriors.

Still the strained and often intolerable situation still exists for the Korean people in its aftermath. With a standoff instead of a hand shake—a vicious cold war has gone on since that time. A sort of an armistice was agreed to on July 27, 1953, but to this day nothing has been truly resolved. Both America and North Korea maintain battle-ready troops at the thirty-eighth parallel. Even so great a holocaust as World War II has not lasted so long.

What would have happened had MacArthur moved across that boundary with the approval of Truman? Would China have risked a war? Would North Korea have made peace and accommodation with the southern half of what was after all a very small country? Would friends have become enemies instead of remaining in the grip of a constantly escalating and receding standoff? Would an eventual union of the country under a democratic form of government occurred?

THE AFTERMATH

While the war went on and soldiers were bleeding and dying on both sides, an ugly stagnation pervaded the peace talks at Panmunjon. It was satirized in later films and a successful television series.

The people of South Korea, a democratic nation, still suffer emotionally from the partition that has divided families as it has divided the country along the arbitrary thirty-eighth parallel of 1944.

Fortunately, they don't suffer too much. South Korea's gross domestic production was estimated at a cool $1 billion in 2007. That is, indeed, one billion dollars! Sitting on the crossroads of Northeast Asia between industrial and financial giants Japan and China, it is one of the small wonders of the economic world.

In contrast, North Korea is the last Stalinist state on earth. In 2006 while its other societal institutions suffered stagnation, it set off a small nuclear blast and has made a heavily publicized launch of a rocket capable of carrying a nuclear warhead in the direction of Japan. The result was less than spectacular, since the rocket demonstrated very limited range and fell ignominiously into the sea.

In his State of the Union address January 29, 2002, President George W. Bush named North Korea part of an "Axis of Evil" including Iraq and Iran, both of whom were believed at the time to have nuclear weapons. The world suffers from the nuclear threat voiced by its Communist regime that remains in power after more than sixty years. Though the leadership of Iraq has been changed through a quick war and a long and exhausting post-war period, Iran and North Korea remain.

Kim Jong-il, the current dictator, is the son of "Great Leader" Kim Il-sung. Ideologically, he preaches eternal war until all governments and economic structures are destroyed and the perfect communist government is achieved. Actually, he is determined to keep his absolute power and attract as much attention as possible to maintain it by keeping his own country terrified that they will be invaded. The former playboy styles himself "Dear Leader" and frequently appears in public in a jumpsuit and platform shoes.

His country remains desperately poor in comparison to South Korea, whose people frequently send supplies to relatives and old friends across the thirty-eighth parallel.

The attitude of the American public has been shaped by the entertainment industry that refused to take the small, long war as a serious engagement. Perhaps because the single country involved and the numbers of men required to fight were so relatively small in comparison to the staggering statistics of World War II. Perhaps also America's capacity for horror has reached a saturation point.

In 1968, *M*A*S*H: A Novel about Three Army Doctors* by Richard Hooker appeared. It was written into an Oscar-winning script by Ring Lardner, Jr., directed by revisionist director Robert Altman with Donald Sutherland as Hawkeye Pierce and Robert Duvall as obnoxious bible-thumping Major Frank Burns. The dark satirical comedy was the third most popular film released in Hollywood that year. No sooner had the lights dimmed on the marquees than it was developed for television and on September 17, 1972, it appeared to great critical success and wide audience approval. The adventures of Doctors Hawkeye Pierce played by Alan Alda, Trapper John, and Frank Burns as well as Nurse Margaret "Hot Lips" Houlihan delighted audiences for more than a decade. On February 2, 1983, the final hour-long episode became the most watched television episode in history with 105 million people tuning in to see some of their favorite people depart forever except in reruns.

With much less success Hollywood has given its take on several serious movies taken from history of the Korean War. While the movies were made long after the hostilities ceased, they remind the audiences of what has become one of the most senseless engagements in the twentieth century. Neither ever found a serious audience.

In *Pork Chop Hill* made in 1981, Gregory Peck leads a 135-man attack on a Chinese communist-held objective. When reinforcements arrive, only 25 men are still alive. The utter senselessness of the war is underscored by the fact that the negotiators for peace argue for days about what shape the peace table should take.

The next year a movie entitled *Inchon* was financed by the Reverend Sun Myung Moon's Unification Church. Sir Lawrence Olivier, arguably the greatest living English actor, was cast as General MacArthur complete with the general's signature corncob pipe. For his part in the film Olivier, one of the foremost actors in the world, chose to use a voice reminiscent of W. C. Fields.

Did MacArthur really sound like the comic actor famous for portraying lecherous drunks? Or was Olivier delivering his own impressions of the worth of the movie? Though it is reported to have cost $50 million to make, it grossed only $2 million at the box office.

Perhaps an utterly horrible war deserves an utterly horrible movie.

Perhaps America will never again find glory in a war of any kind.

12

A NEW KIND
OF WARFARE

THE SITUATION

In the last half of the twentieth century, the idea of World War III or any kind of engagement that might lead to another global war became abhorrent. For the first time, all-out war seemed less than inevitable because such an event could very easily escalate into total destruction of civilization as it had evolved to that time.

The world could never forget August 6, 1945, when it entered with a blinding flash and a mushroom cloud into a new era—the Atomic Era. Colonel Paul Tibbets in the B29 Superfortress *Enola Gay* took off for the Empire of Japan with a single load to be dropped over a single target. A single bomb nicknamed "Little Boy" exploded over Hiroshima, a city of three hundred thousand people. It produced a blast, such as the world had never seen—fifteen kilotons of violence—the equivalent of fifteen thousand tons of TNT. All structures within a mile of ground zero were severely damaged or totally destroyed.

Birds in the air burst into flame. People on the streets and on park benches, soldiers outside their barracks engaged in calisthenics, children on playgrounds, pets in backyards, all crumbled into charred bones. A mushroom-shaped cloud rose and rose and rose into the sky to be carried by the wind over the city and its suburbs. For many hours no one had any inkling of what that monstrous gray pall would come to mean.

President Harry S. Truman immediately demanded the unconditional surrender of the Empire of Japan. Though the Emperor Hirohito was instantly agreeable, the warlords to a man denied that a single plane dropping a single bomb could wreak such destruction. They denied the testimony of the witnesses. They ignored reports that already some of these survivors were beginning to feel ill and weak as they experienced the first effects of radiation poisoning. The official report to the Japanese people was that America had sent a huge flight of bombers that dropped their bomb loads simultaneously.

They lied to their own people.

The following day, August 7, President Truman again demanded immediate and unconditional surrender adding the ominous proviso: "If they do not accept our terms, they may expect a rain of ruin from the air the likes of which has never been seen on this earth."

To his everlasting credit, Emperor Hirohito again tried to persuade the warlords to quickly offer the following conditional surrender terms: (1) the *kokutai* (the emperor, the imperial institution, and the governmental structure) would be preserved; (2) the Japanese government itself was to take responsibility for disarmament and demobilization; (3) the Japanese government would assume responsibility for the punishment of war criminals; and (4) no army of occupation would be imposed on Japan. No one knows whether he believed America would agree to any of those but, in the light of the unmitigated disaster on the main island of Honshu within three hundred miles of the capital, surely they could serve as talking points.

The warlords were adamantine. Hiroshima had not been destroyed by only one bomb. America was bluffing—bluffing and lying.

While their debate raged, one minute after midnight on August 9, Premier Joseph Stalin announced that the Soviet Union had officially declared war on the Empire of Japan. The Soviet army crossed into Manchuria.

Emperor Hirohito could only shudder at the thoughts of an implacable enemy in the south and imminent invasion from the north. The obdurate men surrounding him seemed bent on the destruction of the Empire of Japan. Perhaps they were right. Perhaps the American president was bluffing.

What none among world leaders realized was that no man in America was less likely to bluff than Truman. He was the commander in chief. His powers derived from the American Constitution, which he carried ever in his pocket. On his desk was a famous sign: "The Buck Stops Here."

He did not want another American soldier to die in this war. Additionally, he did not want to have to deal with Stalin and his "Commie bastards" at the conference table. Sure of his course and his conscience, he gave the second command. To this day it remains the most momentous executive decision of all time.

On August 9 at 11:01 a.m., a last minute break in the clouds over Nagasaki allowed Captain Kermit Beahan, the bombardier of the B29 Superfortress *Bockscar*, to visually sight a secondary target on the southern island of Kyushu.

The bomb known as "Fat Man" contained a core of Plutonium-239. It was dropped over the city's industrial valley exactly halfway between the Mitsubishi Steel and Arms Works and the Mitsubishi-Urakami Ordnance Works that manufactured the torpedoes for its highly efficient submarine fleet. Forty-three seconds later, Fat Man exploded 1,540 feet above the ground. The resulting explosion had the strength of twenty-one kilotons of TNT. It generated heat estimated at seven thousand degrees Fahrenheit. Winds bursting outward from the center were estimated to have reached speeds of 624 miles per hour (more than three times the speed of the whirling winds in a Category Five hurricane).

The second disaster could no longer be explained away. Japanese newscasters described Nagasaki as "like a graveyard with not a tombstone standing."

No one knows how many people died that day. Possibly seventy-five thousand. By December, another five to ten thousand had probably died. Dead bodies lay unattended in the street. The sick were everywhere, so many they could not be adequately cared for.

The peace treaty ending World War II, which had been in actuality a continuation of World War I, was signed aboard the battleship U.S.S. *Missouri*, named for Truman's home state.

With it came the most omnipotent assurance that there would never be a World War III. Obviously, no more world wars could be waged. A single wing of bombers could destroy every major city in an enemy country.

And only America knew how to manufacture the weapon. In the months and years that followed unto this very day, America was forced into a role which it had never sought. It became the world's policeman.

Nobody loves a cop.

Great Britain, the former arbiter and peacemaker, was no longer equal to the task. Her once far-flung empire, "the empire on which the sun never sets," was disestablished. To rebuild her island nation's tottering economy along with her shattered cities, she had to concentrate all her efforts in behalf of her citizens across the English Channel from Europe.

One by one, her former possessions, colonies, and protectorates left her fold. The status of Canada changed first. Her citizens became Canadians in 1947. Once the cascade began, the desire for total independence continued, until by 1980, most of the great empire was gone.

Probably with only a twinge of regret our "Mother Country" ceded to its first rebellious child, America, the burden of tamping down "skirmishes, disagreements, conflicts, aggressions." The details as to who were aggressors and who were victims were often murky. The results were far less than satisfying, but so far few dictators, be they communist, monarchical, or religious, have dared to step too far out of the boundaries of their own countries. When such aggression has occurred, America has generally stepped in, backed by the pressure of world opinion, to keep the aggressor in bounds. Perhaps exhaustion has led to reason. The general problems have been civil wars that threaten to slop over onto the neighboring countries.

When problems do occur, although world leaders may hate the idea, they really don't have to ask, "Who ya gonna call?"

In halting these intrusions against the peace and security of the world's people, the Rangers have played a part, although not so significant a one as they once played.

Among the new "highly trained and efficiently prepared forces to lead the way" are the Special Forces. Without any sort of traditions, they quickly adopted the lineage of the Rangers likening themselves as heirs of the justly famous Merrill's Marauders. On April 15, 1960, the Seventy-fifth Infantry Ranger Regiment became officially designated the forebears of the new Long Range Reconnaissance Patrol (LRRP) organization.

Older Rangers shook their heads in some disgust as they saw their highly specialized and exclusionary training immediately become "watered down." Still, they had no choice but to accept the incorporation. As the Marauders had said when promises were broken and they were left in the jungle almost to the last man, "What the hell did you expect?"

On February 1, 1969, the active army LRRP platoons were deactivated and reactivated as companies of the Seventy-fifth Infantry Regiment. They became the new volunteers in a "cost-effective" move, all designated as LRRPs. Eventually additional Army Reserve National Guards were designated Ranger-style companies. Various state guards—Alabama, Puerto Rico, Delaware, Michigan—underwent somewhat more rigorous training to rise to the LRRP designation for Viet Nam. They were Rangers—sort of.

THE ACTIONS

Since World War II ended in 1945, at least nine conflicts, operations, police actions, interventions, rescues, et cetera, have seen the new Rangers in action beginning first with Korea.

In that case, North Koreans with the assistance of the Chinese Communists were determined to take the entire peninsula. While America was able to stop the communists at the thirty-eighth parallel and save the people of South Korea, North Koreans remain today "some of the most brutalized people in the world." They have no political or economic freedoms and are shockingly abused; prison camps, starvations, medical experimentation, murders, and forced abortion are only some of the horrors under which they suffer. Their leader is the son of the man who assumed control at the end of World War II. His administration spends millions of dollars trying to build an atomic bomb that he can attach to a long-range missile.

From 1959 through 1975, America waged a "peacekeeping mission" between communist units infiltrating South Viet Nam, Laos, and Cambodia (formerly French Indochina).

How Douglas MacArthur would have deplored the entire affair! The old General's maxim, "It is fatal to enter any war without the will to win it," was long forgotten. For sixteen terrible, frustrating years, American LRRP units, infantry regiments, and airborne units, as well as many units of the South Vietnamese army called South Vietnamese Rangers fought time and time again to drive the aggressors from the south.

The real tragedy of this operation, which turned into America's longest war, was that it created deep divisions in America. Because of the shocking attrition (58,000 killed in action and the 304,000 wounded in action), the average age of the soldiers gradually sank to some months over twenty-two. The newspapers carried stories of massacres and retreats, of jungle heat and ambushes.

Rather than die for something their parents came not to believe in, young men left America rather than be drafted to serve. The electorate continued to be appalled at the actions in Viet Nam. Equally appalled was newly elected President John F. Kennedy, who in 1961 saw his term of office beset by a war he did not want to wage.

A militant communist leader named Fidel Castro took control of the island of Cuba. Americans were incensed at the idea of an outpost of their most obdurate political enemy and the direst threat to their way of life being established only ninety miles off the Florida coast. The American people might not be in favor of the war in the South China Sea, but the Caribbean called for action.

On April 17, 1961, with the blessing and aid of the president, 1,500 Cuban exiles, who had escaped and organized themselves in southern Florida, attempted an invasion on the Bay of Pigs. Planned and funded by the American military, the landing ended in disaster. Present among the exiles were spies that had been party to the American training. They had learned and even rehearsed the entire plan, all the time pretending to be comrades.

In short, the patriots were ambushed in the water. Many died before they reached the beach of their homeland. Cuban-American relations disintegrated and have remained little changed to this very day. Keeping the anger alive was the Cuban Missile Crisis the next year, when only America's promise of all-out air war prevented Russian missiles from being installed in silos only a few hundred miles from Washington, D.C., itself.

To add to the sense of unease throughout the Western world, in June 1961 communist construction began on the Berlin Wall. In agony, the peoples of West and East Germany watched a wall erected down the center of their beloved capital. More than the zones that had existed since 1945, the wall symbolized a brick and mortar division of Germany into communist and capitalist states. Though Kennedy deplored the wall and visited West Germany to speak against it, he did not live to see its destruction.

In 1963, President Kennedy had passed on his way through the downtown streets of Dallas. At his own insistence, the shield had been removed from the open car, and he was seated on the top of the backseat waving to the cheering crowds. The sun shone brightly down on him and his wife Jacqueline, who was wearing a dazzling pink suit. The Lincoln made a right turn onto Houston Street to take them under the Triple Underpass and out onto the freeway. In the front seats beside the driver were Texas Governor John Connally and his wife, Nellie.

"Peace in our time" had never seemed more certain. Nellie turned with a smile, "Mr. President, you can't say Dallas doesn't love you."

In the public schools, principals turned on their public address systems to let students listen to the live narrative of the presidential motorcade to the huge new Trade Mart, where he was to make a speech.

When shots rang out and the terrified voice Bob Huffaker of KRLD-TV and Radio told them that the president had been shot, some students cheered.

His vice president, Lyndon B. Johnson of Texas, took his place, won the election the next year, and dedicated his term in office to establish domestic programs of lasting importance at home. Meanwhile the Viet Nam War plodded on. The stupid, bloody war and the young lives it continued to cost haunted him. Although he could have done so, he did not choose to run for a second term.

One of the bright spots in the long and deadly struggle was the "Red Devil Brigade," part of the First Brigade (Mechanized) Fifth Infantry Division. Originally a LRRP, in July 1968 they had been converted while still in training to Company P (Ranger), Seventy-fifth Infantry Regiment. In March of 1969, they arrived in Viet Nam and commenced averaging twenty-six patrols a month, nearly two-thirds of which ranged along the Laotian border.

Their standard operating procedure was to patrol for five days within a 6-kilometer "patrol box." On the sixth day they would set up an ambush just prior to extraction.

The most-wanted Viet Cong guerilla leader in that province was Nguyen Quyet. Alerted that he was in the area, the sniper team settled into their position and waited. From a tree line along a creek bank, the senior marksman among them spotted a man moving hunched over at a fast clip. Reasoning that whoever he might be, he was spying on their operation, the sniper killed him with one shot at a distance of twenty yards. The man was incontrovertibly identified as Quyet. With his loss, the Viet Cong guerrillas lost effectiveness and perhaps heart. They were no threat in that area any more.

Before the "Red Devil Rangers" were ordered to stand down on July 23, they had accomplished what the Special Forces had been unable to do in six years. Despite encouraging successes from America's best trained personnel, the war went on for another six years until its humiliating finish.

If we were the world's policeman, we were doing a pitiful job of being it.

Through all the horror, America had in its power the bomb that would perhaps stop it all. One bomb strategically exploded could bring any one of the warring nations to its knees. Because we, more than any other country in the world except Japan, knew its power, we did not use it in retaliation. We had opened Pandora's box once, and against all odds somehow had gotten the troubles returned to their hiding place.

We never used it.

But neither could we win the peace.

In 1970, while opposing the war that had escalated to an invasion of Cambodia, four students were killed and a fifth was permanently paralyzed by nervous, ill-trained National Guard soldiers at Kent State University in Ohio.

A famous movie actress, daughter of one of America's most talented and beloved actors, became known as "Hanoi Jane." She visited North Viet Nam and returned to report that young imprisoned American soldiers were liars when they said they had been tortured, starved, beaten, or brainwashed. Rumors also followed her that the prisoners had tried to slip her messages for their families at home, but she had betrayed them and given the messages to their captors.

More young men left the country for Canada or points south and have to this day never returned. America's returning veterans, rather than being greeted with parades and waving flags and pretty girls running up to kiss them, were spat upon and vilified everywhere they went. The flag—"Old Glory" itself—was burnt in the streets.

After sixteen years, America pulled out of Viet Nam ignominiously, leaving thousands of people who had aided America and been loyal to the cause to face imprisonment and probable death when the communists took over.

It was the nadir of American history.

No one likes a bad cop.

It was 1974, the same year that President Richard M. Nixon, his popularity at an all-time low, was forced to resign from office. He was the only president in almost two hundred years to do so.

Rather than let our military capabilities sink into an irreversible decline, General Creighton Abrams, Chief of Staff of the U.S. Army, issued a charter for the formation of the First Battalion (Ranger) Seventy-fifth Infantry Regiment.

The Rangers were back in business "to be an elite, light, and the most proficient infantry in the world—a battalion that can do things with its hands and weapons better than anyone. Wherever the battalion goes, it must be apparent that it is the best."

They were ordered activated on January 31, 1974. In 1975, the Ranger black beret became their symbol—to be earned, not issued. It remained so for a quarter of a century.

Of course, the Ranger units remained limited in number while the rest of the armed forces suffered from budget cuts and political infighting. From 1977 through 1981, the next president Jimmy Carter, a mild-mannered man from Georgia, had great cause to regret the deteriorating conditions that went along with the exhaustion of the American people who no longer cared about the wars they did not understand.

Then suddenly, they were galvanized into anger and demanded action.

In November 1979, a mob of militant followers of the Ayatollah Khomeini of Iran defied international law that proclaims that the embassy of a sovereign nation is foreign ground within the country where it is located. Screaming that America was the "Great Satan," the mob broke into the American Embassy in Tehran and took sixty-six American hostages. The terms of their release were that the Shah of Iran should be returned from America where he had taken refuge in the wake of an Islamic overthrow of his government. He had already been tried in absentia, found guilty of war crimes, and was to be executed forthwith.

America refused and demanded the return of the hostages now reduced to fifty-three. At that point, Iran refused to honor international law. America imposed economic sanctions. Cries among many of the disgusted and embarrassed American population were to declare war. Even cries of "Nuke, Iran!" were heard.

Still America did not use the bomb.

Months passed with no sign of the stalemate ending despite exhaustive negotiations. Finally, Carter decided that his administration had no choice but to conduct a military operation to rescue the captives. He named Colonel Charlie A. Beckwith, "Chargin' Charlie," a hardened Green Beret and Ranger from both Korea and Viet Nam, in charge of the operation.

On April 11, 1980, the rescue mission Operation Eagle Claw was authorized—and on the April 24 it went forward.

Murphy's Law: "If something can go wrong, it will go wrong."

Later investigation listed enumerable mistakes: bad luck, no backup plan, no rehearsals, and no margin for error.

When one of the eight helicopters developed a cockpit warning light indicating that something was possibly wrong with one of the rotor blades, it was instantly set down rather than take the chance of a crash.

The remaining seven helicopters took off and ran headlong into a giant *haboob*, a blinding dust storm two hundred miles across with an altitude of six thousand feet. No one had thought about the weather. A desert was simply a hot dry place, wasn't it? One pilot immediately experienced loss of his blower system for cooling air. He was forced to turn around and make a run out of the area.

The six remaining helicopters spotted what they thought might be the white bus containing the hostages. At the same time they believed themselves to be spotted from the ground presumably by militants. They set

256

down anyway in a deafening noise and blasts of swirling dust with no idea where they were. As the last two helicopters arrived, one was discovered to have a crippling malfunction. It had no choice but to turn and head for home. With the mission down to five operational helicopters, Beckworth was forced to concede that he didn't have enough space remaining to rescue and transport the hostages. The mission was forced to abort. The hostages were driven back to the embassy. The Iranians who aided in their escape by creating diversions in the streets, by arranging transportation, by spying, and passing messages were never heard from again.

As the five remaining choppers came back to the landing area, one pilot became disoriented by the swirling dust and crashed into a C-130 loaded and waiting to refuel the incoming "birds." The explosion created a mammoth fireball. The five Air Force crewmen in the C-130 died as well as three Marines in the helicopter who burned alive. The other helicopters were abandoned and the entire contingent of Rangers, Delta Forces, and support were loaded into the remaining planes. Their expensive equipment was jettisoned to make room, and they all got the hell out of Iran.

Lost were a nation's honor and its pride, the lives of the Iranian people who had revealed themselves to rescue the hostages, and the presidency. After 444 days of captivity the hostages were released minutes after Ronald Reagan, a former movie actor, was sworn in as the new president, allowing his incumbent opponent only one term.

Carter is reported to have wept.

Every police department needs a strong-minded, competent executive officer.

In October 1983, the Army Rangers were part of a task force that invaded the tiny Caribbean island of Grenada. By executive order of President Reagan, a famous "warhawk," they executed Operation Urgent Fury.

As part of a seven-nation task force, the job was to "conduct military operations to protect and evacuate American and designated foreign nationals from Grenada, neutralize Grenadian forces, stabilize the internals situation, and maintain peace."

Grenada had been a member of the United Kingdom of Great Britain since the Peace of Paris of 1763. In 1877, she became a crown colony with her capital at St. George's, named for the patron saint of Britain. In 1967, she became an "Associated State of the United Kingdom." In other words, she was responsible for her internal affairs, but Britain was responsible for her defense.

Her governmental structure was initially supposed to be democratic after the British model, but "strong man" mentality soon brought troubles. Still she was (and is) called The Spice Isle for her valuable production of crops of cinnamon, clove, ginger, and mace from which nutmeg is extracted. Her spices are exported to 20 percent of the world. Coffee grows wild along with oranges and all sorts of citrus trees.

Such a plum was ripe for "aid from Cuba." Castro sent crews of workmen, who were ostensibly building an airfield at Salines. Best intelligence discovered that it would be an airfield for Cuba to use to possibly bomb important targets or at least to threaten other islands to create Castro's communist hegemony in the Caribbean.

After Reagan gave the executive order, Operation Urgent Fury was begun. Since Ranger battalions specialize in airfield seizures, the First Battalion was ordered to take possession of the Point Salines Airfield, and of much more importance to the American people, to move onto the True Blue medical school campus. American personnel as well as students were attending that school that sat at the eastern end of the runway.

Navy SEALS were assigned to infiltrate the Salines area and set up beacons for an airborne invasion. Second Battalion was ordered to take Pearls Airport.

Unfortunately, all were operating without sufficient information to ensure success and a minimum of risk. The defenders were believed to have Soviet antiaircraft machine guns and 37-mm cannons. The American people were told that some of the least-liked people on the island were the Cuban military advisors and the 635 armed Cuban construction workers.

Like Operation Desert Claw in Iran, too little intelligence and too little basic preparation led to the loss of young lives that didn't need to be lost. Instead of a well-ordered and rehearsed drop of Rangers from three planes, only one plane was able to drop the paratroopers. They employed their buddy system and attached their battle harnesses, secured the reserve chute, and attached the excessive weight of weapons cases on their left sides. Each man carried over a thousand rounds of ammunition. Some rucksacks weighed over fifty pounds. Later studies of the operation would discover that it was a wonder the men did not plummet straight to the ground and die from the fall.

Proving that no jump is ever really safe, one man was towed behind the plane when he tried to jump last. He was hauled in safely, but the next two planes were well past their target drop by that time. Only forty men actually parachuted and were able to organize themselves despite tracer fire. By a stroke of "God blessed luck" none of the Rangers who landed suffered any casualties.

Despite the small force who received various orders and counterorders, the Rangers seized the initiative and cleared the field. They commandeered a bulldozer as well as trucks and tankers. Many vehicles were found with the keys in the ignitions. Those that were not were promptly hotwired and put into immediate use.

A platoon moved to the True Blue campus to secure it in fifteen minutes. One student was injured, but none had been taken hostage. Unfortunately, the Rangers learned, too late, that many of the students were at another campus at Grand Anse.

In the end, in an attempt to get to the other campus, a Gun Jeep Team of five men from Company A was ambushed. Four of them were killed. They and one other man were the only Ranger casualties resulting from the entire invasion.

Then, when everything seemed to be secure and an extraction about to be made, four flights of Black Hawk helicopters each loaded with fifteen Rangers came roaring into the Grand Anse campus. Two landed safely. The third Black Hawk lost control and crashed into the second helicopter. The fourth Black Hawk veered away, but in so doing damaged its tail rotor. When the pilot attempted to land and then take off, he lost control, spun out, and crashed.

A SNAFU caused by poor communications ended in a deadly FUBAR!

Grenada was not a stellar mission for the Rangers, or for anyone, but President Reagan was pleased. (Whether anyone told him about the various mistakes and near mistakes is unknown.) The medical students were all rescued, and America had triumphed again. The president further reported that the Americans had found warehouses full of Cuban guns, military equipment, and ammunition. Everyone was satisfied that Castro's plans to take the entire Latin American world into the communist party had been foiled for the time being.

Clearly, Reagan was pleased to believe that Operation Urgent Fury had averted a communist takeover in the Caribbean Sea. His speech to the American people about Grenada contained the words, "We got there just in time."

How average Americans loved him!

More important, for the Rangers the entire operation had lasted from October 25, 1983, to draw down and return to America on October 29.

Encouraged by his speedy success in Grenada, Reagan turned his attention to what was surely one of the most terrible symbols of the West.

The Berlin Wall remained standing while Germans on the eastern side saw their economy and their currency decline to the poverty level of many third world countries. On June 12, 1989, before the Brandenburg Gate, President Reagan delivered the type of stirring speech that the former actor loved to give. Though he faced the people of West Berlin, every word he spoke (thanks to impressive West German technology) was audible on the Eastern side. His words sounded a death knell for the Soviet threat in Europe. He challenged his counterpart in Russia with the words, "Come here to this gate! Mr. Gorbachev, open this gate! Mr. Gorbachev, tear down this wall."

Reagan was not called "The Great Communicator" for nothing.

Perhaps to the surprise of only the most benighted, chip by chip, the strongest and angriest populace in Europe, forever Germans, long divided by their oppressors, knocked it down. In October 1990, East Germany was absorbed into the Federal Republic of Germany—reunited without a shot being fired.

On December 20, 1989, the forty-first president George H. W. Bush, an ex-navy pilot from World War II, authorized the invasion of Panama to capture General Manuel Noriega, the Panamanian dictator and drug lord. He named the venture Operation Just Cause.

Mindful of the many mistakes of Urgent Fury and Desert Claw, "Task Force Red" of the Seventy-fifth Ranger Regiment was assigned to conduct an airborne assault on Omar Torrijos International Airport and Tocumen Military Airfield complex. Also designated for a simultaneous jump would be First Ranger Battalion and Company C of the Third Ranger Battalion against the Rio Hato base camp. Their action was to be "Task Force Red-Romeo."

Rather than go in unprepared and blinded, the invasion was planned for. Like Pointe du Hoc, large-scale models of each objective were created and studied. Even the place names on the models were Panamanian. The operations were rehearsed to a fare-thee-well on December 14 and 15 in the Florida Panhandle. For forty-eight hours, the Rangers practiced and practiced and practiced against two companies from the 101st Airborne Division that served as the enemy. By the time they were actually ready for the invasion, they were exhausted.

Nevertheless, off they flew, but not too efficiently. Things began to go wrong when the number of C-130 had been underestimated. Instead of carrying sixty-two paratroopers, seventy-seven were crowded in. Many of the Rangers simply fell asleep on their equipment.

Then two hours out from the green light, the companies received word that the operation had been compromised. The Panamanians knew they were coming. Ranger veterans groused among themselves: "What the hell could you expect?"

Still, the order was given for the operation to proceed, but not as scheduled.

Then a second report came back that the planes could not land at Torrijos-Tocumen because a Brazilian airliner was on schedule to arrive at that time. They could not commence the attack until the airliner had landed and all the passengers had been cleared and had picked up their luggage.

For seven hours the C-130s and all the support planes circled the airport. At last, it was announced that (oh, hey, sorry) the plane was already on the ground, but the crew and 398 passengers were still in the terminal.

Though the planes could have landed and discharged their Rangers, the orders were given for the men to jump. The vast majority landed on the concrete runways and on the tarmac resulting in fifteen Rangers being taken out of commission immediately with torn knee ligaments, broken feet, and broken legs.

All for nothing.

Noriega and his men were not at Torrijos-Tocumen. Instead they were traveling in two vehicles in the Rio Hato area. Rangers fired on and disabled the first vehicle, but Noriega escaped in the second vehicle. Later he surrendered after spending two weeks in the Vatican embassy where he had sought asylum.

Various skirmishes between Americans and Panamanians occurred at various times within the eight days of the operation. Four Rangers were killed in action, two by friendly fire. Twenty-seven were wounded in battle. Thirty-four Panamanian soldiers were killed. An unknown number were wounded, and 362 were taken prisoner as well as forty-three civilians. Still it was accounted a success by the press corps. It made headlines for twenty-four hours.

Just Cause was just the kind of war Americans like. In the words of Lieutenant General Lewis "Chesty" Puller, "What the American people want to do is fight without getting hurt. You cannot do that any more than you can go into a barroom brawl without getting hurt."

He was certainly right about the brawl.

On August 2, 1990, Iraq invaded Kuwait in the Persian Gulf. This time President George H. W. Bush mobilized over half a million American and

270,000 coalition troops from the United Nations (UN) for the liberation of the oil-rich country. Kuwaiti oil production was a major artery to the world's economy. Its independence was considered essential.

Saddam Hussein, military dictator of Iraq, had made himself a threat to the peace of the entire world. He boasted that he had weapons of mass destruction (WMD). He had already used some sort of poison gas against the Kurdish people of the northern province of Iraq. When weapons inspectors from the UN came to inspect his weapons' facilities, he turned them away.

Kuwait, an oil-rich, sovereign emirate on the Persian Gulf, tempted Hussein. Obviously, the UN could be bluffed. Without warning, he declared Kuwait a rebel Iraqi state and sent a huge army to take it back into the fold. His regiments were ill equipped and untrained, but the sheer numbers were thought to be sufficient. He could not imagine that anyone would oppose him.

The Operation, called Desert Storm, began on January 16, 1991, and consisted of thirty-seven days of intense, high-tech air bombardment utilizing Patriot Missiles and "smart bombs." The sky over Baghdad was green with explosions that went on and on and on. On February 23, the ground phase began. For four days, American ground forces killed an estimated 150,000 Iraqi soldiers. Almost as many were captured. Many hunted up American forces to surrender to.

One CBS news team, complete with translator, went out to find their own Iraqi soldiers to interview. When they returned with happy Iraqis in the back of their Range Rover, they had not even bothered to disarm them.

Company B Rangers and First Platoon of Company A were deployed to conduct pinpoint raids behind enemy lines searching for SCUD sites, destroying communications, and submitting reports of enemy troop movements. They were brought home less than two months later after acquitting themselves gallantly.

In 1993, William Jefferson Clinton, a man who had never served in any branch of the armed services, became commander in chief of the military. The last nine presidents directly preceding him stretching back to Truman in 1945 had been military men, including General of the Army Dwight D. Eisenhower.

In an economic move, Clinton brutally pared down the military budget, satisfied that those moneys could be spent on domestic programs. The Patriot missiles and smart bombs had shown the world what American military efficiency could do. Why maintain a large standing army? The twenty-first century would be a time of peace.

For five years the world had watched a bitter genocidal civil war between six rival clan factions in the African country of Somalia. The word "country" is significant. Somalia was a geographical entity. It was not then nor has it ever been a nation with the characteristics of a united economic and political force. It is located farthest east on the continent where its geographical "horn" projects out into the Indian Ocean.

But the world's heart began to bleed when CNN made tapes and transmitted them all over the world. Drought produced famine, and some three hundred thousand Somalis perished in eighteen months. The UN proved to be totally unequal to the task of aiding these people.

AUTHOR'S NOTES

The terrible genocide in Rwanda, the starvation, murder, and rape of Darfur, and the descent into economic chaos and resultant terrorism in Zimbabwe are modern examples that prove a rule about charity. A national initiative with government controls and structured institutions is absolutely necessary to equably distribute large amounts of food, clothing, medical supplies, et cetera. Aid delivered but not strictly administered becomes a weapon in the hands of vicious warlords.

Yet the world was caught "between a rock and a hard place." Inaction would have allowed Somalia's woes to spread throughout Africa if they were left unchecked.

General Colin Powell, Chairman of the Joint Chiefs of Staff, was opposed to American military intervention in the region. He insisted too many questions had few or no answers—too little was known and understood about the rival factions and the men who headed them. Sixty years had passed since Benito Mussolini had tried to organize the countries of Africa's horn into an Italian province. With the exception of Ethiopia, all remained in various states of barbarism.

Powell further warned that the mission would fail if purely humanitarian aid was offered. The army must go in with "overwhelming force" to crush the warring bands that had reduced the country to chaos. The UN agreed in principle. On December 3, 1992, following his defeat, President Bush in one of his last acts as commander in chief ordered the mission for humanitarian aid to Somalia. The use of the UN force was to defeat a threat to international security, "to restore peace, stability, and law and order with a view to facilitating the process of a political settlement under the auspices of the United States."

Bush's act committed America. Clinton, his successor, was forced into a quagmire from which there was no clean escape.

The UN wanted a bigger game—peace*making*. These operations were to be labeled operations other than war (OOTW). Twenty-five thousand American soldiers, seamen, and airmen were designated unified task force (UNITAF) in charge of Operation Restore Hope.

Their first task was to figure out who the bad guys were. Almost the entire populace was armed and excessively dangerous. For the first six months, however, everything went reasonably well as the people cooperated out of necessity. They were starving.

Acting from his own inclinations, Clinton, the new commander in chief, withdrew the American part of UNITAF. The UN appointed Turkish Lieutenant General Cevik Bir to begin to build a nation by "rehabilitating political institutions and the economy."

Good luck!

One of the warring chieftains was Mohamed Farrah Aidid, whose name means "one who allows no insult." Disdaining all the UN's efforts, he threatened to throw the UN and its organization out entirely. "We intend to rule!"

On June 5, lightly armed and careless Pakistani forces tried to seize Aidid's radio station. The Somalis had been warned—some said from the Italian consulate, which still had its own agenda as well as pretentions in the area. The Pakistanis were ambushed. Twenty-four were killed and double the number wounded including three American advisors.

The UN wanted Aidid arrested, prosecuted, and punished.

The quagmire deepened as escalation began. More skirmishes occurred resulting in more dead and wounded soldiers. They were not supposed to die. This operation was for *peacekeeping*. For *nation building*.

Two weeks later a pitched battle ensued against street demonstrations that were becoming more and more frequent and violent. The Pakistanis were doing well, protected by a Moroccan regiment on their perimeters. French reinforcements arrived in tanks. The crowds dispersed.

At that time President Clinton announced that "the military back of Aidid [had] been broken."

Aidid must have laughed at that declaration. He no longer needed to win. . . . He only needed to survive to gain victory.

Still, all out war was avoidable until the UN staged a violent act of retribution on July 2. An Italian checkpoint was attacked by Aidid's men. Investigations began immediately. On July 12, a group of tribal elders gathered in a public building in Mogadishu. Present were senior representatives of several clans, religious leaders, professors, former judges, and a renowned poet. They were all seated on rugs in the middle of the floor surrounded by younger clansmen standing against the wall. Probably ninety men were assembled. Not present was Aidid.

Four UN Cobra gunships swooped in for a surprise attack that encircled the building. They began bombarding it with missiles with fourteen-pound explosive warheads. From Black Hawk helicopters men fast-roped down and rushed into the burning building to secure prisoners. An unknown number of important and influential men died that day. Numbers are as low as twenty and as high as seventy-three.

The UN had sought to send a message to Aidid. Instead, they sent a message to the country. Somalia's clans declared war on the UN and America, who had provided the Cobras and Black Hawks. At the same time, the clans united in an unprecedented move against the "invaders."

What could Clinton do?

Who ya gonna call?

America deployed Task Force Ranger, 450 of the best from various Special Forces, Special Ops, and Delta Rangers of the Seventy-fifth Ranger Regiment out of Fort Benning, Georgia. They were too small for an invasion force especially since it was decided to withdraw some of the gunships because they were counterproductive to the peacekeeping initiative.

Nevertheless, Clinton told the story proudly to the American people, "It was late Sunday afternoon, October 3, the nine-year anniversary of the reactivation of the Third Ranger Battalion, Seventy-fifth Ranger Regiment, and 'The Battle of Mogadishu' was underway in the streets below." The first attack of the new forces resulted in success similar to the previous one.

But then the Rangers or at least their superior officers and "masterminds" running the war ignored the advice of a senior leader, Colonel Ali Aden: "If you use a tactic twice, you should not use it a third time." The plan was for an "insertion-and-extraction" action that would require the use of choppers and fast-ropes.

Likewise, a review of Robert Rogers' Rangers' Standing Orders would have shown at least two major violations that should have been evident to the commanders as well as the men. Rule Number One, "Don't fergit nothin'," hurt the men severely in terms of simple need. No one had brought water. When the planned in-and-out raid failed, the grinding equatorial heat added to the Rangers' sufferings. Rule Number Eleven, "Don't ever march home the same way," proved to be even more disastrous. In this case, it can be interpreted to mean, don't use the same tactic twice.

Not just the Rangers but the Somali adversaries as well had the timing perfectly for the fast-rope descents that had been so successful in previous attacks.

At the target site, the situation grew worse as crowds of Somalis hurried through the streets to converge on the prison to rescue twenty-four prisoners, termed "precious cargo." The men quickly pushed women and children in front of them to act as shields against the defending Rangers. One tactic used repeatedly was to jump out of the crowd, fire, and leap back in. Another was simply to kneel or drop flat and fire between the women's legs. Some lifted children on top of their backs.

Then the call came. Chief Warrant Officer 4 Clifton P. Wolcott, pilot of Black Hawk, Super 61, shouted into his mic, "Six-One's going down! Six-One's going down!"

If the reaction in Task Force headquarters was incredulous, the reaction on the street was anything but. With merciless accuracy, rifle fire, hand grenades, and rocket-propelled grenades (RPGs) thundered into the foundering ship. From every window, doorway, rooftop, and corner, the hail descended.

The RPG penetrated the Black Hawk's armor. Until that moment none had ever done so. The Rangers were shocked by the success of a weapon they had regarded as generally infeasible. Moreover, they had not practiced a rescue drill in the case of a downed chopper. Three blocks west, Americans watched the Super 61 crash on the roof of a house within a walled compound. The pilot and co-pilot were killed. Two crew chiefs, a Delta medic, and two Delta snipers were injured.

Immediately recovering, however, Rangers launched three contingency plans: provide cover with Black Hawk 68, deploy the main body of the Task Force from the objective to the crash site, and alert the Quick Reaction Force to deploy to the Mogadishu Airport where the wounded would be taken.

As the survivors crawled from the downed aircraft, Sergeant Jim Smith, one of the Delta snipers, emerged with his rifle as well as his Squad automatic weapon (SAW) and a .45-caliber pistol.

To the rescue came a Star 41 MH-6 "Little Bird," a small extraction helicopter with a clear bubble around the cockpit. The survivors crawled in helped by Smith, who then climbed in himself. The Star 41 took off for the American compound. Thanks to the heroic rescue and Smith's deadly fire cover, only one of the men died from his wounds.

On the far side of Mogadishu Airport, the rotor and three feet of tail assembly of Super 64 disintegrated. The chopper itself began to spin. The pilot fought the stick. Within seconds of impact he radioed, "Going in hard! Going down!" Against all odds, he managed to pull up its nose and land it upright on the back of a shack near the flight line. The entire crew survived.

In the meantime, a sortie had drawn to within sight of Black Hawk Super 64. As a Humvee pulled up to transfer, an RPG detonated under the vehicle. The explosion blew it straight up into the air, but it landed back on its four wheels, undamaged, and still fully functional. The gunner on top whirled his .50-caliber around and eliminated the Somali gunner and the tree from which he fired.

During the return trip, the way grew easier and quieter. Just blocks from the compound, the Americans had a surreal experience. They came out into the middle of an open-air market where crowds of civilians were quietly going about their shopping as if the cavalcade was an ordinary occurrence. Proceeding slowly, the Humvees pulled through the crowd that parted. Through the last hundred yards, the people turned to line the route and applaud.

Evidently not all Somalis were friends and supporters of Aidid.

Still Black Hawk Super 61 remained behind. The Ranger Creed called for the wounded and the dead to be extracted. Though their requests were denied, Master Sergeant Gary Gordon and Sergeant First Class Randy Shugart lived the Ranger Creed and returned. Their rescue mission failed. Their own Black Hawk was shot down, and only one among the Black Hawk crew and the rescue crew survived. Chief Warrant Officer 3 Michael Durant was spared and served as a hostage through eleven days of captivity and pain.

The treatment of the bodies of the casualties was broadcast on television around the world. The raid of October 3 came to be known as "Black Sunday" or "Bloody Sunday" and the "Battle of the Black Sea." Somalis came to call it the "Ma-alinti Rangers"—"The Day of the Rangers." Task Force Rangers suffered seventeen killed, fifty-seven wounded, and one missing during the course of the fifteen-hour firefight.

On the morning of October 4 when the whole world awoke to the outcome of the battle, President Clinton, in a hotel room in San Francisco, watched the images on television including shots of Somalis gleefully celebrating around the burnt hulk of Black Hawk 61. He emerged horrified and demanded to know why he hadn't been informed of the decision to undertake the mission. Whether anyone dared to tell him that he had had full knowledge is unknown. Since he had been the first president in fifty-two years not to serve in some branch of the military, perhaps he had no real knowledge of the cost.

Convinced that he was losing a war, he lost the will to pursue anything further. At this time America, the world's one true Superpower, quit. The courageous sacrifice of Task Force Ranger was for nothing. Their own commander in chief had not the resolution to finish the job.

The Rangers, the Delta Force, the SEALS, and the Special Ops were all called home. They left with the knowledge that men of that stripe always carry with them:

"All gave some—and some give all."

Despite the humiliation, despite reports that Aidid had been struck a mortal blow, despite the fact that his supporters were fleeing the city and his arsenal was near depletion, and despite the fact that other influential Somalis were offering to dump Aidid, the president was adamant. Eighteen dead and one missing was too large a number.

Still the capture of Durant was not forgotten. Robert Oakley, former Ambassador to Somalia under President George H. W. Bush, was dispatched to recover the bodies of the American military and to arrange the return of Task Force Ranger Durant. Oakley offered this piece of friendly advice to his counterpart in the deal making, "The minute the guns start again, all restraint on the U.S. side goes. Once the fighting starts, all this pent-up anger is going to be released. This whole part of the city will be destroyed, men, women, children, camels, cats, dogs, goats, donkeys, everything."

Six days later, Durant was returned along with a Nigerian prisoner of war captured in September.

In 1997, former Chairman of the Joint Chiefs of Staff Powell, who had sat in on all the president's policy meetings on Somalia, stated succinctly, "Bad things happen in war. Nobody did anything wrong militarily in Mogadishu. They had a bad afternoon. No one expected a large number of soldiers to get killed. Is eighteen a large number? People didn't start noticing in Viet Nam until it was 500 a week."

From that point on President Clinton decided to "study war no more."

The Rangers remained an elite force with distinguished uniform tabs and black beret through all the skirmishes, police actions, peacetime operations, et cetera, until 2001. Under the new president, George W. Bush, General Eric K. Shinseki, the Chief of Staff of the United States Army, decided to attempt to raise morale in the army in general. He ordered the Rangers' symbol, the black beret, to be issued (not earned) at large in the army. Unvoiced was the feeling that creation of these special elite forces within the structures of the armed forces was somehow undemocratic, and its presence was limiting enlistment.

When a protest was raised, Pentagon spokeswoman Martha Rudd assured disgusted Americans that the decision was based on fashion, adding that "black goes best with the army uniform." Many Rangers were outraged at having their exclusive symbol issued to general enlisted men without any sort of special training. All were insulted by her denigrating their symbol as a "fashion statement."

One can hope that the spokeswoman's offhand "fashionable" remarks were thoughtless rather than intended to deprecate. For the reader's information, although many women are serving among combat troops in Afghanistan and Iraq today, no woman has yet passed successfully through the grueling training activities to become a Ranger.

Nine months into President Bush's first term, another reprehensible sneak attack occurred. Radical Islamists affiliated with a terrorist organization called al-Qaeda hijacked four jet airliners. It was undeclared warfare. Deliberate destruction carried out by rogue civilians unlike anything imagined because of the cold-blooded mass murders that resulted. The religious terrorists did not consider military targets in the vein of Hickam Field or Pearl Harbor.

The objective was the modern materialistic world that lured people with its luxury and vice. The message was war until all are destroyed. The explosions were a call for a return to the thirteenth century.

The date was September 11, 2001. The date written 9/11—by coincidence or intent—is the emergency telephone number for America. "Call 911" is taught to every school child. Every person knows something terrible is about to happen.

As people in their homes all over the country stared at their television sets at 8:46 a.m. EST, they saw a huge airliner, American Airlines Flight 11, loaded with passengers and filled with highly inflammable fuel fly deliberately into the North Tower of the World Trade Center. Seventeen minutes later United Airlines Flight 175 hit the South Tower.

While television cameras and panicked barely intelligible newscasters and reporters tried to make sense of billowing smoke, falling debris, and bodies, people on the lower floors fled in panic from the burning towers. Americans learned in real time that another plane had crashed into the Pentagon half an hour later. And half an hour after that, a fourth plane crashed in a field in Pennsylvania, brought down by the heroic efforts of the doomed passengers who had heard what was happening through their cell phones and determined to take back the plane or die in the attempt.

The most reliable information available today reports that the fourth plane was bound for the Capitol.

The perpetrators of this attack made little if any effort to hide themselves. Nineteen hijackers had divided themselves among the planes. The twentieth, who had somehow failed to make his assigned flight, was arrested shortly. He identified his associates as Arabs who had learned to fly the planes in American flight schools. The instructors had assumed because of their nationality that they were our friends.

The leader of the plot was identified as Osama bin Laden, the son of an Arab billionaire, who had used his father's money to form a coalition that he called the International Islamic Front for Jihad Against the Jews and Crusaders. Its enemy was first and foremost America, the symbol of commercialism and, therefore, corruption through its control of the world's wealth.

In 1998, the militants had published a *fatwa* first in a London-based newspaper, but later worldwide calling all Muslims to "kill the Americans and their allies—civilian and military—wherever they may be." Their first attacks had been on American embassies in East Africa—Nairobi, Kenya, and Dar es Salaam, Tanzania—for which President Clinton ordered retaliatory missile attacks on al-Qaeda training camps in the Sudan and Afghanistan with insignificant results.

In October 2000, the U.S.S. *Cole*, an American guided-missile destroyer was damaged in the Gulf of Aden. Seventeen servicemen were killed. The attack had seemed hardly worth going to war over.

The deaths of 2,974 people with twenty-four others missing and presumed dead woke up the world to the militant nature of this religious sect. A radical religious group within one of the world's great religions had declared *jihad* (holy war) against the world. The buildings contained offices of over ninety different countries. Their citizens lost their lives as well as the Americans.

Though the damage to the Pentagon was cleared and repaired within a year, the economy of Lower Manhattan has been damaged for years. The

New York Stock Exchange (possibly their eventual target with its capacity to generate wealth and—in their eyes—worldly corruption) was shut down for a week. The airlines suffered immediate losses in the value of their stocks. As of this writing the price of their shares has not recovered.

The American flying public has been subjected to harsher and harsher scrutiny before entering any domestic airplane no matter how "short" the hop. No longer a swift, convenient way to travel, it is preceded by delays, searches, X-rays, and metal detectors. It requires people to move their shoes to pass through X-rays because the thick soles or wedge heels might contain explosives.

The World Trade Center has yet to be rebuilt.

President Bush sent the Third Ranger Battalion to lead the attack in Afghanistan in 2001. Though they have succeeded in sending bin Laden into hiding and ending the rule of the radical Islamic sect, the Taliban, they did not capture the most wanted criminal in the world. From time to time he surfaces in carefully filmed television and radio speeches shown initially on the Arab network al-Jazeera.

Though most of the footage is old, the war continues.

In the meantime, President Saddam Hussein of Iraq took advantage of the world focus on another Arab leader to rattle his saber again. Boasting loudly of his own WMD, he ruthlessly began to destroy whole villages in the northern provinces of Iraq, the homelands of the Kurdish people, who were trying to win independence from his control. His action drew the attention of Western nations to their plight.

Hussein demanded Kurdish oil as he had demanded the oil of Kuwait, when he had begun that war in 1990.

The decision was made by President Bush and British Prime Minister Tony Blair to "disarm Iraq of weapons of mass destruction (WMD) to end Saddam Hussein's support for terrorism, and to free the Iraqi people." Blair further stated that Iraq had failed to "disarm itself of nuclear, chemical, and biological weapons," which were deemed an intolerable threat to world peace.

On February 15, 2003, a month before the invasion, protests were staged around the world against the war. The *Guinness Book of Records* lists a rally of 3 million people in Rome as the largest ever anti-war rally.

The war was another that Americans love (if loving a war is possible). It began March 20, 2003, and was declared ended with the securing of Basra by the British and Baghdad by the Americans on May 1 of the same year. The world watched pictures of giant statues of Saddam Hussein being torn down, looters running through the streets, American soldiers patrolling the streets, manning checkpoints, and generally behaving in a soldierly fashion while searching for WMD.

In 2003, the entire Ranger Regiment was on deployment from the start of what is termed the Iraq War.

To put a period to this most swiftly conducted war was a carefully televised scene of America's own that rivaled anything bin Laden has presented to this date.

On May 1, 2003, the television audience was treated to the sight of an S-3B jet zooming in to make a perfect tail-hook landing on the deck of the U.S.S. *Lincoln.*

America waited.

President Bush, who had been in the air force like his father before him, climbed down to the deck, helmet in hand. Above him, a huge yellow banner had been lashed to the carrier tower: MISSION ACCOMPLISHED.

The entire production was an act worthy of a Hollywood movie. The *Lincoln* wasn't in the Persian Gulf as most Americans thought and perhaps still think. She was off the coast of California. What theater had America descended to? What was the purpose of such a deception?

The war wasn't over. The navy and air force had played little part in it. The mission was not accomplished. And still is not.

Bush left offices five years later with American soldiers still serving in Iraq besmirched by scandals of torture and humiliation within the country. Hundreds of men are still imprisoned at Guantanamo. The military believes that if they were returned to Afghanistan and Iraq, they would instantly join the guerrilla warfare ongoing there.

Most ironic is that in 2005, the Central Intelligence Agency announced that there were no WMD in Iraq.

HISTORY'S ASSESSMENT

History has reeled before the task of sorting out this war, especially since it is ongoing. This author could make no assessment.

13

RANGER TRAINING SCHOOL

One Warrior's Experience

Robert L. Pickett, Lieutenant Colonel U.S. Army (Ret.)

Then I heard the voice of the Lord saying, "Whom shall I send? And who will go for us?"
And I said, "Here am I. Send me!"

—Isaiah 6:8

Rangers Lead the Way!

Rangers have been part of the American military since before the Revolutionary War. They have trained at many locations, often adjusting their tactics to their environment and the equipment available but always using some version of the Standing Orders dictated by Major Robert Rogers. In World War II, Rangers were trained in America, Ireland, Scotland, and India. They fought in many bloody battles across Europe and Asia. Of course, after the war was over, Ranger units were disbanded.

Until the next time.

With the outbreak of hostilities in Korea in June 1950, the Army once again recognized that Ranger units were needed. On September 15, 1950, Colonel John Gibson Van Houten was directed to start training of Ranger-type units at Fort Benning at the earliest possible date. The target date was October 1, 1950, and training actually started on October 9, 1950. A total of eight Ranger airborne companies were trained and deployed during the Korean War along with replacements.

After the Korean War ended, these Ranger units were disbanded—until next time. However, the Army did a very smart thing and retained the Ranger Training School in the Army force structure. Between the wars, Ranger School trained young Army officers and non-commissioned officers in the basics of Ranger operations and leadership. One entire class per year was dedicated to training West Point graduates. These officers and non-commissioned officers were sent to units throughout the Army where they used their knowledge and passed their knowledge and skills on to their troops. And that is where I came in.

I did not really start out to be a Ranger. It was an accident.

While in college I had been in a sports parachute club and made over 130 parachute jumps. When I entered the Army, I requested assignment to the Army Airborne School. Unfortunately the school was full, so I moved on. Years later I was accepted as a regular Army officer and was advised that regular Army officers had the option of attending Airborne School and Ranger School on a priority basis. The young Specialist Four processing me said this option was routinely waived for "experienced" officers like me. However, I really wanted to go to Airborne School, so I did not request the waiver.

When I received my orders for my next assignment (Viet Nam) I had a delay in route to attend Airborne School. I was a little dismayed to see I was also scheduled to attend Ranger school. I went back to the personnel section to tell them they'd made a mistake, but my arguments fell on deaf ears. I have always wondered if the young specialist knew what a favor he did me and how he changed my outlook on life and the Army.

Probably not.

I reported to Ranger school in the best shape of my life, having just finished Airborne school two days prior. The other 199 personnel who started in my class were also in super physical shape, but that didn't matter. By the time we arrived, the Ranger school cadre had eighteen years to perfect the techniques of tearing men down. This is done through a combination of emotional stress, sleep deprivation, and control of the amount of food the Ranger candidate has to eat. The instructors were on a mission when I went through Ranger school. The decision had just been made to start forming Ranger units in Viet Nam, using the Long Range Reconnaissance Platoons assigned to combat brigades in Viet Nam. This decision was implemented in 1969 and the Ranger school at Fort Benning was already in high gear turning out personnel to fill the new Ranger companies.

Ranger school is conducted in three phases; the Crawl Phase is conducted at Fort Benning, Georgia, at Camp Robert Rogers and Camp William O. Darby. The Walk Phase is conducted in the mountains at Camp Frank D. Merrill near Dahlonega, Georgia. The Run Phase is conducted at Camp James E. Rudder located on Eglin Air Force Base, in the panhandle of Florida.

The Crawl Phase consists of two distinct parts. Part I is the assessment period and is conducted at Camp Rogers in the Harmony Church area of Fort Benning. It lasts about ten days. The program on instruction for this ten days includes the requirement to successfully complete the Ranger physical fitness test, the combat water survival assessment, a combined day/night land navigation test; several hours per day in the sawdust pit learning hand-to-hand combat; an individual 12-mile foot march; and the "Darby Mile" run event, a 1.63 mile terrain run with the Malvesti obstacle course negotiated afterward. Advanced physical training assures physical and mental endurance and the stamina required for obtaining basic Ranger characteristics: commitment, confidence, and physical and mental toughness. Additionally, the candidate executes demolitions training and airborne refresher training. Airborne soldiers get a refresher jump from both high performance and rotary wing aircraft and conduct tactical assembly area procedures.

Doesn't sound too bad? Here is how my first day went. We were rolled out of bed at 4 a.m., in formation and sent on a brisk two-mile run only to find we had arrived at the field where we would take our Ranger physical fitness test. So, after the test that includes a timed five-mile run, we were back in formation and ran another mile down the road to take the combat water survival assessment, and another mile back to Camp Rogers and . . . gosh, it was time for breakfast. We had classes much of the rest of the day and a couple hours of hand-to-hand combat that evening. We had homework, which required some memorization, and off to bed by midnight.

A note on the physical training we participated in each morning during this phase. Most of us were used to running in military formation at a pace called the Airborne Shuffle, which will produce a seven- or eight-minute mile. Most of these runs are for only three or four miles. In Ranger school we ran at a pace that would produce a five-and-a-half- or six-minute mile. It was five miles in length. These runs were preceded by about thirty minutes of standard exercises. In most cases the run ended at an obstacle course that took another forty-five minutes to negotiate. Then we could go clean up for breakfast. At the end of part I of the Crawl Phase, our class received about one hundred replacements to bring our number back up to two hundred candidates.

In part II of the Crawl Phase conducted at Camp Darby, the training focus was primarily on patrolling techniques and execution of squad combat operations. We received instruction in field craft, the fundamentals of patrolling and principles of mission planning/troop leading procedures. The fundamentals of combat operations included battle drills, ambush and reconnaissance patrols, and air movement operations. During this phase we conducted a field training exercise where we could practice these techniques.

During this field training exercise our food was cut to one meal per day per man, and we learned about the grading system. At any time a Ranger candidate can be called on to assume the leadership of the patrol. He must demonstrate his ability to plan and lead ten or twelve other very tired, very hungry candidates. These exercises are graded on a GO or NO GO basis. During the entire course if a man gets two NO GO ratings, he will be recycled or simply removed from the course. The field training exercise ended with a twelve-mile force march with all field gear. It ends at the Darby Queen Obstacle Course.

While executing the Darby Queen Obstacle Course, I cracked a rib. We had an eight-hour break, so I went to the emergency room and got an X-ray. The young doctor was going to call the Ranger school and get me recycled. I told him, "No, I will not do that three weeks again." I left the emergency room with a large supply of Ace bandages and a stern warning not to participate in heavy strenuous physical activity for a couple of weeks.

Oh, well, what would you expect from a non-Ranger qualified doctor?

After completing our training at Camp Darby at Fort Benning, we received another eighty-plus replacements and moved to Camp Merrill, the Mountain Ranger Camp in Dahlonega, Georgia. My group went into the mountaineering phase first, which gave me five days to heal a little bit.

While doing mountaineering, we actually got to eat breakfast in the mess hall several days. They made the best blueberry pancakes in the world. A man could gain a couple pounds each meal.

To quote from their website: "The mission of the Mountain Ranger Camp is to train small unit leaders on mountaineering skills, develop their combat leadership, develop their functional skills by requiring them to perform individual and collective tasks in a tactically realistic mountainous environment, under mental and physical conditions, approaching those found in combat."

The first five days of training included three days of mountaineering (lower) where we learned about knots, belays, anchor points, rope management, and the basic fundamentals of climbing and rappelling. Our mountaineering training culminated with a two-day exercise on Yonah Mountain applying the skills learned during lower mountaineering. Each Ranger candidate had to make all prescribed climbs to include a two-hundred-foot night rappel off a cliff.

Guess what? The ropes were only 150 feet long, so everybody had to stop about two-thirds of the way down the cliff and transfer to a second rope, unassisted, in the dark.

Once we had completed mountaineering, we conducted two combat patrol missions against a conventionally equipped threat force in a low intensity conflict scenario. The patrols were conducted both day and night. Our first patrol was a four-day squad field training exercise, and the second was a platoon five-day field training exercise that started with a parachute assault. The one meal per day per man rule was back in effect as was the twenty-plus hour per day operations. At this point any man had to be prepared to become a leader at any time. During these patrols we conducted vehicle ambushes, raided a communication site, and conducted several river crossings.

One of our last missions required an eight- to ten-mile foot march over the Tennessee Valley Divide. I still believe the night patrol when we crossed the Tennessee Valley Divide was one of the longest nights of my life. We were twelve soldiers who had already been on their feet for fourteen hours starting off on a nine-hour ordeal in the dark, all uphill. I came very close to quitting on that patrol but convinced myself to do another hundred paces before I quit, which was followed by another hundred paces and another and another. We were told later this patrol was to test our commitment and see if we could perform after being stressed to the maximum. They do not know how close they came.

The Run Phase is conducted at Camp Rudder. After receiving another sixty or seventy replacements, two platoons of our company conducted a parachute assault from Camp Merrill to Camp Rudder, and the other two platoons conducted a helicopter assault. Training starts the very first day.

Here is a good place to talk about fatigue. Fatigue is cumulative and it becomes the Ranger candidate's greatest enemy. Working twenty-plus hours with just six or seven hundred calories per day wears on a person. Young men recover faster. My class was made up of newly commissioned second lieutenants from the Reserve Officers Training Corps and the Officers Candidate Training Course. Their average age was probably twenty or twenty-one years old. My Ranger buddy and I were thirty-two and twenty-nine years old, respectively. We did not recuperate nearly as fast as the young guys. We moved straight from a patrol in Georgia to a patrol in Florida. We were tired going in.

Fatigue is one factor in accidents. Many consider it to be the most important factor in accidents. Since Ranger school opened, twenty-two Ranger candidates have died in the final phase. To the credit of the instructors, they have not let the casualties dictate a revision or lowering of the standards for the training they conduct. In the last few years the instructors have built an invisible safety net around the training that is close to infallible, but the potential for an accident is there, simply due to the intensity of training being conducted. Safety is a part of every operation order a Ranger candidate gives. It is required, and failure to make it so is grounds to receive a NO GO on his patrol.

After parachuting into Camp Rudder, we spent eighteen days learning jungle tactics. During this time we participated in two patrols; the second patrol lasted ten days. All patrols are conducted "in a jungle/swamp terrain against a well-armed, sophisticated enemy in a low intensity warfare environment. All missions were conducted in a tactically realistic environment under physical and mental stresses that approach those found in combat." Missions included in the field training exercises are airborne and helicopter assaults, small boat operations, river crossings, and swamp crossings.

The Run Phase of Ranger school is just that. As I remember, we spent sixteen of eighteen nights in the field. We did parachute assaults; we did air assaults with helicopters; we did ship-to-shore operations with rubber boats; we did small boat operations of all kinds; we rowed rubber boats up and down rivers and creeks; we did many stream and river crossings using our ropes; and then we navigated the swamps. Not just once or twice. We navigated the swamps, often.

On the afternoon of the seventeenth day in Florida, we conducted a frontal assault against an enemy position. During this assault the instructors tapped some of our comrades on the shoulder and told them to lie down. They were casualties. At the conclusion, the remaining eighty-nine Ranger candidates were made to look at prone bodies of our friends and lectured that this is what the battlefield looked like even after a successful operation. We then went into an assembly area and started planning the next operation, an attack on a village to secure a hostage being held by the enemy. We were told to add realism we would not get our casualties back as replacements. In fact, we would never see them again. They had not met the standard and were gone before we got back to camp.

That night we conducted a successful attack on the village and executed a successful river ambush as the survivors of the attack fled the area by rubber boat with our hostage. We secured the hostage alive. We sat up a hasty defensive position around the village, defeated a counterattack by the enemy on the village, and were feeling pretty good about the whole operation. We had been told this was our last event in the course so every man expected trucks to come down the road and truck us back to the camp for a well-deserved night in our bunks. Then the order came down—no trucks. We were walking out.

The Ranger candidate designated as our leader for this last patrol did try. He briefed that we were going to walk down that nice big, wide, dry road that led straight back to camp. Then he was corrected and told the enemy owned that road. Our only escape route was, naturally, through the swamp. So off we went.

I admit I do not remember a lot about that march. I followed a large chocolate cake, loaded with pecans and about a half inch of icing most of the night. Somewhere about dawn, I was slapped in the face by a big branch and woke up. We were just clearing the swamp, and Camp Rudder was coming in sight. For at least an hour, I had been walking while sound asleep.

I have mentioned replacements several times to this point. The replacements we received were provided to bring us back up to two hundred Ranger candidates at the start of each phase. After the first set at Fort Benning, the replacements were men who had completed the course up to that point but who had been injured during training. Those candidates who did not meet the standards of the course and were quietly removed just disappeared. No instructor would ever mention them again. I have never faulted these men. They were good soldiers. Some people just have more trouble than others dealing with the mental and physical demands of a twenty-hour-plus workday on one or two meals a day (600–1,200 calories), seven days a week.

My Ranger buddy had been injured in the previous class and had been recycled. He was about the first person I saw when I reported for Ranger school; he was a friend from the Infantry Officers Advanced Course. Reed Myrick and I teamed up as Ranger buddies and remained Ranger buddies for the entire course. Reed and I were a little surprised when we were told that we were the only Ranger buddy team in several classes that had gone through the entire course together.

After cleaning our equipment, taking a quick shower, and putting on clean—well, dry uniforms, eighty-nine soldiers got into formation and were awarded the distinctive Ranger Tab. My Ranger buddy Myrick and I were in this group. Not bad for a couple "old guys."

We had a short commencement address. I honestly do not remember much about it. Most of us were still in shock at some level after the rigors of the past nine weeks. I hope it was as good as the address quoted in part:

> The next best thing to staying out of "Harm's Way" is knowledge of what to do when you get there. As the United States military is being called upon to carry the fight for America's safety to an ever-hostile world there is a small group of young men that are taking out a little extra "Combat Life Insurance." You cannot purchase a policy with dollars. The only way to obtain this insurance is to complete "Ranger" training.
>
> An Army Ranger is expected to move farther, faster and fight harder than anyone else on the battlefield. He is expected to use his brain equally to his muscle power. He is taught over and over how to improvise while learning the basic techniques to overcome the objective. A Ranger is ever observant to his surroundings. It is a Ranger's mission is to be the one delivering any surprises on the battlefield.
>
> J.J. Chen
Colonel, Infantry
Commander of the Ranger Training Brigade

I reported to Ranger school in the best shape of my life. When I got home I found that I had lost twenty-six pounds during that nine weeks of Ranger school. The weight came back in about two weeks, but what I took away from Ranger school stayed with me for the rest of my life.

I found that my mental attitude toward a lot of things had changed. I had a lot more self-confidence because I knew I could make myself focus on and solve problems, no matter how tired or hungry I was or how much pain I was in. I learned that pain is relative. It can be suppressed. Pain is not your friend, but it does not necessarily have to be your enemy. In some cases pain is a means to help you focus on what is important and not worry about the minutiae.

I could make myself do things I was really afraid to do. Perhaps this sounds funny when you consider that at this point I had over 140 parachute jumps, 125 of which were free-fall jumps.

I had paid to jump out of a perfectly good airplane at thirteen thousand feet and free fall for over a minute, but climbing a forty- or fifty-foot ladder, then walking across an eight-inch wide plank for forty feet across the shoreline of Victory Pond was a real task for me. Of course we got the good advice of look out at the end of the plank and do not to look down. Sorry, I (expletive deleted) well will look down once in a while to make sure I am in the middle of that plank because there is no safety net. This is not as dangerous as I have made it sound in retrospect. Think of a set of bleachers. Most people can walk the length of a football field on a set of bleacher seats with little or no problem. Still, that thought was hard to focus on while accomplishing this little task.

I had sharpened my small unit leadership skills, something I would need within a month as I reported for duty in South Viet Nam. There I served as an Assistant S-2 (Intelligence) at brigade level and as the interim Platoon Leader for the Long Range Reconnaissance Platoon and later as a Rifle Company Commander. These skills and many more that I had learned in Ranger school helped me survive in combat, made me a better combat leader, and helped me set and maintain higher standards in training.

All of these abilities may have been there before I went to Ranger school, but it took Ranger school to bring them out.

After I retired from the Army I went to work as a civilian contractor at the Joint Readiness Training Center at Fort Polk, Louisiana. The motto of the Joint Readiness Training Center is "Forging the Warrior Spirit." Many times I have thought that the motto of the Ranger Training Brigade should be simply "Forging Warriors." It is something they have done exceptionally well for over a half-century.

After the Viet Nam War, Ranger units were once again disbanded; however, the Army once again reconsidered, and the First Ranger Battalion was activated on February 8, 1974, at Fort Stewart, Georgia. Currently three Ranger Battalions serve in the U.S. Army. They and their regimental headquarters are assigned to the Special Operations Command, so they are truly a national level asset. These units are expected to move within eighteen hours of notification from their home station to any place in the world, and when they arrive, conduct the assigned mission.

The Rangers' primary mission is to engage the enemy in close combat and direct-fire battles. This mission includes direct action operations, raids, personnel and special equipment recovery, in addition to conventional or special light-infantry operations. They may deploy on these missions using a variety of means to include airborne assault, helicopter air assault, ship-to-shore operations, small boats operations, vehicle, by foot or a combination of the aforementioned means.

Since Ranger units were reintroduced into the Army force structure in 1974, they have participated in every conflict to include the attempted rescue of the hostages in Iran, Grenada, Panama, the Persian Gulf War, Somalia, Afghanistan, and Iraq.

These men live by the Ranger Creed and follow the rules set down by Rogers. They are members of a very small society, and above all things they are warriors.

And, yes, you can bet that if I eat at an IHOP/Waffle House type restaurant, I will have some blueberry pancakes. It is my personal, never-ending quest to find some blueberry pancakes that are as good as the pancakes in the mess hall at the Mountain Ranger Camp.

ABOUT THE AUTHOR

Robert Pickett was reared on a farm in Rogers, Arkansas. After high school he attended Arkansas Tech University where he met his future wife, Rexa Lee Lusk, in a Skydiving Club. After completing Reserve Officer Training Corps at Arkansas Tech, he was commissioned a Second Lieutenant of Infantry in the U.S. Army. Pickett served more than twenty-five-plus

The author, in a Jeep circa 1969, in a photo taken at the New Plei Djereng Special Forces Camp in Viet Nam.

years in Germany, Japan, Korea, and Viet Nam. He retired as a Lieutenant Colonel. He then worked for fifteen years as a contractor for the U.S. Army Joint Readiness Training Center which trains U.S. Army brigades; U.S. Air Force units; and special operating forces, including active Ranger units, to work as teams in all levels of military fighting. Now fully retired, Pickett and his wife of forty-six years now live in DeRidder, Louisiana, where he enjoys doing yard work, growing flowers, and working with the local American Legion Post on community service projects.

14

THE GLORY ETHOS

I'll pay you ten thousand dollars if you'll let me go along!"
So spoke Ensign Thomas Gay.

The mission was to sail in a worthless hulk of a boat upriver to the anchorage of one of the most powerful and dangerous ships in the world. For a weapon they were carrying a jerry-rigged torpedo that would explode at the end of a pole. The pole would be directed manually under the hull of a giant ironclad; somehow it would not explode prematurely thereby blowing the hulk and the crew to eternity. The mission would probably end in the deaths of them all. Yet Gay would pay any price to go along. He did not count that the lieutenant had barely one chance in ten thousand to complete the mission. For his flag and his country and above all his leader, he would give everything to join the band.

And the leader answered, "You're on—I need another madman on this expedition."

This night was "the big adventure." The danger didn't matter. This chance would never come again. He would have given ten thousand dollars for it. He would be willing to face the danger, even to give his life. His name is remembered even 150 years after the night the mission was successfully completed—a small price to pay for glory.

During the Viet Nam Conflict, a Lieutenant John W. Gay, Jr., led a six-man insertion. For two hours they were behind lines. Before they were extracted they had killed three North Vietnamese soldiers.

In Somalia, a SEAL Petty Officer John Gay placed suppressive fires down an alley to rescue a fellow soldier Specialist Aaron Hand. Taking command of a Humvee, Gay ordered the driver to stop for nothing. In the alleys of Mogadishu, they encountered ambush after ambush, with Gay firing at every possible target. Finally, they encountered a roadblock of fifty-five-gallon drums set in the roadway in the middle of piles of debris and set ablaze.

Sure that his vehicle would not be capable of moving off its tire rims if it came to a stop, Gay never faltered. He ordered the driver to ram it!

The Humvee burst through. The remainder of the convoy followed as Gay led them back to the K-4 traffic circle.

The author could find no lineage among the three men, but the name seems to indicate a blood relationship. Indeed, if they were not brothers in blood, they were certainly brothers in spirit.

They were warriors. Adrenaline pumping. Lips peeled back over their teeth in wolfish grins. Risking everything and delighting in the risk.

Warriors are invulnerable. Wounds—they don't feel them. Caution—only a word. Mission—whatsoever the objective may be.

Brothers. "He today who sheds his blood with me shall be my brother" (*Henry V, IV,* iii, 60). Warriors' comrades are those who march beside them, who share the privations with them, whose face they see hanging above them to rescue them or to comfort them before their eyes close forever. The regiment are volunteers carefully selected by their mind-set, the strength of body and character, and the desire above all else to reach the highest, to do the most, to be the best.

The leader. "Praise and glory on his head! For forth he goes and visits all his host. . . . A little touch of Harry in the night" (*Henry V, Chorus,* 31–22,47). Mosby, Darby, Marion, Puckett, and Rudder. Merrill, Cushing, McCulloch, and, first and foremost, Rogers. The patrol that slips through the rising mists. The battalion that moves through the swamps chest deep in oozing black water, their rifles held above their heads. The sweat-streaked group covering each other's back as they move down the dusty streets of Mogadishu and Baghdad. The regiment. "All in the valley of Death Rode the six hundred" (Alfred, Lord Tennyson, "Charge of the Light Brigade").

Patriotism, duty, honor. "Failure" is the enemy's word. Self-sacrifice—a necessary act. So "Take one with you" (Winston Churchill, from an undelivered speech written to be broadcast to the English people in the hour preceding the Nazi invasion).

"Ethos" is the Greek word for character. In this sense it refers to a system of conduct, to moral principles.

The U.S. Army Warrior Ethos is a set of standards that all U.S. Army Rangers (the premiere Seventy-fifth Ranger Regiment of the U.S. Army) are encouraged to live by. Developed in 2003, it is meant to be the core embodiment of the soldier's mission:

> I am an American soldier—protector of the greatest nation on earth—sworn to uphold the Constitution of the United States.
> I will treat others with dignity and respect and expect others to do the same.
> I will honor my Country, the Army, my unit and my fellow soldiers by living the Army Values.
> No matter what situation I am in, I will never do anything for pleasure, profit, or personal safety which will disgrace my uniform, my unit, or my Country.
> Lastly, I am proud of my Country and its flag. I want to look back and say that I'm proud to have served my Country as a soldier.

In 2005 it was revised and incorporated into the *Soldier's Creed*. The most current revision is give here.

> I am an American Soldier.
> I am a Warrior and a member of a team.
> I serve the people of the United States
> And live the Army Values.
> I will never accept defeat.
> I will never quit.
> I will never leave a fallen comrade.
> I am disciplined, physically and mentally tough, trained and proficient in my warrior tasks and drills.
> I always maintain my arms, my equipment and myself.
> I am an expert and I am a professional.
> I stand ready to deploy, engage, and destroy the enemies of the United States of America in close combat.
> I am a guardian of freedom and the American way of life.
> I am an American Soldier.

FURTHER
READINGS ABOUT
RANGER BATTALIONS

Adams, Henry, and the Editors of Time-Life Books. *Italy at War.* Alexandria, VA: Time-Life, 1982.

Astor, Gerald. *The Jungle War: Mavericks, Marauders, and Madmen in the China-Burma-India Theater of WWII.* Hoboken, NJ: Wiley, 2004.

Bass, Robert D. *Swamp Fox, The Life and Campaigns of General Francis Marion.* Orangeburg, SC: Sandlapper, 1959.

Baxley, Charles. "Ancillary Actions, Battle of Camden Project." E-text.

Brinkley, Douglas. *The Boys of Pointe Du Hoc, Ronald Reagan, D-Day, and the U.S. Army 2nd Ranger Battalion.* New York: William Morrow, 2005.

Brokaw, Tom. *The Greatest Generation.* New York: Random House, 1998.

Cameron County's Historical Markers and Brownsville's Heritage Markers Trail Guides. The *Brownsville Herald* and the *Valley Morning Star.* Brownsville: July 23, 1999.

Churchill, Winston S., and the Editors of Life. *The Second World War, Vols. I and II.* New York: Time Inc., 1959.

Darby, William O., with William H. Baumer. *Darby's Rangers: We Led the Way.* Novato, CA: Presidio, 1980.

Fehrenbach, T. R. *The Battle of Anzio: The Bloody Beachhead That Turned the Tide of World War II.* www.e-reads.com, 1962.

———. *Lone Star, A History of Texas and the Texans.* New York: Macmillan, 1968.

Holbrook, Stewart H. *The Swamp Fox of the Revolution.* New York: Random House, 1959.

Huffaker, Bob, Bill Mercer, George Phenix, Wes Wise, and Dan Rather. *When the News Went Live, Dallas 1963.* Lanham, MD: Taylor, 2004.

Jeffers, H. Paul. *Onward We Charge, The Heroic Story of Darby's Rangers in World War II.* New York: NAL Caliber, 2007.

Lane, Ronald. *Rudder's Rangers.* Manassas, VA: Ranger Associates, 1979.

Leckie, Robert. *"A Few Acres of Snow," The Saga of the French and Indian Wars.* Edison, NJ: Castle, 1999.

Lock, J. D. (Ltc.U.S. Army). *To Fight with Intrepidity, The Complete History of the U.S. Army Rangers 1622 to Present,* 2nd ed. Tucson, AZ: Fenestra, 2001.

Mauldin, Bill. *Bill Mauldin's Army, Bill Mauldin's Greatest World War II Cartoons.* New York: Random House, 2003.

——. *Up Front.* New York: World, 1945.

McHenry, J. Patrick. *A Short History of Mexico.* Garden City, NY: Dolphin, 1962.

Moen, Marcia, and Margo Heinen. *The Fool Lieutenant, A Personal Account of D-Day and WWII.* Elk River, MN: Meadowlark, 2000.

Moser, Don, and the Editors of Time-Life Books. *China-Burma-India.* Alexandria, VA: Time-Life, 1979.

Noonan, Peggy. *Patriotic Grace, What It Is and Why We Need It Now.* New York: HarperCollins, 2008.

Puckett, Colonel Ralph (U.S. Army Ret.). *Words for Warriors, A Professional Soldier's Handbook.* Tucson, AZ: Wheatmark, 2007.

Robinson III, Charles M. *Texas and the Mexican War.* Austin: Texas State Historical Association, 2004.

Roske, Ralph J., and Charles Van Doren. *Lincoln's Commando: The Biography of Commander W. B. Cushing, U.S.N.* New York: Harper Brothers, 1957.

Scully, Everett G. *The Story of Robert E. Lee.* Portland, ME: L. H. Nelson, 1905.

Summary of the Second World War and Its Consequences, An Alphabetical Reference Book, Persons, Places, and Events; Scientific and Military Developments, and Postwar Problems in Preserving Peace. Chicago: F. E. Compton, 1946.

Tarassuk, Leonid, and Claude Blair, eds. *The Complete Encyclopedia of Arms and Weapons.* New York: Simon & Schuster, n.d.

Webb, Walter Prescott. *The Texas Rangers: A Century of Frontier Defense.* Austin: University of Texas Press, 1996.

Webster, Donovan. *The Burma Road: The Epic Story of the China-Burma-India Theater in World War II.* New York: Farrar, Straus and Giroux, 2003.

Wert, Jeffry D. *Mosby's Rangers: The True Adventures of the Most Famous Command of the Civil War.* New York: Simon & Schuster, 1990.

INDEX

ABOUT THE AUTHOR

Mona D. Sizer is a child of World War II. Her father, her cousins, and her uncles all did their parts, small or large, for the war effort. Her mother, the only Sunday operator at the telephone company switchboard, was the first to learn that Pearl Harbor had been bombed and alert the rest of the small Texas town. Besides hearing news about D-Day, the Burma Road, and Darby's Rangers almost as they were happening, Mona is a longtime student, reader, teacher, and writer of history and biography. She lived and taught on Ramstein Air Force Base in Germany and traveled extensively in France and Italy. She is the author of thirty-five works of fiction and non-fiction and recently the editor and contributor to *Tales Told at Midnight along the Rio Grande*. She lives in the Rio Grande Valley of Texas.